14.99

BEYOND THE BBC

BEYOND THE BBC

Broadcasters and the Public in the 1980s

Tim Madge

MACMILLAN

First published 1989

Published by
THE MACMILLAN PRESS LTD
Houndmills, Basingstoke, Hampshire RG21 2XS
and London
Companies and representatives
throughout the world

Typeset by Footnote Graphics,
Warminster, Wiltshire

**Printed and bound in Great Britain at
The Camelot Press Ltd, Southampton**

British Library Cataloguing in Publication Data
Madge, Tim
  Beyond the BBC: broadcasters and the public
  in the 1980s
  1. Great Britain. Television services
  I. Title
  384.55′4′0941
  ISBN 0–333–39427–5
  ISBN 0–333–39712–6 Pbk

To Oliver
'All these are thine, but thou art more than all'

Contents

List of Tables

Acknowledgements

The research project which forms the basis for what follows was a considerable undertaking, spread over a number of years. The whole effort would never have got started were it not for the continuing interest in broadcasting (and now telecommunications) policy matters shown by my good friend and mentor of the past ten years, Jeremy Tunstall, Professor of Sociology at City University, London.

Once the research was under way many people made invaluable contributions; most wish to remain anonymous. I can only say thank you to that small army of interviewees and confidants – well over 150 – who over a period of five years sustained the BARRTA project with immensely valuable assistance, in talking to me, in providing documents and in opening doors.

The first doors to be opened were unlocked by the persistence inside the BBC of one man – John Cain, formerly Controller, Public Affairs. John has become a good friend over the years; it was he who saw an opportunity both for academics and for the BBC, which he loves so dearly, in letting this project get under way. His careful guidance through the labyrinths of BBC procedures in the early months ensured that I got far more access to broadcasters and their private musings than I – or he – could have dared hope. I owe him a great deal – so in fact does the BBC because his firm belief that the old and trusted ideals of public service broadcasting are indeed worth saving have changed my own views, as *Beyond the BBC* will witness. And that has much to do with the access I have been given and the mode of discourse of the BBC: cultivated and civilised discussion, at least with me!

David Barlow, who took over John's minding role also deserves many thanks for the help and advice he gave. In particular he was able to get me into parts of the BBC other researchers have not reached. Pam Mills, formerly Head of Special Projects, BBC Broadcasting Research, has been of immense help. At a critical moment earlier in the study so was David Holmes, formerly BBC Secretary. His able successor, Patricia Hodgson, took great care to see that I got what I wanted and cast a lively and informed eye over drafts. Stuart Young, BBC Chairman now deceased, and Alasdair Milne, former Director-General, were willing interviewees and most helpful, as well as forthcoming, as was Brian Wenham, former Managing Director, Radio.

Alan Protheroe, then Assistant Director-General, noted my presence at a News and Current Affairs meeting as an English-speaking sociologist; coming from a Welshman that might have a double edge as praise or otherwise but I thank him for letting me in.

There are many more names I could mention; one stands out: Tony Raymont, who from very early on has added a dimension of wit and laughter to what could so easily have become a ponderous journey. Three people did provide a different but much needed form of help: Elana Varon, Lorraine Predham and Linda Block, some of my Tufts University students who acted as invaluable – and unpaid – research assistants in the latter stages of drafting the book; to them much thanks.

So many doors were opened that I have to acknowledge that my eventual disappointment at not getting to either Board of Governors or Board of Management meetings is itself a recognition of just where I did go – more or less at will. If the book that follows at times berates the BBC for being too secretive still at least some of that secrecy was swept aside in my own passage through what was, and remains, a fascinating organisation.

Writing in 1988 I can reflect how much longer, and with what greater effort, the final product took; its birth was not easy. Finally, I own a great and lasting debt to two people: my wife and my first son. Nicola happily took upon herself the main task of providing for us all while I wrote the early drafts; Oliver provided me with endless amusement. I hope he will one day be amused – in the nicest possible way – by what follows.

TIM MADGE

List of Abbreviations

ACTT	Association of Cinematographic and Television Technicians;
ADG	Assistant Director-General
BAFTA	British Academy of Film and Television Arts;
BARB	Broadcasters' Audience Research Board
BARRTA	Broadcasting and Accountability: Responsiveness and Responsibilities Towards Audiences
BBC	British Broadcasting Corporation
BCC	Broadcasting Complaints Commission
BCNI	Broadcasting Council for Northern Ireland
BCW	Broadcasting Council for Wales
BMRB	British Market Research Bureau
BoG	Board of Governors
BoM	Board of Management
BSS	Broadcasting Support Services
BRD	Broadcasting Research Department
CE	Commissioning Editor
CEAC	Continuing Education Advisory Council
CPU	Community Programmes Unit
C4	Channel Four
DBS	Direct Broadcasting by Satellite
DDG	Deputy Director-General
DG	Director-General
GAC	General Advisory Council
IBA	Independent Broadcasting Authority
ILR	Independent Local Radio (ie commercial)
ITCA	Independent Television Companies Association
JICTAR	Joint Industry Committee for Television Audience Research
NTF	National Television Foundation
NVALA	National Viewers and Listeners Association
PCS	Programme Correspondence Section
S4C	*Sianel Pedwar Cymru*
SBC	Scottish Broadcasting Council
TAM	Television Audience Measurement
VHF	Very High Frequency

Introduction

Beyond the BBC is the end product of a two and a half-year research project – the BARRTA project. BARRTA (Broadcasters and Accountability: Responsiveness and Responsibilities Towards Audiences) started out from comments made in the Annan Committee Report about the broadcasting advisory councils. Among other things the Report said there had been widespread concern expressed by various bodies giving evidence, including the advisory councils themselves, about the role they played inside or on the fringes of broadcasting. Annan concluded that one of the weaknesses of the present general advisory structure is that it is remote from most members of the audience.

The original intention was to test that assertion by looking at the membership of all the broadcasting advisory councils, both in the IBA and in the BBC, by observing them in action and by attempting to assess how their deliberations were used, if at all, by programme makers; and to determine if any programme-making policies came from what the councils said. In January 1981 when this proposal was first put to the BBC it seemed a simple enough request and one which would cause little difficulty. Without boring the reader with all the twists and turns of the plot, it was not until January 1983 that the author finally saw his first advisory council in action. For the record it was the BBC Midland Regional Advisory Council, meeting in Pebble Mill. It is also fair to record that on this occasion there was considerable nervousness all round: the representatives of the BBC, unsure of what they had let loose; council members unclear who I was; myself feeling a little as if I had been permitted to witness a deeply significant and highly contentious event in the secret history of broadcasting.

This particular episode I relate because it does illustrate the continuing nervousness with which broadcasters face the public: I, a specialist member of that public on the occasion I have recalled, but a lay person in broadcasting terms, was allowed to peep under the heavy folds of the professional broadcasting curtain. I later discovered many members of the advisory councils felt as I did: nervous; uncertain; privileged; to be allowed, however much at arm's length, into these hallowed portals.

It is not an exaggeration to see broadcasting as a latter-day

1

religion. *The New Priesthood,* an early book on exactly this theme, by Joan Bakewell and Nicholas Garnham, captures this mood perfectly through extended interview with the new priests. Garnham, significantly, is now a professor of communications, having forsaken his early career for older, but nowadays no calmer, pastures of academic theological dispute. Bakewell still graced late-night BBC2 territory, as arts correspondent for *Newsnight*, at least early in 1988.

Broadcasters, as we shall see, cultivate an envy and awe at the same time as they seek to exude a bonhomie with their congregations. They need ordinary people to accept the rite and mysteries of their enactments. Too fanciful? Not entirely. Broadcasters are the most accessible part of a greater religious mystery of the twentieth century: science. In the magic of the radio or of the colour television and video cassette recorder, the mass public can hear and see part of what science mostly hides away. Broadcasting is science and technology made manifest and in that sense it is a scrap of the prophet's robe for each of us to hold.

But broadcasting demonstrates something else. It appears to give instant access to the real world. It substitutes, in one sense, information for action; it creates for some a learned helplessness; it brings violence and death into the living room and asks us to forget or to laugh it off with a comedy sketch. It also often seems to have a predisposition to confuse the issue – and those at large who would seek to understand it.

It also enlightens, widens horizons and brings colour into otherwise drab everyday lives. It creates fantasies and it entertains. In short it is a paradox and those who would seek to unravel its tangled web first have to accept that there will be many lacunae, many impossible connections to make; to accept the *Gestalt* of sudden revelation combined with the banality of the daily output. Broadcasting mirrors everything – nearly so – as the cliché would have it; except, it tries too hard perhaps to be the Holy Grail, the panacea for our information needs, and our apparently endless desire for more, more, more by way of entertainment.

It is, so the next two hundred pages will argue, still too secretive of its operations by half, considering how much it dissembles populist sentiment while we sit vulnerable in our homes. But, so this argument goes, maybe that secretiveness is related to broadcasting's own concern that, like the Wizard of Oz, to uncover the secret is to reveal a small event masquerading as a cosmic wonder.

The BARRTA study concentrates on the means broadcasters say

they use to be accountable to the public. Defining accountability, attempted in the first chapter, is not easy and I have on the whole adopted the view that it means what people want it to mean. Broadly, however, accountability is only partially possible or even desirable in a rational broadcasting system. Iconoclasts, hoping for a sustained attack on broadcasting's current mode of discourse with the public, should stop reading here.

But there is a strong strand of critique in what follows. If broadcasters ought not be foolishly accountable they should none the less be as accountable as possible – and that means more than at present. The bedevilling and besetting disease of the English way of life – secrecy – should be ended. I believe that open government in broadcasting is as important as it is elsewhere and needs to be applied to broadcasting employees, as of course to the paying public.

The mushroom theory of management – keep in the dark and feed shit – is still too evident in broadcasting where, dare one be élitist and say it, staff are often well above average in intelligence and commitment. In the BBC, hierarchies sit increasingly uncomfortably with public announcements about creative freedom (which, thank God, still exists). Belatedly, the BBC is tackling its immediate problems of the failure to utilise half its staff – women. It has still (in mid-1988) to *show* seriously that it has the same commitment to racial minorities.

The 'public' consists of audiences for programmes, although accountability ought to take note of those who choose not to listen or watch. Most of the fieldwork for the study was with the BBC because the BBC is still the centre stage for any discussion in the UK of the nature and meaning of public service broadcasting. It also purports to do more for its audiences and for the public (as licence fee payers) than do commercial broadcasters in the UK or elsewhere.

Early on I approached the IBA, the Independent Broadcasting Authority, for permission to undertake a part of the whole study within commercial broadcasting – in particular their own structure of advisory councils. As with the BBC negotiations were protracted. In the end the IBA side of the original research project was dropped. It became clear the IBA did not see their advisory structure as being in any way open to researcher scrutiny.

As it happened, Channel Four began operations in the autumn of 1982 and after some thought it seemed to be a good opportunity to make a more limited comparison between the oldest public service broadcasting system and what purported in its pre-existence to be the youngest. Channel Four also originally appeared to be offering the public more access – whatever that was supposed to mean.

What the BBC eventually offered was far in excess of what I had originally asked for. It might legitimately be asked how this squares with the overall impression (still true in 1988) that the BBC is highly secretive about its internal workings? Why, in short, did they agree eventually to let me in? To this I have only partial answers; among them are the fact that a senior BBC executive believed – and persuaded others – that a well conducted piece of research could do no harm. Other partial answers surround the growing belief in the early 1980s that the BBC needed to show it was not as secretive as people generally thought. Accountability too was on the agenda, following the Annan Report.

The limited research proposal of studying the advisory councils had, however, touched a sensitive nerve. The summer of 1981, for example, had witnessed what can only be described as a row inside the most internally prestigious of the BBC's advisory councils, the General Advisory Council, when one member, a passionate advocate of nuclear disarmament, had called for a vote on the question of whether the BBC should finally show *The War Game* after 20 years of stalling over its transmission. This was unprecedented but might have been passed over had not the member then written to the *The Times* about it. This breached one of the then existing prime rules of conduct amongst advisory council members: that their advice was sought and given in confidence. I had had dim intimations of what was happening but only subsequently realised what a shock-wave this single incident sent through the centre of the BBC.

The result for the BARRTA project was delay. When I eventually heard from the BBC they suggested a different piece of research altogether, something much larger but potentially much more interesting. It was that if I was truly interested in accountability I ought in fairness to the BBC to look at *all* the mechanisms they considered to be a part of their taking account of the public: these included the advisory councils, but also letters, telephone calls, formal audience research in general, public meetings, back-up to programmes, feedback programmes on air, the Community Programme Unit, BBC Education. As I happen to know the source of the suggestion I do know it was a genuine offer made in order to circumvent internal opposition to my being allowed in at all. In the event I accepted the challenge and I was allowed in. *Beyond the BBC* is part of the result. Over the time I was within both the BBC and

Channel Four I accumulated a vast amount of data. Inevitably, only some of these data have been used in writing this book.

What I have tried to do is to use the bulk of the data as background, to inform me as fully as possible as to the mood of broadcasters in the 1980s, and the mood of the audiences they seek to serve. The book which follows does not often directly quote a source, especially an oral (interviewed) source. Many people have contributed to this book; most are anxious to remain entirely anonymous. Many have put their careers at some internal risk by being prepared to be brutally honest about themelves, their aspirations and the future of the organisation they work for. Out of their willingness to help me has come much of what follows.

To all those people who have helped, and to the BBC as an organisation, I would like to offer a sincere appreciation of the time, effort and anxieties they have contributed. If what follows is occasionally upsetting to some of them then I have to say my intention is not to destroy what I believe to be a unique and extraordinarily creative cultural body. But all has not been well and the attacks have mounted. In times like these a careful critique may help, not hinder.

Of course this is the point at which to say: the interpretation, the use I have made of all that accumulation of facts, figures and opinion, is entirely my own.

Part I
Opening and Closing Doors

1 Public Service Broadcasting and the Public Interest

The first of January 1987 saw the 60th anniversary of the start of the British Broadcasting Corporation. Diamond Jubilees suggest continuity, the certainties of a fulfilled purpose and an agreeable retirement. For the BBC few of these can be applied, yet it is likely that it will at least *continue*. How far its presence in the future will be changed by events in the immediate short term; how far, indeed, it will be able to maintain its present position at the leading edge of British and world broadcasting, seems now to hang on the extent to which it can adjust to a different environment – political, economic, social and technological. From its own history we can work out how powerful is its ability to emerge from this kind of challenge intact, if altered.

When the BBC enjoyed its zenith in the public imagination it existed in a much more certain world than we have now. Arguments would rage over exactly when that zenith was: probably from the 1930s through to the 1960s at least. This period is really the age of radio – and its decline – and it gives pause for some thought that in a sense the BBC indeed was and remains best at a certain kind of radio, most obviously continuing on Radio Four but manifest in other parts of the output too, like some local radio.

Discussion of the peak of popularity in the public imagination also gives rise to questions surrounding the relationship of 'the public' to audiences, mass or otherwise, and to a much trickier question: how popular has the BBC been at any time – and with whom?

Myths – as manifest even in the title of Briggs' second volume of the *History of British Broadcasting: The Golden Age of Radio*, have a redolence hard to escape. Yet we can surmise that, by and large, the BBC did enjoy a huge measure at least of public *acceptance*. This lasted well beyond 1960. It lasts still although now the terms of the debate are shifting all the time.

Of course, what we might mean by 'public' and 'popular' is social and political élite acceptance and approbation: the toast, not of the Old Kent Road but of the Establishment, of the Surrey hills and Oxbridge. Some of that remains but in some of the stockbroker belt the BBC is now a ripe plum, ready – if not long overdue – for rich picking.

It is impossible to separate the history of the BBC from that of contemporary Britain. It is a measure, in fact, of the degree to which the Corporation remains politically astute, that it is able to shift its position as subtly as does the British Constitution. And it is a measure of the failure to respond that the BBC is in some form of domestic (and therefore painfully public) trauma. But part of the central problem for the BBC has become the ground on which it makes its stand. That ground, the indefinable but so crucially important middle, has affected and afflicted political life at large over the past decade.

But is there really a *crisis* for the BBC; has there ever been, in the period from 1982 to 1988? Apart from the overworked nature of the word, crisis implies something very serious indeed.

The BBC has certainly been going through public and private agonies – some would say of indecision – over its future direction. The débâcle over direct satellite broadcasting has diverted and delayed the BBC. And it has had too many domestic rows, perhaps symptoms of a management malaise which had been developing for many years. Looked at dispassionately the BBC has entered what systems theorists are happy to call a 'turbulent field'. The organisational 'flow' becomes disturbed and this sets up the kind of whirlpool in which uncertainty of direction can be fatal. But to imagine as one recent writer did (Leapman, 1986) that this means the Beeb (as he insists on calling it) is doing down the drain, is absurd.

Part of the turbulence, however, is generated by pressures arising from the public, divided as they are into many sets of audiences: mass or otherwise. Knowledge about those audiences, their preferences, prejudices and idiosyncracies, has become more and more important to programme makers as competition has grown for their attention. Whether any of the activity now directed at those audiences, in particular by the BBC, leads to meaningful exchanges is hard to establish. The significance, in the history of broadcasting, of the growth of real interest in audiences, and not entirely as ratings fodder, is unquestionable.

When things were more certain, when broadcasting was in its earlier phases, audiences counted for much less. But this was not just an attitude on the part of arrogant broadcasters but of arrogant British society, of which BBC employees, at the sharp end, were fairly representative. The BBC at the beginning made public pronouncements the like of which would be howled down today. But then so would many of the contemporary statements made by all kinds of public authority. In the 1920s the general public were not considered to be a part of 'public life'. Although still excluded from many areas of real power and decision-taking – at least in politics – today the public at large are given a more sophisticated, if possibly more cynical, exposition of what is going on. The problem of authority in a popular democracy may never be resolved. As with other physical representations of different kinds of authority, the BBC is hoist on the petard of one set of definitions of populism – to which of course in many of its own programmes it subscribes.

It is in the general attitude of authority to the public that the BBC's earliest clues to its own behaviour can be found, not in their having a monopoly. The question of the BBC's monopoly dominated its first 30 years, half its life in fact, just as the question of its continuous growth to its present size, set against a slackening, then falling real revenue, has dominated the second half. But the issue of the monopoly was continuously overshadowed by its presence.

The BBC was able in those early years to use its power to concentrate much more on its output than it has in recent years when its own future has come to dominate much management thinking. It was then much smaller in size than it is now. Programme policies could dominate the proceedings, rather than political manoeuvring, or building site priorities, or what the Press thought of it all. All these things were on the agenda of meetings in the 1930s but they never give the impression of taking over. In the 1980s the opposite impression can be given.

The system *was* stable. Instability within the broadcasting system began with the onset of ITV and in particular by the failure at the time by BBC managements to acknowledge, other than in asides, that 'the competitor's' existence was destabilising. The story of the early days of ITV, and its slow but inexorable erosion of the BBC's television audience, has been told a number of times and need not, in the details, bother us here. But that experience for the BBC had a long-term corporate effect; and it has coloured the BBC's present.

Most of the present management missed the actual moment of the toppling of the BBC from its previously unassailable position (for example, Dick Francis, asked to resign as Managing Director, BBC Radio in May 1986, had been in the BBC for 27 years: that is he started in 1959, at the time when BBC television was at its lowest audience-level ebb). But all had witnessed the BBC's response, its aggressive 'relaunch' through its television (and then radio) service in the early 1960s. It was that relaunch that had inevitably to diminish the importance of the Reithian 'ideal'. Once diminished it began its own decline as a central corporate ideology, to be dragged out periodically in death-like pallor to re-proclaim its truths, but in reality replaced by the newer, much more pragmatic ideology of 'professionalism'.

Reithian principles, in the 1980s, can look pretty reactionary. They have one advantage: like all absolutes they are hard to attack from without. The creeping pragmatism of professionalism, aside from being very hard to identify (and therefore defend) can nevertheless be made to stand for all things. It was for this reason that the BBC floundered in 1985 when it had suddenly to despise advertising all over again. Apart from misreading its own history (Reith never despised commerce, he merely thought it inappropriate for the BBC to dip into it), the BBC failed to insist on the broader cultural reasons for keeping advertisements off its airwaves. In any case many of its more astute critics pointed to its self-advertising: its use on air of 'commercial' breaks between programmes to hype its own output, and its increasing activities in the market-place for merchandise: videos, T-shirts, books – and that BBC computer.

The growth of the commercial side of BBC operations was no great deal. Once again it was consistent with the belief in many quarters of the need for business in the macro-economy, to get itself back in the market-place. The BBC reflected the impetus of the macro-economy: art imitated life. The desire to become a more aggressive purveyor of its goods and services was, of course, a reflection of another kind.

By the late 1970s the BBC was no longer able to rely on a natural increase in licence fee revenue, the saturation of colour television sets having been more or less accomplished. As governments found themselves squeezed in the larger economy by revenue deficiencies set against increasing demands for intervention, so the BBC was squeezed – on the one hand by a lack of funds, or their increase; on the other by demands of services and for their improvement. In the climate of the times, inflation took its toll, as did the post-war philosophy of year-on-year wage increases. Strong unions and the inherently inflationary nature of television set, in the case of the BBC, against high wages in commercial television, combined to ensure that the squeeze on its revenue was acute.

Additionally, by the late 1970s other, more subtle, pressures were increasing. Internally BBC management structures were creaking – despite efforts to change them through the late-1960s McKinsey

Report. The most instructive source of criticism here comes in the Annan Report (1977), which clearly believed the BBC's management was a mess. There was by then a problem of recruitment too. Senior producers simply did not want to be pushed into a management system they had begun to despise (seeing it more and more locked into the single issue of money and how to save it).

Few of the really bright programme-makers wanted to get into a situation where they had to balance the books by turning down their former co-producers' requests for money to make programmes. Some were tempted and rapidly retreated (like David Attenborough). Others fled to the financially rich management pastures of ITV. Yet this period was one when the BBC needed more than ever to find the talented manager who would be able to fight the real battle: not about ratings, not about DBS or the expansion of local radio, but about the central crucial principle of public service broadcasting. It was less ill-luck, more complacency borne of 50 years survival, that resulted in the BBC by 1980 being faced with an internally weak management and an externally strong and implacable enemy, Mrs Thatcher's first Government.

ENTER THE DRAGON

The significance of the 'Thatcher Phenomenon', to take the title from a belated BBC radio documentary about it may, as is now suggested, not be in what she directly achieved but in a fundamental shift she occasioned in attitude. Towards the end of a difficult century for Britain, when we had lost so much power, and so much morale had dissipated, when instincts tended to a continuation of 'business as usual' and a quiet life, Mrs Thatcher acted like a very cold douche indeed. Whether the long-term result will be that we continue as a nation to sink slowly into the oblivion of past glories and no future, or whether we will re-discover – or just discover – a future, any future, remains in doubt.

But the first two Thatcher Governments did drastically alter one seeming absolute of British political, economic, social and even cultural life since well before the Second World War: consensus. As it happens the BBC's entire rationale is based on that single notion, along with its innate ability to identify where that 'central' consensus is at any time. Consensus, acting slowly, allows organisations like the BBC to adjust relatively gradually to those changes. As a plank of civilised living consensus is forgiving and flexible. The first half of the 1980s showed what happens when that plank slips – or is misplaced.

The BBC had already decided it needed to adjust its own consensual awareness in one important way. As it now needed more and more to increase its revenue base by putting up its single product price – the licence fee – it turned to its consumers in a frantic effort to persuade them it 'belonged to them' and was worth saving. In particular it wanted to show what good value it gave. Its early diffidence in this matter gave rapid way to an increasingly hysterical vulgarity of approach, so typical of hitherto-remote British institutions which realise they need to be closer to 'the people'. (This affliction, caused partly by the continuing pressures of that singular British ailment, social class, may yet affect even the Royals.) In the case of the BBC this left a large proportion of the public unmoved, mystified or even, in the case of its more middle-class professional clientèle, shocked.

The BBC's misfortune, in the matter of its funds, is that the licence fee is not understood at all by those who pay it, and hardly by many of those who administer it, or those who decide how large it should be. In the past this obfuscation has been a curious strength because the very obscurity of its true nature has prevented much interference by Government. It worked because it went up rarely and then uncontentiously. Now, with all governments obsessed about the level of central government spending (the licence fee in this context is seen as a tax, and a regressive one at that), the mystery is unravelled a little but only so far as to discomfort the recipient.

The licence fee is a *poll* tax levied on *households* wishing to receive *broadcast* signals. The BBC is nowhere mentioned on the actual document held by each household, and a Government could, should it so wish, divert the entire sum into the exchequer. In the bad old days it did take a large chunk as a broadcast tax. At the same time as governments wish to retain control through taxation of what the public can and cannot do with their television receivers, it is the BBC who has to put up the case for increases. As the BBC receives the bulk of the revenue raised (only losing a 'collection' fee) this, it could be argued, is fair. It is not, insofar as the licence fee in reality is a fee enabling the British public to receive *all* broadcast material, commercial as well as BBC. In a fairer world ITV and commercial local radio would promote the value to the consumer of the licence fee, not leaving it just to the BBC to do so.

This point is not an academic one. As has been amply shown by the arguments that raged back and forth over the Peacock Committee and its report (see Chapter 12), commercial broadcasting in Britain does extremely well by having and keeping a monopoly of advertising. The first disturbance of the system, with the coming of ITV, was rebalanced in the 1960s between BBC and ITV sharing, as they did, the audience.

TURBULENT FIELDS: POLITICAL, ECONOMIC, SOCIAL AND TECHNOLOGICAL CHANGE

What then, has finally created the turbulence in the system? We have already seen that a major structural change in Britain – the denial, if not destruction, of consensus – has altered the field in which British broadcasting as a whole operates, with clear-cut implications for the BBC. Then there has been the failure of the management of the Corporation to attract as many of the top programme-makers to the ranks as has been necessary for its own future.

Technological changes have also increased the turbulence. First the implementation of a policy on colour television, now a couple of decades since, resulted in considerable cost increases, not all borne by the increases in licence fee or the separate, higher, Colour Television Licence Fee. Over time, the onset of various new studio and outside broadcast camera technologies has also put additional burdens on the BBC budget. These changes are expensive and increasing in number so that making any decision now may mean increased spending which has then to be repeated when the next package of improvements arrives.

Because of ITV and the consequent competition for audiences, the BBC has to play at least part of the game which involves giving the audience the very latest technical wonders, like Quantel, like live action using light-weight cameras, like the expensive transmissions live via satellite of news and especially sport.

As well, technology has provided audiences with a much greater potential choice in broadcasting, entirely outside the control of the broadcasters. With the video tape recorder the public can, and do, hire the latest films. On-air broadcasters then have to compete harder – and at a higher price – to show those same films. The same is begining to apply to sports events and to a host of other, hitherto cheap, events which now may sell rights to those slow-growing but dangerous rivals, cable and satellite.

Although cable broadcasting is likely to be extremely sluggish in growth, its long-term potential is high. Evidence from those homes already on cable in the UK suggest existing on-air broadcasting is hit as audiences choose the usually less-demanding entertainment of Sky, Music Box or the Lifestyle channels.

Loss of audiences will have a potentially more damaging effect on ITV than on the BBC but, given the unitary structure of the broadcasting system, the BBC is vulnerable. At base, its own privately voiced fear is that the audience, fragmented between large numbers of channels, will simply refuse to pay a licence fee for what it perceives to be just a part of the output, most of which appears to be free.

Direct broadcast satellite television (like the 1989-launched Sky) pose a threat, much greater because more instantly globally available, than cable or the vcr. Technology, then, has thrown a very large spanner in the works.

The final element of turbulence has been created by the BBC as much as by anything. It is the subject of this book: accountability. The BBC's new approach to its audiences and to the public at large may be seen to have begun with the licence fee campaign of 1979. The attempt to bring the public directly into the debate about the level of funding of the BBC has changed forever the BBC's relationship with that public. Once slogans like 'It's Your BBC', and terms like 'BBC shareholders' become vogue they cannot be removed from the public domain.

Accountability, in the loosest sense, is part of consumerism. Its rise through the 1970s has been well charted. Like the public's right to know, the public right to complain (for that is what it has mostly meant) – and to get real redress – is enshrined increasingly in legislation and in a host of quangos, courts and tribunals. Even Government has conceded a little through the establishment of various Ombudsmen.

Broadcasting had its range of techniques well before fashion intruded in other areas of public life – notably the advisory councils (see Chapter 2 *et seq.*). The value of these early efforts in the climate of the new consumerism was rapidly eroded. By the late 1970s demands were made – and partially met – for statutory bodies to investigate complaints within broadcasting. The growth of pressure groups, both outside and within broadcasting, asking for 'real' changes in attitudes towards audiences assisted those who wished to bring broadcasting in line with consumer rights. Two problems have remained intractable. First, what is the nature of the good being consumed? If a creative good then how to measure its value to the consumer (if indeed 'consumer' is the right term at all). Second and absolutely crucial, the freedom of broadcasters to make the programmes they wish, without undue hindrance, is a part of the general freedom of the Press. Curb that, so the argument runs, and you are well on the road to the absolute society, authoritarian government, and all the ills those bring in their wake.

We are, of course, back to consensus. Where it operates – and ultimately it too operates only by general consent – these problems are marginal to a central agreement that good faith, trust and 'balance' will out. Broadcasters suffer more than most when that trust gives way to a suspicion that what they do is not in my interests or yours.

When the BBC brought the audience card into play it triggered all this and more. The pressures were already there and were to grow as Thatcherism implanted in the public mind the notion that the consensus was no more. Incidentally, the same ruling philosophy suggested large public bodies in any way associated with central government funding were to be deplored; and that public 'rights' were to be invested in their ritual destruction. At the same time I am not suggesting that Thatcherism, and a sudden surge in the BBC's concern for 'accountability' were directly linked. The BBC turned to its audiences as a logical (if belated) outcome to its own problems – notably the financial one. But the beginnings of the new interest of BBC management in audiences had much to do with the erosion of ideas about consensus. Whether or not Mrs Thatcher's Governments are the result of that erosion, or to what extent they began the serious work of undermining consensus is not for this book to discover, interesting a question though it is.

The audiences invited by the BBC to come and look round its operations – and approve – were, are, a Trojan Horse. The truth about accountability is that the BBC neither wishes to be, nor can be, fully *accountable*. As Mary Warnock (writing when a member of the IBA) perceptively put it some years ago, *accountability* necessarily involves both a degree of power to impose sanctions and a general right to know. The BBC (and British broadcasting at large) acknowledge neither as far as the public are concerned; nor, at present, would they wish to do so.

Part of the central argument in what follows charts how, in that case, the BBC can revise the enormously complex system of accountability it has at the present time, and how it can argue, publicly, that is it indeed *accountable*. It is also an argument of this author that while the BBC should come much cleaner about what it is really trying to be (*responsible* and *responsive*) it ought to permit of Warnock's second category, the general right to know. This should apply to BBC employees across the board as well as to the rest of us. The new BBC Director-General, Michael Checkland, seems committed to a form of BBC *glasnost*. More internal communication, and a simplified management structure, along with financial autonomy, *and* accountability, have all figured prominently in his efforts to re-organise the corporation.

Setting the limits, at any one time, to that right to know, is properly the job of the BBC Board of Governors; managing the output is that of the Board of Management and the twain should complement each other but not be confused by either body. The power to impose sanction should remain with Parliament (not governments) and in that sense broadcasting (and not just the BBC) should be controlled, albeit loosely, by the central institutions of democracy.

The problem was that all this had become horribly confused. But, as has been argued throughout, this confusion was not unrelated to the growing confusions of British society at large. We seem to have lost our way while resolutely charging at full-tilt through the jungle in a direction set by a forceful, if cartographically ill-equipped, Government. In broadcasting, uncomfortable parallels to the larger confusions abound. To this can be added a feeling that technological change and the easy assumption that this automatically brings enlightenment is a danger in itself. For broadcasters, with their intertwining futures in those technologies, all this spells yet more uncertainty.

What follows, then, is an exposition of one part of modern broadcasting in Britain: the desire and intention to bring the audience a little closer to the programme makers. The degree of success is limited, as has already been suggested in part, by a confusion as to why the audience are consulted at all, and to what real end.

The book also examines one part of British broadcasting – Channel Four – that was set up (unusually, in law) to be different. It poses a model which the oldest part of the system, the BBC, arguably could usefully follow; whether that is an argument is indeed examined.

The BBC is, and remains, the heart of British broadcasting. It is true that it has been under fierce and, for it, most hurtfully *unfair* attack. It has defended itself, weakly but with a slowly growing belief that it still has a central purpose in British society. With that this author concurs. Indeed what the BBC has kept alive, in the dark days of the 1980s, is the cultural certainty that consensus, in developed democratic social systems, is better than conflict in ordering public affairs. If the BBC is remembered and respected for that alone, and kept going because of it, then its invention will have been worth while. All the evidence, however, suggests that it will be around long after current political and economic fads have been forgotten.

2 Origins

Engineers invented British broadcasting, not programme planners and makers. These men of wit and vision stamped one word firmly into the history of broadcasting in the UK, a word that has remained engraved especially in the heart of the BBC: quality. P. P. Eckersley, that much under-rated founder member of the BBC, says in *The Power Behind the Microphone* that ' "publicists" often say the creation of the BBC was a "far-sighted measure of sociological planning". In fact it was nothing of the sort; the BBC was formed as the expedient solution of a technical problem ... scarcity of wavelengths'.

Eckersley, whom Reith sacked for being involved in a divorce case, was much concerned about getting the service technically perfect so that listener could 'forget about the technique of the service'. He explained that three major problems were: (1) Elimination of interference; (2) Production of good quality (sound not programmes); and (3) removal of channel scarcity. This was a far cry from what later became the BBC's central guiding ethos – *programme* quality.

Engineering has remained apart from the programme side with its own training, codes and hierarchy. Engineers judge broadcasters by their own standards and they judge management too. With the onset of digital and other highly technical modern equipment engineering has become more arcane, not less, to the average programme maker. The technical control rooms in broadcasting studios and in transmitter halls are temples dedicated to the state of the art. Few have dared challenge engineering judgements. In the BBC the engineering departmental hierarchy has tended to be a law to itself; many at the top have been inside the Corporation since teenage; their loyalty is total, their own judgements – of Director-Generals for instance – absolute. Charles Curran, DG from 1969–76, was thought to have understood their problems; Hugh Greene, his immediate predecessor, did not. Reith, incidentally, had trained as an engineer.

Where did the audience come into this picture? The traditional view is that they were not so much cultivated as force-fed. Reith's own vision, best given in his early book, *Broadcast Over Britain* (1926) explains in great detail the plan he had for 'enlightening' the public with the wonderful technical means God had given him. But broadcasting as a medium needs to know in rather more detail than inspired piety provides whether anyone listens (and, later, watches) and from the start the BBC (Company) received letters both of approbation and attack. Reith was canny enough too, in quickly setting up a religious and an education advisory panel.

By 1926, when the BBC was still a company, not yet a public corporation, there were panels on spoken English and on music. Although Reith did not allow these committees much power (except the one on spoken English) he did, according to Briggs (1985), attach the utmost importance to their work. But, also according to Briggs (though the general evidence is overwhelming), 'Reith and those of his colleagues who shared his sense of mission were unimpressed by what became a seasonal round of newspaper polls which showed what the public "wanted"'.

Reith believed that radio could cater for minorities and that these, already to be numbered in tens if not hundreds of thousands, could be built upon. Broadcasting, in short, could draw people out and into fields and interests they might, left alone, have never discovered. Today this all looks dreadfully paternalistic, but it fitted – just and increasingly awkwardly – with the tone of the age.

The BBC was founded over that short period when ideas about a national culture based on a particular – and to us perhaps very narrow – consensus were pertinent (Middlemas, 1979; Scannel and Cardiff, 1977). It was also founded as a public corporation during a wave of enthusiasm for large central public bodies (culminating in the nationalisations of the late 1940s). It came to represent the best model, in many respects, though it grew simultaneously in the view of others to express the worst aspects of sizeable and monolithic bureaucracies.

All this cannot be separated from changing ideas about popular democracy, particularly in view of the international political climate between the two world wars. Democracy – meaning one adult, one vote – did not arrive in Britain until 1928; strictly speaking it did not come until 1949 when both the business and the university votes (allowing some people a second vote in general elections under certain conditions) were ended. In any case its meaning has changed so much since the Second World War it is now difficult to imagine the attitude of people living under 'democracy' in the UK in the 1920s. Class – social position – was much more rigid, although cracks were appearing in its fabric. Arguably it is still too important in the late 1980s: one of the hardest jibes for the BBC today to counter is that it is still overwhelmingly middle class, and thus espouses a single and

TABLE 2.1   *Principal Events in UK Broadcasting History*

1922   Broadcasts from Writtle.
       British Broadcasting Company set up.
       Licence fee set at 10 shillings.

1923   Sykes Committee recommends licence fee as means of financing
       BBC.

1924   One million radio licences.

1925   National radio technically possible.

1926   Crawford Committee recommends BBC set up as public corpora-
       tion.

1927   Baird television experiments begin.
       BBC Royal Charter for 10 years.

1929   (Prague Conference agrees international frequency allocation).

1931   Commercial radio broadcasts to Britain from France.

1933   Radio Luxembourg begins broadcasting to Britain.

1935   Selsdon Report on television service.
       Ullswater Committee begins work.

1936   Ullswater Committee report.
       BBC starts world's first continuous high definition television
       service (after Baird fails)

1937   Second BBC Charter for 10 years.

1939   BBC goes on to war footing; television service closes down.

1943   Hankey Report (on post-war funding of television).

1944   BBC voluntarily introduces '14-day rule'.

1946   BBC starts Third Programme (radio).
       BBC television service re-starts (with London victory parade).

1947   BBC Charter extended for five years.

1948   (Copenhagen Conference on frequency allocation).

1949   Beveridge Committee starts work.
       BBC television five year plan.

1951   Company formed to develop commercial television.
       Beveridge Committee Report.

1952   BBC Charter (4) for 10 years.
       One million television licences.

1954   Television Act: ITA set up.

1955   Commercial television starts.
       BBC VHF (FM) radio starts.

1957   14-day rule ends.

1959   Worst-ever BBC television share figures.

1960	Pilkington Committee starts work.
	BBC experiments with local radio.
1962	Pilkington Committee Report.
	ITV national coverage completed.
	BBC Charter extended for two years.
1964	Pirate radio stations start.
	Television Act.
	BBC2 starts.
	BBC Charter for 10 years.
	Clean Up television campaign starts (Whitehouse).
1967	First BBC local radio station (Leicester).
	Suppression of (most) pirate radio stations.
1968	Colour television begins (BBC).
1969	ITV colour television starts.
1972	IBA set up; to oversee Independent local radio as well as ITV.
1973	Commercial (local) radio begins.
1975	Parliamentary radio broadcast experiment begins.
1977	Annan Committee Report.
1982	Broadcasting Act.
	BBC Charter for 15 years (?).
	Fourth channel starts.
1982	Report on cable television (Hunt Report).
	Report on direct broadcasting by satellite (Part Report).
1985	Peacock Committee Report.
1988	Government announces three national commercial radio networks to be set up.
	Commercial television franchises to be sold off.

singular view of the world and its works, a *Weltanschauung* at variance with mainstream reality.

Although it is true that this 'middle-class bias' is inevitable to public bodies like the BBC, and although it is true that middle-class professionals may well have as good an idea as any that what they do, or provide, is good for everyone, the paternalism that this equally inevitably implies sits uneasily with current populist thinking. The BBC is an easy target here too, because its output is aimed at the entire audience, working class and middle class, young and old. The middle-class character of the organisation cannot easily be separated from its output, however universal its appeal. This matters rather more for the BBC than for the many other organisations for which it is undoubtedly true because the BBC intrudes into everyone's home.

The strenuous efforts made in recent years to remove from the air the 'BBC voice' are potent witness to the recognition that both class and education in more traditional sense have to be abandoned if the BBC is to hold both the new middle ground and about half of its audience, as well as trying to keep a regional balance. (The southern bias of the BBC – if it exists – is of course part of the 1980s debate about the 'two nations' of North and South but it has always been a problem for the BBC.)

The significance of broadcasting, and thus its public prominence, was recognised more or less from the beginning of the BBC as a public corporation. That corporation was the result of the deliberations of the Crawford Committee, meeting in 1926, which thought the BBC already to be in charge of something of great educational and social significance. The Committee considered that: 'We are deeply conscious of the magnitude of the issues involved, – not merely as regards their scientific or mechanical aspects, but still more in relation to their ultimate impact on the education and temperament of the country'.

This had been expressed slightly differently, but no less fervently by the Sykes Committee, three years earlier. 'It may be', they had opined, 'that broadcasting holds social and political possibilities as great as any technical attainment of our generation.' They had gone on to say that broadcasting was clearly of great educative value. Before the first Royal Charter had made it manifest then, the BBC was perceived by many as a kind of educational institute of the air, a forerunner of the Open University. Entertainment was mentioned but almost, one feels, *en passant*. And in the climate of the 1920s education was something your elders and betters instructed you upon, not asked how you felt about.

In taking this road the BBC lost a portion of its audience, if indeed it ever had them. They were the listeners who were to turn to commercial radio, after it arrived in the 1930s, in great numbers. Such has been the dominance of the BBC in the early history of British broadcasting that only relatively recently has a re-assessment of the history of broadcasting enabled a better (if still incomplete) understanding of the significance of the early commercial radio broadcasts to the UK, beginning in 1931 and continuing until the Second World War.

Those early transmitters were located in northern France but the audiences lay in southern England. Radio Normandie catered for the listener from the start – the casual 'low-brow'. Its real triumphs came on Sundays when Reith's monstrous and cold Presbyterian personality settled like a pall of winter on the schedules. When Radio Luxembourg joined Normandie in 1933 with a much more powerful transmitter the BBC became seriously worried. Competition, often vaunted as a latter-day problem for the Corporation, has in fact been around from most of its life. The crucial question in the pre-war period is were the listeners served or not? Curran and Seaton (1986) argue that perhaps the BBC, for all its high-flown talk of education and enlightenment, did the job rather well: by 1934, they say, the BBC was broadcasting more vaudeville and light music than any other European station, although they do not say on what their data are based.

Certainly the BBC did not believe it was failing in its avowed task of education. Much of the resistance to any systematic form of audience research was founded upon a sincere belief that such research would inevitably dictate programme policies. As early as 1930 the Programme Board had discussed the possibility of research. But there were outbreaks of real disdain. One BBC employee said that with listener research the real degradation of the BBC was to begin – we know what listeners *like*, said this same wit, 'the red-nosed comedian and the Wurlitzer organ' (reported in Briggs, 1985).

Nevertheless the BBC had reported to the Sykes Committee that:

The Company frequently invite expressions of opinion from listeners, and receives thousands of communications in response. We are informed that on the last occasion of the kind 78 per cent of the letters showed that the writers were satisfied; 20 per cent expressed the opinion that there should be more or less of some particularly class of matter; and two per cent were condemnatory.

Briggs suggests that interest in listener habits grew slowly which seems to be at odds with this comment. From the late 1920s onward, as the total audience grew at a phenomenal rate (based on the numbers of licences taken out) the BBC took an increasingly close interest in who was listening. The Programme Correspondence Section, answering listeners' letters, was started in 1924. Letters were acknowledged with 'punctilious' care – a tradition which continues to this day. In 1927 the BBC was getting 50 000 letters a year (it is now estimated to total several million). Most of these early letters praised the BBC. There have been persistent themes among protest letters. Current incumbents of the BBC (or any other broadcast) letters department will not be surprised to learn that bad language and any reference to vivisection excited the most angry response 60 years ago.

By the mid-1930s, with a huge national audience but also with growing commercial competition, the BBC finally decided to start an audience research department. Robert Silvey was appointed to run it in 1936. He left his stamp on BBC audience research until well into the eighties. The BBC was, of course, not so interested in audience *size* as in audience attitudes to programmes. Silvey set up daily surveys and 'Listening panels'. The BBC had also appointed a General Advisory Committee in 1935 – much like the House of Lords in composition. Advisory Councils continued to increase in number. When the Ullswater Committee came to report on the BBC in 1935, there were in total 27 of them. Many were regional variations on the central theme. Thus, apart from the central religion council, there were six regional councils as well; similarly for adult education, where there were seven.

The Ullswater Committee, which included Attlee, were worried by the middle-class bias of these advisers:

> Our concern as to the composition of the Advisory Committees is derived from an interest which we regard as vital – the benefit of listeners ... We are anxious to secure representation for the views of the general public as well as of experts in each category of broadcast subject – the views, that is to say, not only of recognised leaders in their respective professions ... but also of listeners, not only of public speakers but of their audiences, not only of the older, but of the younger generation ... etc.

Part of the implication here is that all advisory councils should have some lay members. This has still not been fully implemented in one vital respect: the struggle to get more young people and fully paid-up members of the working class on many of the present councils continues.

The development of programme policies remained closely guarded inside the corporate heartland. Categorisations of the audience into 'bundles' reached apotheosis with the division of the BBC's radio output after the Second World War into the three services of Home, Light and Third. William Haley, the Director-General, in introducing this system, explained that there were indeed three categories of listener: the high, middle and low brow, for which these networks had been designed. People, even in the post-war euphoria of socialist democracy, were still to have a place – and to know it.

Haley, an opinionated self-made man, a journalist who went on from the BBC to edit *The Times*, was convinced in his own fashion that by dividing the BBC into three he would be giving the public what it wanted. But the most damaging outcome for the BBC was that by diverting scarce post-war money into a third national radio network Haley had to neglect the nascent but expensive television service. His decision ensured that the best television people began to look elsewhere for a future; the emerging commercial television lobby got one of its biggest fillips when BBC staff of the calibre of Norman Collins and Ian Orr-Ewing despaired of any future in the BBC and left to join the burgeoning lobby for 'independent' television.

But in the mid-1940s the BBC was facing another problem: the whole question of its monopoly. In the contemporary political and social climate this became a major issue. State monopoly was beginning to be feared by many; media monopoly more so. The first Royal Press Commission had a brief to examine this in the Press; the Beveridge Committee, enquiring into the BBC, came to see the question of the BBC's monopoly as the main issue.

Beveridge, who had felt himself slighted by the BBC because he had not been invited to contribute to the Wordsworth centenary, became personally convinced that a centralised monopoly could and did operate a 'blacklist' of people it did not want on the air. The political opposition, the heavily-defeated Conservative Party, also seized upon the BBC as an example of the dangers of State control. The Labour Government had tightened controls after the war as the sterling crisis deepened. Labour ministers used the BBC to 'sell' policies via the agreement with the corporation over what were known as 'ministerials'.

These short broadcasts carried no automatic right of reply by the Opposition, unlike party political broadcasts, and the Labour Government was making about one 'ministerial' every three weeks by 1947, occasioning great alarm amongst Conservatives who also saw, however, an opportunity to compare the Labour Government with the Soviets. This image, also picked upon by George Orwell in *1984*, was of a Stalinist propaganda machine. Although, forty years on, some of the rhetoric looks faintly ridiculous, at the time what it was describing was all too real. It was that a monopoly broadcasting organisation was open to abuse by governments – by the State – and that it was, in the context of post-war Europe, doubly dangerous. The Nazis had captured broadcasting; the Soviet Union had never let it go. In Britain the austerity of the post-war settlement under a radical government was matched by what was increasingly judged to be BBC arrogance – which many thought under the control of the Left.

For the audience the BBC was simply remote: the enormous growth of broadcasting as an institution before and especially during the war; its importance as a means of disseminating news and ideas (and ideology) – all this created a feeling that the BBC was not just out of touch, it was becoming untouchable. Audiences, as the general public, have been mostly ignored in these debates (witness the promise by Government of a 'great debate' over cable development in the 1980s.)

When the commercial television lobby began in earnest it set up a Popular Television Association – countered by the National Television Council. There is precious little evidence that either ever had any real public support, or sought it. Christopher Mayhew, who helped found the NTC, admits that it was a public relations device to get information into the Press. Because the public is hardly ever (in any meaningful way) consulted about broadcasting – especially the eventual decision to allow commercial television – it is very hard to establish what public 'mood' existed. But commercial television was popular when it came and audiences flocked to it.

Having had a monopoly of the audience for such a long time, the BBC were now to find the pain of loss unbearable. It was becoming plain by the end of the 1950s that the BBC was institutionally moribund and that the mass audience was apparently firmly wedded to ITV. The BBC, said one staff member of the time, was run by a gang of old men. They would talk a little about a problem and then walk down Portland Place to their club for lunch. There was no sense of urgency. The loss to the BBC, brought on by competition, had been two-fold, first, simply in terms of numbers and the unpopularity of BBC output. BBC television was staid, stale and stuffy in the 1950s; radio was in what appeared at the time to be terminal decline. Second, the BBC itself had an image of that same remote, stuffy establishment senility that was to bring down so many public personae, and so many public institutions, in the 1960s.

What changed the BBC was its recovery of an audience and this also led to its current problems. But it is hard to imagine how else the BBC could have changed in any way in order to have got back the critical 40–50 per cent of audience it believed it needed to justify the continuance of the licence fee as a universally levied tax. All the old fears of original sin flood in at this point for, so the argument goes, once you introduce competition for audiences you have inevitably brought public service broadcasting into the market place. Gresham's Law – the bad driving out the good – begins to operate with a vengeance. But audiences had dropped to disastrous levels.

By 1960 the BBC was getting regularly only 30 per cent of the national audience; on several occasions this dropped to a paltry 27 per cent per week. The incoming Director-General, Hugh Greene, was faced with having to reverse this. Later, he says, this amounted to a determination on his part that the BBC would, as he put it, throw open the windows and let in a breath of fresh air. The coming of BBC2 in 1964 helped this process by giving the Corporation a second channel on which it could experiment.

The effect of Greene's management style was to encourage in television the same iconoclastic outpourings of youth which external contemporaries were about to unleash at large on British society. BBC television did not entirely lead Britain into the swinging sixties but it was in the van for once. Programmes like *That Was The Week That Was* were watched by millions as well as appealing to cult minorities and they helped to shape the attitude people brought to television.

The onset of television satire, along with well-remembered drama series like *The Wednesday Play*, and various near-the-knuckle comedies, led to the emergence of the first real consumer broadcast lobby, Mrs Mary Whitehouse's National Viewers and Listeners Association (NVALA). It was typical of the prevailing attitude in broadcasting that she was banned from appearing on BBC television, and by Greene himself. Hugh Greene has been lauded by many commentators as a 'saviour' of the BBC and its version of public service broadcasting.

Irrespective of programme output, and Greene's personal impact upon it, the BBC had already received paeans of praise from the Pilkington Committee, reporting in 1962. The BBC gained as much as anything from being contrasted by the Committee with the young and brash ITV. Compared with the first commercial programme companies the BBC could only appear to be a highly responsive and serious-minded broadcasting organisation. Its mode of address in its dealings with the Committee was equally circumspect while ITV, including even the ITA, appeared hell-bent on antagonising.

It is questionable, looking back, as to how far Greene's regime drove down the barriers of public taste well below what the majority audience would have chosen themselves. This lowering of the barriers to what is acceptable continues to this day, although in some areas of television they have been re-erected. This issue is central to accountability.

ITV has always been regulated by Act of Parliament, leading to a potentially more restrictive regime – enforced by a nervous ITA (subsequently IBA). Satire came late to commercial television in the UK for this reason. The BBC has had the additional and vital freedoms implied by the Royal Charter. Greene, in some respects, was the first to capitalise on them. As the sixties wore on he was of course following, not leading, the iconoclasms of 'swinging London', although some of the first prompting came through broadcasting.

Television producers and managers argue that they are highly responsive to public taste and do not attempt to override it. What they do is to nudge the audience towards listening to and watching programmes in which their prejudices are challenged. There is no doubt that there is pressure through playrights and drama producers to push to the limits, on more than odd occasions, what audiences will find tolerable. There is no easy answer here. British broadcasting reflects British culture. The 1960s saw massive fractures in the fabric of what had become an over-stuffy society still obsessed with past glories, wrapped in the fabric of social class. But these fractures had already appeared in British society after the Second World War and during the loss of the Empire.

Changes there had to be and the BBC's own programmes became part of the message. Few would want now to return to the hypocrisies of the 1950s, although there were apparent stabilities as well. At the same time the opening of windows, undertaken with such insouciance by Hugh Greene's men, has led to much agonising over the effects of television on, for instance, young people. It has led to the partially successful efforts of Mrs Whitehouse in getting the question of censorship back on the political agenda, even to the point where senior cabinet ministers appear to embrace it. Broadcasters have been accused of irresponsibility because they failed in the past to recognise that television might just be having more of an impact than mere vaudeville.

The greatest irony over what happened to the BBC in the 1960s was that the opening of windows was never intended to allow the public directly to express a view: even in the 1960s they were perceived as passive witnesses to the wonders of the box. Producers by and large did not expect audiences to bite back; hence the opprobrium heaped on Mrs Whitehouse's head.

The audience was regained for the BBC; by the end of the decade it was regularly 'winning' the weekly share game (albeit that with two channels it had a natural advantage). At the same time it was still distant with its audience. It is possible to speculate this was as much to do with the nature of television as anything. Television by the 1960s had become a massive industry with huge overheads. It worked on a kind of ersatz Hollywood star system where the public were allowed to gawp in awe at whatever new television personality was thrust at them. Radio had had its personalities but, as the 1970s were to re-discover, it had a personal touch television could not reach – perhaps can never reach.

Winning the audience back worked for the BBC but at a bigger price than expected. What Hugh Greene and his executives and producers developed was a theory of professionalism: that is, public service broadcasting as conceived by Reith had to give way to a new definition. That definition was that the only reason for having the BBC was that it understood public taste and responded to it (rather than was led by it). The nature of that response was professionalism.

The model that came to dominate was that of journalism. The BBC adopted for its general programming a view that went like this: What are good programmes? What we understand them to be – viewed from our professional eyries. The audience, under this system, was given what it wanted but in a laundered fashion. There were inevitable middle-class assumptions here too but larded with the sixties style of irreverent superficiality.

Of course, to describe a gigantic broadcasting organisation in such general terms is to invite immediate retort: But what about . . .? The BBC made many good programmes during this time. If an irreverence ruled at Television Centre, egged on by Broadcasting House, there were also producers who made stunning social documentaries like 'Cathy Come Home'.

The underlying problem, not obvious at the time, was that by shifting the philosophic basis of the BBC from the absolute values of the Reithian system, the mandarins of the sixties let in value-relativism. Everything, potentially, was up for discussion, including our system of broadcasting. It is possible to argue that this had already been challenged successfully by the breaking of the monopoly in 1955. But ITV, although popular with the mass audience, had been much berated by the Pilkington Committee in 1962 and was beginning to reform itself. In any case, unfairly perhaps, ITV has always been let off the values hook by being commercially financed. The BBC had assiduously espoused values as part of its bedrock. For nigh on twenty years few have challenged internally what those values might be. As an example of this, by the 1980s fewer and fewer senior management meetings had agenda items asking fundamental 'purpose' questions. They were far too busy looking at the accounts.

Audiences might well have begun to return to the BBC had the latter merely tinkered with programme policies, not effectively thrown them out. But Greene was an iconoclast, a kind of Reithian in reverse. The threat may have been an ITV taking all the audience (unlikely though that ever was) but Greene used it to de-construct the BBC. Reith, still alive at that time, may have understood this. He first rather liked Greene; later, he could not bear him.

The 1970s were a period of relative calm in broadcasting. Although punctuated by the deliberations of the Annan Committee, the turbulence of technological and political controversy which has characterised the 1980s was missing. For the BBC, audience levels for television remained satisfyingly high. And with the slow but sure growth of BBC local radio, as well as the discovery of the networks by a new generation of radio listeners, all seemed well. As Radio One regularly took the honours as the most listened-to radio station, the BBC could relax.

Yet hindsight would suggest that the 1970s were uneasy times. The Annan Committee, much ignored in its elaborate and messy conclusions, did point to problems soon to appear for all broadcasting. In describing the cosiness of what they called the 'duopoly' they unconsciously drew attention to its over-neat parcelling up, cartelisation, of broadcasting and its audiences. A growing mood of agitation was saying that radio was not local enough (a still unresolved issue) and that, at least for producers outside the programme companies and the BBC, there was simply no real work available. The corporate video had yet to develop; as indeed, had the surge of ownership of video cassette recorders. Cable too, was an unknown quantity; even more so, direct satellite broadcasting.

The first big change came with Channel Four, as it happened, disposed finally by a Conservative Government of a markedly radical view. William Whitelaw, at the time Home Secretary, effectively cashed all his political chips in getting it set up as it finally was. When the BBC came up for discussion, much later, he was powerless to defend it from repeated attack, as also from the vagaries of the Peacock Committee.

Channel Four has posed a central challenge merely by being the youngest service in British television. It is no accident that it wants to believe that its audience profile is heavily weighted to the younger age groups, a result of deliberate programme policies from within the channel. (In fact this weighting is not real: its audience profile matches the other three channels – most people watch it some of the time.)

The recovery of the audience, perhaps its re-discovery, has in part been effected through Channel Four. There is also a recognition that what audiences want, what they will accept, is growing more and more apart from what broadcasters continue to offer. The onset of a vastly increased choice may finally make this clear.

Channel Four has its own problems, however, where audiences are concerned. Not least among them is the degree to which a small company like Channel Four can genuinely take account, in any other than the most superficial way, of what audiences want. The channel uses pressure groups as its primary focus in this respect, the second level of a two-step flow of communication, removed from the audience proper. But these pressure groups represent pressures, not people, and although Channel Four had built up strong loyalties six years into its life, its original purposes are being lost in the daily pragmatics of scheduling and programme making.

There *is* a two-way process going on, though. Broadcasters have been able to assume that, as far as audiences go, what they have offered as accountability, however jejune, has been out of the goodness of their, the broadcasters', hearts. For many years, possibly overawed by the sheer technological mastery of the airwaves, the bulk of the public accepted it. The apparent passivity of an audience sitting at home, tired after a day's work, may also have added to this. But as technology enters the home, as its mysteries devolve into the video cassette recorder, as that same technology offers choice, so the public begin to ask consumer questions about output, about content – and about control. Indeed, modern technology aims to give them control, through the vcr, the remote button, through massive channel choice delivered via cable or satellite.

Another factor enters the equation, altering the balance between BBC broadcaster and audience for all time: money. As the natural increase in licence revenue bottoms out to a constant sum so the BBC has to rely more and more on the public's willingness to pay. The BBC recognised this in 1979 when it went public for the first time on the licence fee campaign. In effect it asked the licence payer to accept the accounts – and by implication the programme policies on which those accounts rested. As it happens, more and more programme makers are beginning to ask what their relationship is with their audiences. The public are no longer willing to accept the pure dictates of broadcasters – or anyone else. Evidence is growing of a kind of moral turpitude among some broadcasters when it comes to setting programmes against truth. The public mechanisms of accountability have grown.

Fuelled in this area at least by the Annan Committee, itself worried deeply both by the impact of television and by the apparent lack of control (including self-control) exercised within the broadcasting industry, various means have been employed by broadcasters to give semblance to listening to the public, along with some genuine attempts at feedback. Feedback programmes, public meetings, more advisory groups and a better use of them, all contributed to a re-discovery of the audience, along with – most important of all – an apparent determination by broadcastings' managers, at least in the BBC, to re-align their central relationship with the general public. This public (not necessarily the same as an 'audience') is being asked to accept the BBC on different terms – carrying great dangers for the corporation, incidentally.

But while the BBC may talk of shareholders – may even come to believe it – the very idea of a mass audience is being challenged all the time. Technology undermines schedules; audiences, ever more sophisticated about what they want, and when they want it, do the rest. In Channel Four, with its knowledge of the small audiences it aims to get for most programmes, this is less a problem. For the BBC, believing as it still does, fiercely, that it has to retain around a 40–45 per cent minimum mass audience to be viable, the problem grows.

3 Theory and Practices

'... the Secretary of State ... may from time to time ...'

It is the underlying assumption in Britain that broadcasters are free to do what they want – apart from constraints under the law. Thus broadcasters may be sued for defamation, may commit contempt of court, can incur penalties under the Official Secrets Act. Broadcasters and journalists have no additional legal rights to those of members of the public; they do enjoy certain custom and practice privileges, in Parliament, in local authority meetings, in the courts.

Broadcasting, as it happens, was born on a tide of extraordinary caution and restriction. Since the 1920s there has been a slow and not always clear-cut shift towards greater freedom. Sometimes broadcasters have shot themselves spectacularly in the foot as did the BBC when it voluntarily agreed in 1944 that it would not broadcast any matter likely to come up for discussion in Parliament in the following two weeks. The '14-Day Rule' stayed in force 'voluntarily' for more than a decade; the BBC Caversham archive is littered with letters sent back and forth between the BBC and politicians. The BBC of course was trying to argue a way out. Needless to say, having been handed such a plum example of self-censorship politicians fought with great tenacity and cunning to keep the rule in force.

Naiveté like this cost the BBC dearly. Broadcasting, and television especially, is a politician's dream; it is also his nightmare. The ambivalence of the relationship is everywhere to be seen and heard. On the one hand politicians fondly believe that if only they had unrestricted access to microphone or camera they could convince the electorate of their worth; on the other they know with a politician's instinct that in a democracy to have such total access and thereby control, is to destroy the credibility they crave.

The result is the daily battle for the hearts and minds of broadcasters and through them audiences, the general public. The struggle revolves around the constant whingeing by politicians that they are not treated fairly. Hence their ludicrous clinging to party political broadcasts flying their unrestrictedly partisan flags in the face of overwhelming evidence that the audience finds these broadcasts among the least palatable of all the output. But broadcasters are not innocents in this game. Their desire is for good radio or television. To suggest that their business is entrapment is to go too far but it would perhaps be fair to suggest that they do want to see politicians act out pre-set dramas. 'Professionally' this is known as 'good broadcasting'.

Both sides might be accused of wilfully failing to understand although it can be difficult to disentangle the truth of the sometimes excessive remarks made on both sides about the motives of the other. More probably neither side perceives what radio or television, as media, may do to the political process. Indeed, this is at the heart of a constantly problematic relationship in democracies, for no one appears to have tried to assess whether broadcasting makes a material difference to politics. Can extended serious current affairs output contend with the growing entertainment output except, ludicrously, to mimic it?

Formally, broadcasters *are* accountable to Parliament. That is where the BBC and the IBA report each year. Parliament (and through it ministers of the Crown) has absolute power to do what it will with broadcasting in the UK. Again formally, the fact that it does not in general overtly try to influence broadcasting except through Acts of Parliament, fully debated, is a part of what democracy means. So when Leon Brittan wrote to the BBC to suggest that their film of two extremists in Northern Ireland would, if shown, be against the national interest, he transgressed an admittedly unwritten rule. His transgression may have contributed to his eventual loss of job. (For the full story of this incident see Chapter 9.)

In practice formal accountability is not the key; as with so much in the British Constitution reality and power lie elsewhere, in the informal structure. There we find a continuous struggle between broadcasters and politicians.

There is an important difference between the two parts of the British broadcasting 'system'. The BBC is governed by Royal Charter guaranteeing its rights and specifying its duties. Over time these duties have multiplied – the requirement to provide increasing numbers of advisory bodies, for example. Nevertheless the BBC has a permissive existence. The commercial sector is controlled by an Act of Parliament. Acts are restrictive on the whole, telling people what they may *not* do. The reason for this considerable difference between the IBA and the BBC is that when commercial television was mooted it was decided that in order to curb what were thought to be its likely excesses a tighter regulatory rein was needed.

The original Act has been much amended, most recently to take

account of the very different arrangements planned for Channel
Four, and for planned developments in both cable and direct satellite
broadcasting. It remains the case, however, that the IBA does in
theory operate in a much more controlled environment. Although
politicians require access to all broadcast media they have always
concentrated their maximum efforts behind the scenes on subverting
the BBC (this is not, I believe, too strong a word to describe the
process).

There are a number of reasons for this. First, the BBC is centrally
organised and located. It runs national networks as well as regional
and local services. Second, it has frequently described itself as the
national instrument of broadcasting and has been keen to point this
out to all and sundry. And so officially it continues to be, a salience
which suggests that whatever else may happen to it, it will not cease
to be the primary broadcasting organisation in the country. At the
same time the BBC has become more coy about the relevance of
being designated the 'national instrument of broadcasting'. Third, it
has maintained a high prestige. It manages, although less obviously
than in the past, to exude a mystique, a fainter and fainter perfume of
real power, born from its heady days as the unchallenged doyen of
broadcasting services. MPs almost certainly still prefer to appear on
the BBC, although ITN's *News at Ten* and *Channel Four News* must
now run it close seconds.

The regional structure of ITV also stands in the way of its being
perceived as the more important service to be seen on although this
does not apply to the News. The regional structure is even more true
of local radio, both commercial and BBC, although the trade-off here
is that individual MPs can talk most easily to their local constituents.
The result may be a perception of the local and national broadcast
system but little appreciation of the regional.

Finally, and how important is this factor is hard to determine, the
BBC plays the same kind of institutional power game as does
Westminster: the BBC likes to believe it is close to the centres of
power – in the absence, one can surmise, of having money-making as
an institutional goal. This is demonstrated by BBC officials in
explaining how easily they could be put through to Number 10
Downing Street and is similar to the senior Fleet Street journalist's
boast about how many private telephone numbers he or she has of
VIPs.

If politics is the art of the possible broadcasting provides – or seems
to provide – new possibilities of power, of influence, of legitimation.

Its technology confers the latter in a frame which listeners and viewers assimilate as reality. Politicians, governments, all of the state apparatuses, have realised the potency of a technology which enables an individual to speak simultaneously to a whole population. From the beginning of broadcasting, then, the means of its organisation and accountability have been of the greatest concern to Government and to the whole political system.

Until very recently European political systems have had the perfect 'neutral' device at hand to help them maintain a grip on broadcasting: frequency shortages. This technological imperative has international overtones reaching across the world. Successive British governments from the mid-thirties, have been able to say their hands were tied by international agreement, not domestic expedient. The BBC has been prepared to go along with this in order to obstruct, in particular, commercial radio. It consistently produced data in the 1960s which purported to show that any extension of the number of radio stations was impossible. What they did not reveal were the engineering assumptions built in. More recently the potential onset of frequency glut has created a dilemma for the Conservative Government who have ostensibly wished to authorise community radio. The frequency argument no longer applicable, the new wisdom was until 1988 that such stations would be unable to police their own airwaves, relying as they must on amateur broadcasters who, it is suggested, would lard the air with obscenities and incitements and, more seriously, contempts prejudicial to trials. Although there may some truth in this it is equally possible to see the underlying concern to be one of Government control – or lack of it – over the airwaves. Nevertheless, the Government, late in 1988, agreed to authorise the first 26 community radio stations.

But there have been other means used to maintain forms of political control on broadcasting. The most important of these has been the concept of 'balance', a term which has been taken to mean a strict reflection of the two-party system of British government. This has of course been challenged by the emergence of fringe nationalist parties in Scotland, Wales and, most awkwardly, Northern Ireland; and by the growth of Liberal, latterly SDP and Alliance and now Democrat support. This last development has posed a different order of problem as it is not inconceivable that a coalition may form part of, if not a whole, future Government.

Balance has indeed been used to inform more than just party politics. It has been used in the structuring of the whole system: as a direct restriction on programme output (Channel Four have had continuous problems with the IBA, as opposed to the Broadcasting Act, on this question); between public service and commercial impetus; between centre and periphery; professionalism and accountability; integrity (of broadcasting) and access.

None of this suggests that broadcasting in the UK does not operate within a framework organised to enhance certain kinds of freedom but it is to suggest there is a considerable area of grey in which definitions are unclear, under attack from one side or another. The political arena is the most critical, far more important to both the BBC and the IBA (and by extension, eventually, even to Channel Four) than any individual member of the public, or any collectivity, any pressure group or lobby.

Because broadcasting is a central part of the political process primary accountability is implicit in the working arrangements between broadcasters and politicians. It is for this reason, among others, that both sides get so upset when they perceive the 'rules' to have been broken. The same applies to broadcasters, when MPs try to debate programme 'content' in terms of the incumbent Government acting on it in some way; and politicians when they believe that the BBC (in particular) has transgressed the line on balance – such as over its coverage of South Africa (in 1986). The system of broadcasting may be likened to a continuum: closest to the central political processes lies the management of the BBC; further away the IBA. Programme makers swing closer and further away depending on their output. Current affairs producers may find a pressure exerted almost continuously at one level: mundanely, to have a spokesman from each of the main parties on a topic; more controversially, senior editors may be under a different, longer-term pressure to ensure 'balance'. This pressure is likely to be well internalised by now. Part of the problematic area of the socialisation which goes on in British broadcasting – and especially in the BBC – is the extent to which rules are incorporated into an individual's belief system. Broadcasting of necessity enforces a constant time restriction. Unless ideas like balance can be made effectively a part of a producer's moral code then trouble will not be far away.

At senior levels too there will, on many political issues, be direct pressure from the main parties exercised by telephone calls and by a constant, trickling form of lobbying through lunches, suppers, cocktail parties, asides at meetings. The BBC is in the political arena in every sense. Its past demonstrates – some would say this was the problem – how well corporate wisdom kept the BBC safe in these shark infested waters. It has, however, relied upon its internalised instincts to ensure that its finest unassailable defence is political 'impartiality' – a term which has come to replace the cruder concept of 'balance'. Alas that the 1980s, in the re-definition of politics into combative form, have dictated that balance itself should emerge as a highly political idea, even as new political parties.

Broadcasters may be too easily seen by outsiders as victims in these processes, constantly under threat. Yet they have great residual power: they set the agenda, they edit the tapes; they schedule. To politicians this can look like a great amount of freedom. The belief that broadcasting is also highly influential is also a factor here. Broadcasters and politicians are in agreement that the medium is powerful, whatever research evidence there might be to the contrary.

The area where politicians have had most impact has been at policy level: they can change the arrangements and the relationships; they can move key personnel under the system of patronage which enables prime ministers to appoint governors to the BBC, members to the IBA. In previous research I spent some time examining how this had worked in practice. Certain curiosities came to light. Principally, it has been Conservative governments which have been responsible for what I categorised as 'nodal' decision-taking in broadcast policy.

A Conservative government had introduced the BBC; permitted commercial television and commercial radio; finally introduced Channel Four, planned for cable and, in 1985, permitted the public to tune satellite dishes to pick up any DBS signal they could locate. Labour governments by contrast have tinkered, dealing more with personnel and with paper than with hard change. Similarly with the enquiries into broadcasting. Of the eight major ones so far (including Selsdon and Peacock) Conservative governments have ordered four (I exclude Ullswater under this heading although the National Government was dominated by the Conservative party; the Labour party have ordered two, but one (Beveridge) was initiated after pressure was brought to bear through the Conservatives in Parliament; back-bench Tory MPs had wanted an enquiry effectively from the end of the Second World War.

It is worth asking why this should be so. In the period under question Conservative governments have been more in evidence; in those 63 years there have been Labour governments for 20 years, National governments or coalitions for 15 years; Conservative governments for 28 years. But this is not an overwhelming difference;

until 1979 there was a rough balance. There have always been accidental factors in the way broadcasting policy has been made: technical changes, international pressures; more importantly, domestically, defence pressures. To keep a domestic electronics industry alive and well in the 1950s for instance, commercial television was permitted, ensuring that the Japanese invasion (then not even on the horizon) was kept at bay for a further decade.

The Labour party has tended to be in government at times when broadcasting is going through a settled phase. In the very early days, in the 1920s, the Liberal party was in decline, the Labour party still flexing its national political muscles. The formation of the BBC suited the Labour party as it appeared to represent an ideal type of nationalised body and more likely to espouse socialism under the imperative of balance. Later, the Labour Government of 1950 was already dying when Beveridge recommended far-reaching devolution as a solution to the BBC's monolithic centralism. In the 1960s Wilson's governments were over-extended on the economic front; the introduction of BBC local radio, in return for the BBC starting Radio One as a successor to pirate radio, merely reflected the conclusions of the Pilkington Committee. Finally, although it was a Wilson government which ordered the Annan Committee enquiry, once the report was delivered vacillation in the Home Office made certain it would be a Conservative government which disposed of the fourth television channel, although this was an 'accident' of the electorate in 1979.

Description alone does not help to explain the dominance of the Conservative party in the central decision-taking process of broadcasting policy (neither does Whitelaw's throwaway remark to the author during an interview for earlier research, that it is all down to 'denationalisation'). One hypothesis has been that broadcasting policy may best be understood, other than superficially, as the exercise of influence over two forms of consensus: what I have called elsewhere the contingent and the absolute. The former is constantly fought over and is the stuff of everyday politics; the latter consists in those values certain kinds of society will generally adhere to because they represent a kind of social bottom line. Of course these two may come into question, as indeed may – some would say already has – the whole notion of consensus.

The assumptions to be made are that broadcasting does have an impact at the level of social values, and that the Conservative party is somehow aware of that in a way that the Labour party is not. From

TABLE 3.1　*Main broadcast committees of inquiry*

Committee chairman	Dates of meetings	Report date	Recommendation	Result
Sykes	1923	1923	Licence fee as revenue	Agreed
Crawford	1926	1926	BBC as public corporation	Agreed
Selsdon		1935	BBC should develop television	Agreed
Ullswater		1936	Party political broadcasts should be allowed	Agreed
Beveridge	1949–51	1951	BBC should be regionalised	Not implemented
Pilkington	1960–62	1962	BBC to get third television channel	Agreed (BBC2 1964)
Annan	1974–77		Numerous but C4 should be 'publisher'	Agreed (eventually) but most of report ignored
Peacock	1986	1986	British broadcasting should move to 'consumer sovereignty'	Being implemented

archival evidence in Conservative Central Office and elsewhere it is clear Conservatives have long thought broadcasting to be an important technology for the propagandising of their view. Conservative Central Office were the first to train personnel in television interview techniques. The BBC, unconsciously or not, took part in another crucial element in much Conservative thinking, namely the concept of One Nation. What better way to demonstrate that idea than through the nationally co-ordinated broadcasting processes of the BBC?

Conservative governments have used broadcasting, and continue to do so, in order to develop ideas about their general policy. Thus the coming of commercial television was linked quite openly with the heralded onset of consumerism and twenty years later Edward Heath was able to develop themes around the need to revitalise business, especially small business, parallel to a policy on commercial radio. And now Channel Four helps to develop small businesses, albeit this time within the industry, while showing in its performance the exercise of Thatcherist economic constraints, market economy accounting *and* diversity of output (by providing another kind of market place).

Cable and satellite policies are designed with the same outcome in mind. They also, it is said, offer 'choice', which has come to have a mystical significance within the Right of British politics similar to balance within broadcasting. At the same time the second Conservative Government of Mrs Thatcher apparently walks an awkward protectionist path in trying to get direct broadcast satellites engineered under British specifications. This is perfectly consistent with Conservative party philosophy, if apparently inconsistent with their public position.

All of this points to a close understanding by the Conservative party that broadcasting is important, very important, to the political system not just because of its coverage of politics but because it also 'sells' social values. In terms of attitudes towards broadcasting, and the BBC in particular, the general rule has been broad Conservative party support. That this was lost at Westminster in the mid-1980s, certainly in large part, is due to the fissure between what the new Right have been able to determine as central Conservative party ideology, against the old values of the BBC, many of which were conservative in tone and outlook.

Conservative MPs are not unanimous. For instance in 1986 there were probably three groups differing considerably over what they wanted to do about broadcasting: about a third felt that the BBC should continue as it was, including finance through the licence fee. A further third, many among the intake in 1979 and especially 1983, believed that the BBC should in some way be sold off. The final third were worried about the direction they perceived the BBC to be taking. This may have been based partly on the general perception within the Right in Parliament of the line taken by the BBC in the Falklands crisis.

In short, it was possible by 1985–86 to argue that the BBC had become to many Conservative MPs a kind of political opposition. First, it had kept open all kinds of national debate, which the Labour party had signally failed to do, wrapped up as it was with its continuous set of internal problems since the early eighties. The BBC can be seen in one real sense to be *the* official political opposition since the mid-1980s. Second, the BBC still represents one of the more public examples of a part-nationalised industry (albeit a very specialist one) which by and large both succeeds and retains a large measure of public, if passive, goodwill. It is, therefore, a symbol of what the Conservative Government would like to curtail, if not totally remove.

Third, and most dangerously according to some Conservative party ideologues (and ironically those of the Left as well), the BBC expresses in a form of living symbolism the possibility of a consensually organised society of the kind they themselves have attempted to erode. The tradition of public service itself cuts into the heart of the newer, more abrasive, philosophy that says the market is all. Even ITV and ILR are brought into this equation because their form arises from that of the BBC; that is, they have certain rights (monopoly of advertising sales, monopoly of franchise areas) only because the BBC does not have them.

The Labour party in the past 20 years has also concluded that the BBC is 'a problem', although the instinct of the centre of that party is to leave well alone. For many years it was the inherent belief of the Labour party that the BBC was relatively neutral that kept Labour criticism to a minimum. The experiences of the Labour Governments between 1964 and 1970 have been used to explain subsequent Labour party dislike of the BBC and the Annan Committee was a direct result (setting it up for the second time was one of Wilson's first acts in 10 Downing Street in 1974). But since then the Labour party has changed. Arguably it has no direct policy on the mass media, although publicly members of the Shadow Cabinet support the maintenance of the BBC. In fact an incoming Labour Government would be likely to make substantial changes in future funding arrangements and, as soon as feasible, in the composition of the BBC Board of Governors. It was a Labour Government proposal to hamstring the BBC with Boards of Management in the 1978 White Paper.

The emerging third forces in British politics, the Democrats, the SDP – even the Greens – have also much to criticise in the BBC, notably that it fails to give them enough credit or, more critically, air-time. This, although it is a symptom of a political malaise which for the Democrats reaches right back to the nature of the single non-transferable vote, again does not help the BBC.

Broadcasters in the mid-1980s had won substantial freedoms from the political system. All this was threatened: more than any the BBC, at the heart of the system, was no longer perceived as inviolate, though neither the brilliance of Conservative government propaganda nor Labour Opposition spite alone was the danger. In larger part it was a failure by broadcasters to come up with anything other than the same increasingly tired justifications for what they did. Coverage of politics by broadcasters was patchy. The tendency of broadcasting as a medium (more true of television than radio) to entertain at all times did not help serious debate. Although some political programmes had notable successes others appeared to denigrate the changing fortunes (and views) of politicians as examples of at best feeble-mindedness, at worst culpable deception of the electorate. Broadcasting, when it did this, arguably brought democracy itself into contempt.

The political system in the UK is highly secretive and there is always a temptation to use this as an excuse to personalise and trivialise. But broadcasters have had ample opportunity to prevent that from happening. They, like the Press, had decided to turn much political coverage into a circus, a long-running faintly amusing soap opera. When programmes like *Real Lives* are made – not, perhaps, a particularly good film – they do at least try to open a window in the stuffy hot-house of parliamentary-led politics. They point to political issues crying out to be be ventilated before an audience itself disillusioned with much political hot air.

It may be that television is a medium which inevitably and inexorably falls into the amusement mode of discourse – see especially Postman (1986) on this question. Competition for audiences, however, lay behind much of the trend; competition not just between channels but between programme tranches as well, the common assumption being that if politics is intrinsically not interesting to audiences then its coverage, at least, has to be pure jazz. The judgement, growing by the 1980s, was two-fold. Audiences did not applaud political coverage; neither, it seems, did they much applaud politicians, other than those who could perform well on television. If that is the case part of the problem is possibly that the very high levels of exposure of politicians in broadcasting lends weight to a law of diminishing credibility. Anthony King's thesis of government overload is important here because media exposure would limit space for action even further.

Equally, politicians caught in the media spotlight feel strong pressure to say anything rather than remain silent, to regret a loose tongue at leisure. (The fall of Edwina Currie, late in 1988, illustrates this to perfection.) In all this, broadcasting can legitimately claim it is not entirely at fault. But as I have already suggested, not to have developed a sufficiently tight code of ethics, not to have been aware that to hide behind 'professional' judgements in an area where the whole question of professionalism is in doubt, is to court disaster. Politicians are themselves the last of the great amateur tradition in British public life, and it shows.

The nature of broadcasting, then, is that it is locked alongside and into central political processes; of necessity it is inside the State though trying to pull free. It has been suggested that part of the problem is that, unlike the Press, broadcasting has not yet had an opportunity to fight the great fight for liberty. Such a view is cosy but false. The British Press never fought that fight; like broadcasting it has suffered for it. There has been much rhetoric about the extension of Press freedom; much hyperbole. History suggests that the Press ducked the bigger battles in favour of compromise, and a share of the Establishment's fireside – begrudgingly bestowed.

Like the Press, broadcasting's room to manoeuvre will be determined by its economic freedom. The BBC, in having to return time and again to governments for licence fee increases is restricted in its freedom to operate, even in a benign climate. But the climate has been anything but benign for some years and the first signs of what that means are now writ large. Part of the changing climate has been the development of an external body of control on broadcasters: the first of these was the Broadcasting Complaints Commission.

FREEDOMS, RESPONSIBILITIES, JUDGEMENTS

The Broadcasting Complaints Commission was set up as part of the 1981 Broadcasting Act. It had been preceded for some years by BBC and IBA internal formal complaints procedures. But, as with the early police complaints procedures, public disquiet continued over how impartial a procedure could be when it was run and presided over by the colleagues of those accused. The majority of broadcasters are horrified at the potential scope of the BCC and by its intellectual and even emotional separation of 'understanding' from their daily problems. They seek – and see – constant references in the complaints with which it deals evidence that it is extending its brief to embrace their daily progamme making. In broadcast management some fear it will become more and more prescriptive. With events of late 1988 these fears have been realised: prescription is joined by active proscription and, for the first time since 1945, broadcast freedom is actively being eroded.

Of particular worry has been the number of attempts by the National Front (one partially successful) to get complaints heard by the Commission. There is concern too among producers at the number of complainants who have appeared in investigative programmes, and the possible effect this may have on nervous broadcasting executives.

The BCC is limited in scope, however, in one vital area. It can only deal with complaints from the public where individuals or organisations have been directly involved in a programme. Mrs Whitehouse, in short, may complain that a programme dealing with her organisation treated it or her unfairly; she cannot complain specifically or generally to the BCC that broadcasts are getting more violent, or ruder.

Legally, the BCC was set up to 'consider and adjudicate upon complaints of unjust or unfair treatment in sound or television programmes actually broadcast by the BBC and the IBA on or after 1st June, 1981; or of unwarranted infringement of privacy in, or in connection with the obtaining of material included in, such programmes. This function extends to all such sound and television programmes, including advertisements and teletext transmissions and programmes broadcast by the BBC's External Services'.

In the first year of operation of the BCC 114 complaints were received; 91 were deemed outside the BCC's jurisdiction. In the next year (1982–83) they received 243 complaints, of which 188 fell outside their jurisdiction. In 1982–3 the Commission dealt with 30 out of a possible 52, some being left over from the year before; nine were subject to full adjudications and another 21 were, basically, not dealt with. Of the nine, three were upheld, six dismissed. The Commission's Annual Report suggested that the BCC was concerned in all these cases (as also with those it did not eventually deal with) at a lack of care by broadcasters over editing, editorialising and a failure to keep contributors aware of the way a programme was developing. Broadcasters, seeing such comments, worry even more that the BCC is straying from its strict legal ground into areas of its own making, namely the prerogative of programme making. What, they might legitimately ask, do BCC members know about editorialising?

This debate is in the heartland of formal accountability. It spreads out into less formal areas because the public, although not necessarily knowing the technical terms of debate, are increasingly and dangerously conscious of how a programme can be altered by technical means. The word which people at large use to describe such means is distortion. From the broadcasters' side this can appear to be ignorance of the problems they face in getting a programme on air.

But bodies like the BCC and the Press Council will continue to attract professional brickbats while they remain in the shadowy uncertainties of just what constitutes a profession, or professional practice. Broadcasters do themselves harm when they fail to define this adequately, or retreat into jargon. Both the BCC and the Press Council (with much weaker powers) run the same gauntlet from professional journalists in many pronouncements. The BCC is still feeling its way across very tricky ground. Needless to say it is given generally minimal help by broadcasters in this task.

The public has a right to protection from the excesses of over-enthusiastic programme makers. Broadcasting is big business. All too often it has trodden over-heavily on the sensibilities of those it exposes – and few so exposed have much idea in advance of what the public gaze can do to private lives. The BCC is a blunderbuss but it is at least a warning to the wilder parts of broadcasting. On the negative side it can be and is used by fringe groups to try to push a cause.

The positive side is that some of the public at least seem to realise that the Commission exists and that they might be able to use it. The limitations to its powers are probably set at about the right level. Were its jurisdiction to be extended to anyone who had a complaint against what they saw or heard, it would have to be a very large organisation indeed and its myriad judgements would fail to have much impact. But practical accountability on a day-to-day basis remains – and should remain – with broadcasters who, nevertheless, need to be instructed in the ways in which they should operate to remain professional. Bodies like the BBC have been set up both because of public disquiet over broadcasting's often perceived insensitivity, and politicians' perceptions that to curb broadcasting may be popular.

Until broadcasters can bring themselves to exercise sanctions against their own through fully accredited professional associations, much as medics or lawyers do, then it is arguable whether they can assume the mantle of a distinct profession. Many of those same broadcasters would argue that they have no desire to emulate either doctors or lawyers, that what they do – in the public interest – has to be protected as far as possible from the encroachments of committees, however well intentioned. The exercise of professional judgement by broadcasters is always going to be a tricky thing to pin down. We are in the field of art more than science here and art is notoriously a matter of taste.

This would apply most of all to the newly-proposed watchdog for violent and sexually-explicit content in broadcasting, the Broadcasting Standards Council. One way or another, a body of this nature has been on the agenda for many years. The events of the late summer of 1987 in Hungerford when a lone gunman killed 15 people and then himself, simply crystallised public and private fears. It was symptomatic that broadcasters made no attempt to point out how weak, if existent at all, were the links between content of programmes and audience behaviour. In a classic 'moral panic' emotion and sentiment finally won. The capitulation of the BBC in particular, was total, with a number of senior BBC managers making fools of themselves on air in the immediate aftermath of the killings. For a moment it seemed as if reason itself was suspended, while outraged public opinion sought atavistically for any target. Television was the obvious answer, and responded with the required *mea culpa*. It will take time to see if this further intrusion into broadcast freedom will serve any useful purpose; inevitably it has affected programmes and altered the broadcasting climate such that the kind of artistic iconoclasm British television had sustained against all the odds is seriously damaged. The reaction to Hungerford may well turn out to be British broadcasting's last stand in the long-running fight to preserve and maintain itself as the world's leader in broadcast drama – if that in part means the ability to challenge the cosy assumptions of mediocre middle-town.

4 Making Programmes

> '... there are two jobs worth having in the BBC:
> Director-General or producer.'
>
> (BBC programme-maker)

To concentrate on producers, as this chapter does, is not to deny or denigrate the many tasks, the many roles and parts played by the army of people who go to make up broadcast productions. But as the quotation which starts this discussion highlights, the role of producer is perceived by most broadcasters as the critical one.

There are curiosities about it, singularities which we have to explore before we can address the questions surrounding public accountability (and producer *responsibilities*). Anthony Smith in a paper prepared for the Annan Committee, 'The relationship of Management with Creative Staff' (1977) says that in the UK the British producer scarcely exists as a separate entity (as compared, for example, with his status in France). Part of the problem, says Smith, is the distinction to be made between directors and producers – not least in management/union agreements. 'The agreement between the ITV companies and the ACTT does not refer to producers at all ...'. In the BBC, meanwhile,

> ... there are various grades of producer, all of whom may need but not involve deploying a *directing* skill; the Editor, the most senior of these, tends to merge his function with that of head of department ... The result is that in Britain the producer is placed far closer to management (and the management tends to have far more collective experience in production itself) ... (than in foreign systems) ...

Smith concludes that the producer is a 'creative official, as well as a creative professional'. This has its rewards as well as its dangers and both are exemplified within British broadcasting. It means that producers are able to exercise more judgement (within the BBC this comes down to the referral-upwards system); it also means their decisions are informed by particular cultures of assimilation to broadcasting's own ideas of itself at any time.

Much of the mystery which surrounds production in the UK may be explained here. Producers themselves often claim they do not understand what it is they do. As the socialisation which takes them into the role of producer is often subtle and long-term their response is not unreasonable. The danger is that this process of creative assessment becomes one of self-justification for either arrogant indifference to audiences or a crippling (because irrational) self-censorship.

Producers vary in what they do, the job of a radio producer being different from that of a television producer, for instance. Just as a television producer making drama programmes will do a very different job to one making documentaries. They also vary enormously in their attitudes but there is a containment of those attitudes within the framework created by, say, the BBC – its past, its present and, in the sense that all current work is future-directed, its future too. But producers work within a particular ethos depending on where they work within broadcasting. Specialisms abound, the extreme perhaps being areas like natural history, or drama.

Assessing what to produce can be very hard:

> A lot of the time you are dropping stones down a deep well and hoping to hear the echo. I listen to my next door neighbour or what people think in the pub. I am quite often thrown by the response I get.

> (Drama producer)

There are also differences of approach between the BBC and ITV companies, and Channel Four, in the ways they deploy their production staff, but the similarities override any of these. British broadcasting has become more, not less, seamless over time. The annual national and international awards ceremonies are testimony enough to the parallelism of BBC and ITV production.

Within the BBC there is a tension that is different: the one occasioned by size; the creative professional may feel he or she is at odds with a sprawling bureaucracy. As BBC broadcasting has grown it has divided into many parts. Malcolm Muggeridge describes the process eloquently: 'The BBC came to pass silently, invisibly; like a coral reef, cells busily multiplying, until it was a vast structure, a conglomeration of studios, offices, cool passages along which many passed.' C. S. Lewis (quoted by Smith, 1973) suggests it was, briefly, a democracy before its early ideals were swallowed up in Reith's (and others') gloomy determination that broadcasting must serve virtue and virtue alone.

First, we should not forget, there were engineers; then there was a

nascent bureaucracy; then programme-makers. And if this seems to
be a harsh judgement the record betokens it. The script they followed
was mostly written after the event: in the early days broadcasting was
very *ad hoc*, mostly *ad lib*. Rapidly, because the medium was
perceived to be a crucial element in a modern state, another script
came to be written so that now it is almost impossible not to believe in
the rightness of the way broadcasters do their daily tasks. As
broadcasting has lengthened its shadow so it has been diverted, too
often, from the primary purposes set out by programme-makers. It
may well be that the final judgement of history is that it is a trivial
pursuit, given too much weight in the councils of the wise, a bauble
and not a crystal ball. But programme-making *is* one agreed purpose,
not politics or economics or social change. All those latter three have
bedevilled broadcasting and those who operate its parts.

The BBC, as the 'national instrument of broadcasting' has been
most vulnerable to delusions of grandeur. It has become so good at
playing this game that outsiders can believe the game is reality. But as
one perceptive observer had it in 1986, what BBC officials,
executives, senior staff, all have in common is an ability to seem
'connected', rather more than they are. It took a series of financial
and political hiccups to convince it, corporately, that in the 1980s its
only hope lay in a revival of what it did best: programme-making.
Yet, some producers were arguing, following this apparent revelation
by the Director-General in 1985, the emphasis on programmes was a
cynical ratings-chase all over again. At that too, arguably, the BBC
was best.

The key to programme-making lies with the producer. He (still
unusually she although the balance is changing) *is* the programme in
its early stages, the sole repository, in many cases, of what a
programme may become. The role often combines in one person the
authority for the direction a programme will probably take. It is a job
much misunderstood outside broadcasting precisely because it covers
so many possibilities. That, among other things, is why people love
the work: it creates scope for enormous freedom. This, however, is
within the learned constraints of the organisation. There are two
other curbs: the first financial, the second institutional, for despite
there being, certainly in the BBC, a belief and acceptance of
internalised norms, there is a large administrative net. Wedell (1968)
points out that the tension this induces is neither new nor confined to
broadcasting. What he could not add is the comment, ten years on,
by the Annan Committee that, again discussing the BBC, 'what

differentiates the BBC from normal industry is that it is producing thousands of one-off jobs, each of them unique'.

This may exaggerate, but not much. Programmes, even within a series, have their special individual characteristics and their unique problems. It is the diversity of output in and between programmes which determines the need for particular kinds of people to produce. Too much can be made of this but, within the older BBC, the ability of the organisation to pick these brilliant young men and women was a legend. The trouble has in part been that the BBC still believes it picks them although, as with any other large establishment, the mediocre both get in and survive, often to an astonishing extent. On the whole they are middle class, university-educated, neither of which categories should surprise: their social composition reflects, and is reflected in, the bulk of the output and the origins of the organisation they work for.

Channel Four is no exception to this: indeed – possibly because of its small size – the middle-class self-righteousness of its corporate view is what strikes an observer so forcibly. Moreover Channel Four has capitalised on the notion that somehow its programmes are not made in the same way as the BBC's. By and large, of course, they are.

Although Channel Four uses a number of independent producers, nearly all of them are fully-trained professionals; a high proportion in the beginning, in fact, ex-BBC. Channel Four at no stage hands over anything like editorial control. Indeed, where well-used production companies are involved, whenever a serious problem over content arises, Channel Four snatches back whatever loosening of the reins had been applied. An important example of this occurred in 1986 over a programme made by Diverse Productions attacking the IBA, Channel Four's legal parent. The commissioning editor banned the original showing saying that the programme was 'unbalanced', ironically the classic reason given for such actions by the BBC.

What has happened is that all British broadcasting suffers from socio-cultural centrism (to use an ugly neologism) which constitutes the middle ground of opinion. Not for one moment does this imply that any single producer might not be extreme in his or her views, left or right. But it does imply that overall there has been an effort at institutional balance and impartiality. The accepted master of this process is the BBC. The BBC has of late chosen this ground on which to stand and fight. The inability to perceive its shifting or undermining nature is attributable to any number of causes, many of which are explored in this book. The sincerity and necessity of the stand are not in doubt. Yet by the mid-1980s it was the very existence of this consensual centre which was challenged – by the two main political parties and, apparently, by the behaviour of people in the streets and in the voting booths. The vain efforts of the SDP-Liberal Alliance, not to break the mould but to re-form it, teetered on the edge of success, never quite regaining those older certainties. The BBC was forced into political controversy, as I have already argued, by simply being there.

Krishan Kumar (1977) has developed this 'middle ground' theme at some length. The thrust of his argument is that holding it constitutes the parameters of a very narrow debate about what is 'good' broadcasting. Kumar is discussing presentation, primarily, but his words apply with some force to the whole set of processes which make up programme-making. He believes that this position taken by the BBC, which it holds with increasing difficulty, stems from a consideration of the precarious nature of its institutional position. As it has been so often caught up in controversy it has maintained an institutional balance by insisting that it is, indeed, in the middle of any particular argument.

The emphasis on professionalism, with its overtones of what amount to an academic detachment, has enabled the BBC to present a public face of dispassionate aloofness. It is this persona that can so infuriate the non-broadcaster as its manifestation can all too often appear to be arrogance; it also poses a dilemma for the 'new' BBC – the BBC of the 'shareholder', and of the populist programming face.

Many – most – broadcasters believe they are 'professionals'. As with the debate in journalism at large, there is a dispute over the meaning of this term – if indeed it has one meaning. In broadcasting there is to begin with a separation of 'professions' between the engineers and the programme producers. There is also a separation between the craft areas, including lighting, props, cameramen; and the research, direction and producing fronts. Again, younger broadcasters would reject the term 'professional', seeing in it an implication of precisely that detached aloofness which they desire to break down, between themselves and their audiences. Richard Hoggart, writing 20 years ago in *The Listener* said 'clearly professionalism has to be better defined by the broadcasters themselves so that internal criticism improves; and criticism from outside needs to be much more informed, responsive and varied'.

Broadcasters mean very different things by professionalism, often determined by their programme field. To journalists it can mean careful factual checking against a very tight deadline; getting a story across at all costs; being cool under (sometimes real) fire. To drama it can mean authenticity; to current affairs balance of argument or, where appropriate, advocacy. The professional, in the last case, *knows* when to advocate, when not.

Producers are proud of their knowledge concerning their audiences; there is considerable evidence to show that the majority know less than they think they do (see Chapter 5). What they think of as audience preference comes, more often than not, from a reading of letters, possibly from phone calls and from the ubiquitously mentioned man in the pub:

> The main thing is living in open societies. When I go to parties I don't meet 17 broadcasters, four journalists and half a dozen actresses. My circle is headmaster, computer man, restaurateur, greengrocer ... I am not willing to say 'yes sir', 'no sir' to anyone who writes to me. I take it that it does come back to your instinct for professionalism. Your accountability to your own conscience. The BBC is blessed by a high number of people who care.
>
> (Senior BBC producer)

Burns (1977) points out that the word 'professional' has 'extraordinary wide currency in the Corporation. In context of programme production, and of the BBC's relationship with its audiences, it seems to have three separable, though not distinct, meanings'. These are: (1) The opposite of amateur; (2) Qualified by long specialised training; (3) Indicating a code of behaviour related to the 'client'. But, Burns says, the client is rarely thought to be the audience but the programme-maker's superior. He suggests that the insistence of professionalism, at one level, is the need for self-protection, or to shelve consideration of the implications of a mass audience possibly running into tens of millions.

Producers do produce for their superiors who, after all, have an immediate set of sanctions to bring to bear. They also produce for each other's approval. But it would be grossly unfair to suggest that they do not have any conception of a mass audience. The problem is to reduce its enormity to human size. Letters, phone calls, the man in the pub, are all ways of doing just that. (To put the problem into some perspective, a 1986 Saturday children's show received in one run over five *million* letters.)

Burns' study, the fieldwork for which was done twenty years ago,

describes a BBC much more certain of what it was; even he draws out
the neuroses of change, of unfulfilled purpose. Part of those neuroses
even then were related to size. Part were related to a realisation that
broadcasting was potent, although few then (or now) would have
cared to indicate how the brew could be reduced to rational analysis.

Producers, although less obviously than actors or presenters or the
so-called 'personalities', have an image attached to them. In a
different way, but no less glamorously, so have all broadcaster
personnel. The public has become used to the acclamation, through
the Press, of broadcasting as part of the twentieth century's Roman
Games. Broader political, economic and social circumstances are
lending weight to the broadcasting managers who wish to get the
public more inside the system. For the BBC this is primarily
defensive – ensuring that people understand what they pay the
licence fee for. In commercial broadcasting, including Channel Four,
it is good business to allow the audience to join in – up to a point.
Accessibility, if not accountability, is marketing policy. The processes
of history at large are determining that the public will wish to know
more and more about broadcasting. How much more is a matter for
fierce internal argument. Keeping the mystery alive is a strong
argument (as it is with theatre and special effects in film). But the
clamour of the times is for more knowledge, not less, at whatever
price.

Programme-makers also inhabit a world where they are coming
under other kinds of scrutiny; under increasing pressure from their
own heads of department to be, in one sense or another, accountable.
Their responses are highly differential, largely dependent on their
proximity to the audience, and on their institutional position. Thus,
on the broadest possible scale, radio programme-makers are more
likely to respond, and respond quickly, to audience pressures than
are television programme-makers. But within radio there are great
differences. Radio Three, whilst retaining a generally good relationship with its tiny audience, does not pride itself exactly on
'responding'. The relationship is at best teacher–pupil. Radio Four,
not least because it produces programmes like 'Feedback', is better.
On this scale BBC local radio is likely to be best. The level of
response is also related – although not necessarily cynically – to
self-interest. Radio is much more competitive than television; and is
indeed in competition with television. Radio audiences have already
begun to fragment, especially in the evenings. In television the two
classically remote areas are drama and light entertainment. There are

no hard rules in all this, just observational surmise. Programme-makers clearly have an overriding need to be free from insistent pressure from audiences to do this or that; the standard defence by programme-makers on not responding is that it would take far too much time.

Additionally most would say that the purpose of their employment in broadcasting is to make 'professional' judgements about what audiences 'need'; or to put that another way, and to reiterate Reith, 'few people know what they want, fewer what they need'. This is not to suggest that programme-makers can or do operate in a vacuum; they are extremely good at assessing public desires and public needs. As television programmes and the more elaborate radio series take up to two years to pass from idea to finished product, second-guessing the future is a highly developed art. The output shows programme-makers as quite often uncannily accurate sooth-sayers, scheduling programmes – and not just long-planned documentaries – just as a news event covering the same topic breaks.

Sometimes they are too good, in drama for instance, when a play planned long before may mirror an unpleasant and immediate reality. Programmes dealing with the growing nuclear threat, and with the NATO and Warsaw Pact 'windows of opportunity' were made years before the Reagan–Gorbachev summit. The *Real Lives* programme 'At the Edge of the Union', shown at last in the autumn of 1985, pre-dated by just a few weeks the Anglo-Irish Agreement and showed the kind of bigotry and extremism in human terms that the Accord is supposed to circumvent. There are many other examples. Producers and many of those assistants, researchers, secretaries, inside broadcasting 'read' the world intensely for signs of what will be, as well as what is, and what has been.

Mis-reading does occur. Although programmes can be close to audience concerns, and in current affairs this can be more easily done than in, say drama, many can seem irrelevant. Given that programmes can cost huge sums of money, and given that once a commitment has been made a programme will generally roll on its way, untrammelled by additional argument (unless over any unforeseen escalation of costs), the chances of being transmitted are nearly total. Whether an audience at that time wants that programme is another matter. Part of this mis-reading of audiences – and it is hard to know how often it happens – is because programme-makers are, by and large, poor users of the tools they have available: principal among these is audience research (see Chapter 6). There is a strong tendency to read audience research data for the good news, not the bad. Programme-makers thus become obsessed by the raw number of total watchers or listeners and by what are known as AIs (Audience Appreciation Indices). The latter is a sophisticated and well-tested attempt to give more information than simply how many watched or listened.

Thus it is professionally acceptable that many science programmes will not get mass audiences; they ought, however, to get good AIs, providing that those who chose to watch or listen did so with enjoyment. Programme-makers rarely get beyond this point. But they can, if a programme of their making is not doing as well as they believe it ought, indulge in one or more behaviours. The first is to look at what was running against it on the other channels. It may be true that a strong programme on the other channel can take away ratings points; it would not affect AIs of course. But schedulers are trying to set strong against strong, weak against weak so the validity of this excuse is always dubious. Second, and frequent, is the denigration of audience research and its personnel. Until recently in the BBC this was common and had a certain force because of the idiosyncratic nature of parts of the BBC Audience Research Department. Since the unified system of BARB (Broadcasters Audience Research Board) this has not been so acceptable a defence – although it is still tried.

Curiously, those ex-programme-makers, heads of department, controllers and above, also indulge in knocking the audience research they expensively commission, sometimes publicly. The result is that some programme-makers have a very poor view of audience research and an even poorer understanding of what it might achieve for them, for example in pre-testing programmes or programme ideas. There are honourable exceptions, chiefly in educational broadcasting, where different arrangements between broadcasters and part of their audience (teachers) ensure that much more thought goes into programme planning.

The older attitudes are changing under growing pressures. More and more producers are turning to the battery of methods now available at not much cost to give them some idea of what their audience both wants and is capable of absorbing within one programme. Needless to say science, health and continuing education are in the van of this movement. But the *That's Life* production team made changes to its style after audience reaction testing by BBC audience research staff, as did the BBC news.

One problem for producers is suspension of disbelief in test results, especially if they appear to fly in the face of received wisdom built up over years. If a programme works, goes this argument, leave it alone. Poking into audiences' motives might lead to a failure to innovate, to be brave. Not everyone will agree to a change before they have seen or heard it. Would *Monty Python* or *Not the Nine O'Clock News* ever have been transmitted if the public had been asked in advance about its views?

But programme-makers will point to statistical inconsistencies; others will lament the times when having two sets of figures (in the pre-BARB days; sometimes contradictory because they used different methods) at least meant you could legitimately challenge those which were least favourable to yourself – or dismiss them both *because* neither agreed.

Tracey (1978) has argued, using political programme producers as a sample group, that producers have in truth no interest in the audience at all: 'the manifestation is of a relatively closed world festooned with a number of vaguely formulated but unsubstantiated assumptions about the audience'. This is too harsh. Producers manifesting that degree of cynicism or indifference in their output would not last long. It is encouraging indeed to witness precisely the opposite. But the dilemma remains the organisation of an essentially creative activity within a framework set by a dangerous mixture of bureaucracy, money and conditions of political power. There has to be as well a 'correct' level of assessment of audience requirements which should in no way interfere with the exercise of critical judgements.

Inevitably these judgements will often appear to be prescriptive. Audiences of course matter. But they are not a homogeneous mass making demands. Over the years they have been extraordinarily tolerant as programme-making has grown from its infancy. Their collective sophistication is now immense and programmes are made which simply could not have been 'read' correctly a few years ago. Unquestionably the pressures on programme-makers have been growing. Since the 1960s these pressures have taken a number of forms: Financial; Institutional; 'Professional'; Political; Social; Audience.

Financial Pressure

The major problem for programme-makers has been costs. Broadcasting, radio or television, has been explosively expensive. Although many radio programmes have tiny budgets (a few hundred pounds, other than staff costs), and many television programmes are also relatively cheap (a few thousand an hour), many are hugely priced. BBC drama, per hour, in 1985 was costing around £250 000; ITV drama was thought to be at least 50 per cent more.

The trade unions were continuing to milk broadcasting dry. They operated many practices similar to (if not borrowed from) national newspapers. The attitude was that television, especially, could afford to pay through the nose. For the BBC, although it had traded on its position in the national culture to persuade many staff it was worth working for despite lower rates of pay, this was all potentially fatal.

The BBC, whose accounting system had been built over many years, and which many observers thought to be quaint, was not overly profligate; neither was its real spending so far out of line with other organisations of its size. Its central problem was its income, fixed as it was so tightly to the licence fee. There were many areas where spending could have been controlled more tightly. But producers and programme-makers at large feared that the easiest to cut were future programme commitments because they involved paper transactions rather than tackling awkward-to-lose existing jobs. It was partly to counter these fears that the Director-General's office issued a statement in 1985 that the BBC was still committed to programme-making as a first priority.

Institutional Pressure

At the same time, and partly as a response to growing financial pressures, programme-makers have been under greater management controls. The BBC has operated a system of 'reference up' for its producers which at its best creates the room for them to make the programmes they want, subject to the constraints already discussed. This policy, which was laid down by the Board of Governors, is designed to ensure that producers are free, but keep the obligation to refer to their line manager any policy issue they cannot resolve.

Of course this helps reinforce a 'middle ground' culture. In the climate of increasing pressure upon the top management of the BBC from outside, it may result in a kind of institutional abuse. While there are large numbers of 'case law' directives and 'guidelines' coming down the line from senior management, some producers may feel, not an obligation to managers above in reporting problems, but an obligation to protect their nascent programme from senior interference.

Within the BBC there is a feeling that on certain questions (and
Northern Ireland is the most prominent) the multiplication of
'guidelines' and imprimaturs now informing any attempt to make
programmes in these areas, will lead to a form of indirect censorship.
This takes the form of 'good idea, but not just *now*'. Part of this, and
equally serious, has been the institution's own growing caution, born
of the twin fears that it will upset Government and/or its audiences.
In the words of one senior producer 'it dies the thousand deaths of
the coward'.

In Channel Four the pressures also exist: first, the company
operates a fierce accounting system which gives commissioned
producers very little room to manoeuvre. Second, there is a form of
ideological coercion, subtle but ever-present, which tends to give
programmes a sameness of outlook. This 'oppositionalism', a form of
radical liberalism without any apparent political direction, is as
powerful a force as anything the BBC can muster against its own
programme-makers. If a judgement is to be made it is that programme-makers in the BBC are still much freer than programme-
makers working for Channel Four; but that in the BBC those
freedoms are constantly under attack. In Channel Four the freedoms
available to the commissioning editors have not begun to emerge as
any kind of a potential problem.

Professional Pressure

The simplest to explain but the hardest to pin down, this pressure
stems from the best side of British broadcasting which is its
commitment to excellence. Over the years the standards of
programmes, taken overall, has improved immeasurably. But the
immediate effect is that all programme-makers are looking over their
shoulders to see how they may increase what might be called the
'slickness' factor. In high quality drama this may be laudable but
where it is applied to a radio station output or to the Community
Programme Unit it is less so. There is, contained within this desire to
be seen to be making better and better programmes, a highly volatile
cost inflation, which bears back on the whole structure.

This is the awards syndrome, itself encouraged by managements
anxious throughout broadcasting to 'prove' that excellence is alive
and encouraged *here*. The number and classes of broadcasting
awards, both national and international, have been steadily growing
as broadcasting itself has grown. Traditionally the BBC have always

scooped the pool. Since the 1970s, with increasing financial pressures and, perhaps more importantly, lessening organisational will, the BBC had been gaining proportionately less and less awards each year. Suddenly, in 1986, the BBC nearly swept the board. There were good programmes but the suspicion remains that award panels, anxious to help the BBC at a time when it was under fierce attack, and when the Peacock Committee had not yet reported, were tilting the balance a little to prop it up.

The pressure remains – if anything it grows in proportion to the relative lack of success. The coming of Channel Four, with its innovative approaches, has made the situation much worse for the BBC. The effect is to distance programme makers further from their audiences, who probably care little for whether a particular programme wins an award or not. The running of the annual BAFTA awards ceremony, among others, live or semi-live on television, is of dubious interest outside the industry.

Political Pressure

Political pressure there has always been: its increase on programme-makers comes from a growing recognition by the political system that broadcasting may have great social purpose. Although it would be wrong to suggest that such pressure exists on all programme-makers at all times, equally it would be wrong not to recognise its presence in current affairs, news and, perhaps surprisingly, in drama.

Drama programmes throw into sharp relief many of the political questions of the day. Almost by definition drama playwrights tend to be oppositional, radical, often overtly left-wing. Their output is meant to stimulate viewers and listeners; their eyes and ears bring the uncomfortable into focus. 'Tumbledown', transmitted in 1988, demonstrates this desire in drama, to think the uncomfortable, to force audiences to look at what they would prefer to forget.

Direct political pressure is very rare. But retrospective pressure there is: a programme is broadcast, is roundly condemned; next time the programme-makers, aware of what happened last time, may exercise more caution; if they do not their immediate bosses may do so on their behalf. To call this process self-censorship is too strong but it is constantly there. It is my view that the BBC has become more timid; that some of the dramas, for instance, that it might have shown in the 1970s would no longer be acceptable. Part of the existing threat to the BBC is that companies like Central now make plays like 'Made in Britain' and that they are prepared to run them in peak time. The argument in reverse is that without the BBC as a model such plays would not be made by commercial television; again, perhaps, the BBC re-took the lead in this field by showing two Alan Clarke plays early in 1989, 'Elephant' and 'The Firm'.

Social Pressure

Programme-makers have become more conscious of the world at large and their responsibilities, though it was always true that a large part of the output took consideration of the world and its problems: broadcasters as a group have always espoused a very public social conscience. Since the late 1960s there has been growth of another related pressure on programme-makers; it is to understand the medium in which they work; and as a concomitant of that to recognise its limitations and its inherent if not fully understood ability to change attitudes.

The issue of the power of broadcasting, and of television in particular, lies outside the remit of this book. Nevertheless broadcasters have become more and more aware of the dangers associated with their chosen form. Equally they have begun to recognise the limitations of content. Television has a certain shortsightedness: it purveys crude broad-brush emotions, not finely-tuned argument. It is long on spectacle, short on specifics; extremely powerful when conveying a simple idea, weakest when attempting a subtle philosophy. On the other hand radio does lend force to the imagination and it has increasingly been able to concentrate on the smaller, committed audience. The visuals of television, its immense power to inform a worldwide audience, the technology and who controls it, all come back to the programme-makers' door.

Audience Pressure

Finally then, to audiences and the completion of the circle. Audiences *do* exert pressures. As we have seen these may stem from the ratings; they may stem from physical contact. Most ephemeral of all but in the long term among the most telling, the pressure may come from that very antenna-like sensitivity a programme-maker has of what audiences demand, or may like to hear and see in the coming months and years.

Part of this sensitivity is derived from a number of quite well established and formal mechanisms designed to gather intelligence. They have, in the main, a secondary (and recent) overlay of formal accountability placed on them. Part of their primary purpose has always been defence of the programme-maker *against* the cruder forms of public pressure, and a means for the programme-maker to respond to that public through *post hoc* knowledge of what was right and wrong about a programme already produced.

One of the more recent developments, not yet much used by programme-makers, some because they mistrust its source, others because they do not know it exists, is projective testing: asking an audience sample what kind of programmes it might like dealing with a subject; how they should be organised; what contents they should have; and who ought to present them.

Meanwhile programme-makers muddle on, the security of their belief in their profession under attack as the public is exposed to more and more broadcasting. It is the greatly under-estimated expertise of that huge audience that broadcasting research has been at pains to tap, all in the name of better programmes.

Producers and their assistants are not the only creative staff who count, of course, but they do exercise an enormous influence over all broadcast programmes. They are among the most privileged people to work in British broadcasting and most of them know it. They are the front line of programme-making and it is on their continuing commitment to making the best programmes they can, given the available resources, that British television and radio prospers.

But it is the case that that commitment is not wholly audience-directed. It has, as we have seen, many dimensions. The question here is not dissimilar from most consumer goods. Buyers there too have little initial choice when it comes to deciding what should be made available. Subsequently people may or may not choose to buy and thus a market-place which responds to some form of demand begins to function. Broadcasting is not so different, despite its artistic pretensions – but then neither is fine art. The more interesting questions then, is not whether audiences count with the makers of broadcasting but whether they are seriously considered as consumers in the active or passive sense. To understand that, programme-makers would have to look much more closely at the mass of research data already extant which tells us a great deal about audiences and how they behave. On the whole neither programme-makers nor broadcast-executives bother. Their surprise when their own researchers tell them about the 'real' audience out there is manifest – and revealing.

What, then, do we know about the audiences for broadcasting? Read on . . .

5 The audience *is* out there

What do you think of it so far?

A paradox of broadcasting is that while audiences have been much studied, and British audiences top the league table for breadth and depth of studies, the largest amount of all this effort is devoted to answering the least interesting question. That is how many people are watching what at a particular time. More interesting questions, why people watch or listen when they do; how people make their choices; and what they make of what they watch or listen to, although asked of samples, are analysed poorly. Of late these questions have come to be recognised as the truly serious ones about broadcasting if we are to have any understanding of what it is that audiences want from broadcasting in an age of proliferating choice.

What is clear is that one way or another audiences are fascinated by broadcasting. This began with radio, reaching a crescendo in the late 1930s, peaking again perhaps in the early 1950s. Then radio personalities were like film stars. Television displaced some but by no means all of that simple worship. Today it is possible to discern that the mass audience, while 'loving' some of its television personalities, may also have a much better understanding of what that relationship is and of the clay feet of those worshipped.

This intimacy with broadcasting and broadcasters is exploited through devices like the television personality – constructs not dissimilar to, but far more potent than the older Hollywood stars. Individual members of the mass audience do identify considerably with, for example, soap opera characters. The perception by the audience of soap opera characters is probably one of realism – that is, they believe in them and in their 'real' existence. The relationship deserves more research. One such exploration was in Dorothy Hobson's pioneering work on *Crossroads*, ATV's (now Central) long-running serial – now defunct – about a Midlands motel. Hobson discovered that her sample of the very large audience for this programme did have a close identity with its characters although there was rather less than expected fantasy in this. People, while accepting the fictional conventions of the television soap opera, nonetheless were able to create a sense in which those fictional portrayals became part of their intimate lives. In some ways the very

66

crassness, the stereotypical, clichéd poverty of dramatic art or even artifice in such soaps gives them an added verissimilitude: after all, how many 'real' people talk the way a Pinter character, or even an Iris Murdoch hero, does?

This point about audience choice and attitudes touches upon another significant problem about those who produce and manage broadcasting, and those for whom it is intended. It is still the case that in the late 1980s the vast majority of those connected with broadcasting have middle-class backgrounds and tastes; along with an often highly developed sense of 'art'. Television – and some radio, i.e. network BBC Radios Three and Four, are bedevilled by a covert struggle between rank populism and high culture. There is perhaps only a hint but it is there, of a secret snobbery towards much of the more popular television output. Indeed some of the overt debate within television – both BBC and commercial – of late has been between those who see the possibility at least of television as art and those who see it effectively as commerce (as in buying and selling audiences to advertisers). Audiences are hardly noticed at one level in this argument, although of course they are targets for both groups. The terms of the debate – although its rancour excludes the word more often than not – are the old ones: giving the people what they want, or trying to lead them on to better things (as defined by the providers).

At one extreme the argument leads to a view that *all* television (usually the prime target) is bad for us and should be banned. Jerry Mander's *Four Arguments for the Elimination of Television* sits at one end; much more serious a proposition (that television destroys 'true' culture) is put foward by Neil Postman's *Amusing Ourselves to Death*. Both these authors concentrate exclusively on the United States where, British broadcasting managements frequently iterate, things are very different. Well, so they are, but not *that* different. And indeed one so far unsullied principal of European – especially British – mass media is what happens in the US today will inexorably happen to us tomorrow, in however attenuated a form.

Postman is a cogent thinker and his central thesis is that we have embraced that part of Aldous Huxley's *Brave New World* which suggested that the tyranny of the future would not be imposed from above but absorbed from below. The new slavery would be self-inflicted. Postman says so it is, and that it is all done through television which has progressively reduced all debate, all discourse, all meaning, to entertainment. Show business, he says, is what television does best – possibly the only thing it can do – and the result is the loss (if I read him right) of the pain of learning, cured by the new panacea of the tube. Many would agree with this analysis. Yet it flies in the face of just about everything we know to be true about audience responses to broadcasting, as opposed to the responses of the élite: politicians, educationalists, theologians, sociologists, journalists and moralists at large.

The subject of audience attitudes to broadcasting is entirely a fascinating one. There are strong grounds for believing there is a quasi-religious element; a kinship with the Royal Family perhaps, in the UK, with all the overtones of mysticism that relationship entails along with its equally religious overtones. It is worth noting that in the latter case, too, clay feet are an inevitable part of the continuing story, and that the Royals have recognised, if not exactly welcomed, their soap opera alter egos.

What we have then from audiences, is a complex set of attitudes directed at the 'others' as portrayed on screen and via the radio set. Certainly the latter (radio) pulls its audiences in this way. The mid-1980s' surprising rediscovery by Radio Four listeners of *The Archers* is a good case. What motivates more and more people to start to tune to an already long-running five-times weekly serial is a mystery. Yet *The Archers* has become a vogue again.

Broadcasters would argue, with some justification, that this new interest develops in small ways – out of casual conversations in pubs and work-places – which accumulate in a hyperbolic audience curve like the spread of a rumour or of smoke through a building. They cannot so easily answer at what point this happens, or why. Script changes help. *The Archers* is part of a long radio cultural heritage. It has the advantage of being familiar, yet it is changing. Sex helps too: the injection of more of that magic ingredient (Brian's affair with Caroline; Shula's marriage to Mark; Sophie's, now Ruth's, innocence to be snatched by David) has undoubtedly boosted flagging ratings. Old listeners die away, possibly disgusted – at least irritated – at these changes; new ones arrive and, like all mass media, the programme achieves that inevitable but vital revamping it has to have in order to keep going. Many other programmes do the same. Mainstream US television is posited on the basis that once you find a formula that works kick it to death over many years. *I Love Lucy, Highway Patrol, MASH, Starsky and Hutch, Kojak* are a few examples in thousands.

The problem, of course, is that broadcasting was borne on the wings of art, and of life through the news. It has never quite sorted out the punctuation between its music hall insouciance and its serious purpose and the two functions have often been confused. Thus the BBC, the more serious in intent if not in realisation, has pushed its news service towards the stage: the *Nine O'Clock News* is in presentation much less serious than it once was; on *The World at One* (Radio Four) in the mid 1980s, the Christmas schedules for BBC radio were solemnly read out as 'news'. Other broadcasters commit other but equal sins.

THEORIES

There is no shortage of theories of audience behaviour, based, as many are, on extensive study of the mass audience and all its sub-cultural parts. Much early research was carried out in highly artificial laboratory environments, most notably the mass of psychological research concerned with the effects of violence. Other research has relied on recall – not just of what was listened to or seen, but how respondents felt while they were engaged in watching or listening.

A considerable research effort has been put into defining the possible framework (or, for Tracey (1978) its absence) between programme-maker and audience: how, in short, does the programme-maker figure out who his or her construct is for? McQuail (1969), addressing this question falls back on G. H. Mead: 'a community that has no common interest, no co-operative activity, is one in which you could not communicate . . . The process of communication cannot be set up as something that exists by itself . . . the social process is pre-supposed.' As with many researchers before him, McQuail gets stuck on the question of how on earth the two parties do in fact communicate, other than in a purely formal sense.

In a later work (1987) McQuail attempts to put some form of framework on the relationship. He says there are four ways of looking, formally, at audiences. First, they may be perceived (and commonly are) as an aggregate of spectators, readers, listeners, viewers. Second, they may be perceived as a mass. Third, they may be perceived as a public or social group and, finally, as a market. What McQuail is at pains to point out, following the 'uses and gratifications' school, is that audience experiences are active, rather than passive. The evidence grows that audiences also have a social relationship with mass media, rather than an isolating one. The missing link is between audiences and what might be called 'purposive' activity.

Although audiences 'think about the media ... as if they could be useful ... What is missing is extensive independent validation that much media use is prompted by consciously or unconsciously formed motives'. Much of the official audience research data gets no further down this road than asking the most superficial questions about the reasons for watching or listening to a particular programme. Special projects in the BBC audience-research department have taken a deeper view but there is little exploration of the 'motives' for using broadcasting. It is always possible that, as with motives in other aspects of living, these are not susceptible to other than impossibly expensive psychological (and individual, tentative) examination.

PRACTICES

The astonishing fact is that after all the research that has been done into audiences we still appear to know very little. It is as if each generation of broadcasters and broadcast researchers, facing the same problems as their predecessors, conspire tacitly to tear up the account so far and demand a new one. Every now and then, however, new insights creep in; sometimes these have an impact out of all proportion to what they reveal. Peter Collett's Oxford television study is one now well on the way to being a legendary project, although the data it produced are similar to those produced in the USA in the 1960s (and therefore significant for that reason alone).

Collett studied 20 homes and the way they 'watched' television. The novelty of the approach, courtesy of modern technology, was to install a television camera in 20 modified television receivers so that the camera recorded what went on in the room when the television was switched on. In order to help the analysis the playback tape also recorded in real-time the programme being 'watched' and a digital clock enabled a frame by frame analysis of the television picture set against the audience reaction. Apart from providing themselves and other researchers with years of material to analyse in any detail required, Collett's own first results suggest that, as we might have suspected from our own behaviour, television 'viewing' is as liable to distraction as is radio listening. People go on doing what they have always done in their homes before any broadcast media intruded.

They are of course brought back to the attention of the screen when given cues – dramatic music, noisy advertisements, loud voices. These 'effects' have been intuitively exploited for years in every kind of thriller and cops and robbers show. The most significant point is that television programme makers are producing their work for viewing in a climate in which maybe a majority of people are only intermittently engaged with it. People are 'skimming through the book' glancing at the illustrations, rather than reading line by line. Collett points out in *The Listener* for 22 May 1986 that whereas the old methods of television audience measurement by means of diaries (not strictly true, in fact) were used extensively the results can now be seen to be widely inaccurate. Even the newer means using electronic keypads registering 'presence' can only indicate just that; attention to what is on the screen is simply not known.

The Collett study fits well with a presentation given by the former head of the BBC's Broadcasting Research Department's Special Projects section, Pam Mills, at the 1985 Biennial Royal Television Society's meeting in Cambridge. Mills called the paper 'Beyond Head Counting'. It analysed audience data to indicate how people used their media in the home, and looked at the broader question of how audiences chose what they watched. She dealt with the technology available, with the programme factors (why they watched one thing rather than another) and with the environment in which they were watching.

Taking technology first: although some 40 per cent of homes now have a second set there is very little simultaneous use of both sets. On a July Saturday in London, for example, for every 100 hours of first-set viewing, there were 47 hours of second-set viewing. But 29 hours of this was at a different time. Of the 18 hours that were simultaneous 11 involved both sets tuned to the same channel. Only in seven hours was the second set used for choice. A quarter of the homes with second sets were tuned simultaneously to the same channel.

In the then 30 per cent of homes with video cassette recorders (the figure in 1988 was nearer 60 per cent) these are mostly used for time-shifting rather than to watch pre-recorded tapes. Video ownership does not increase significantly the amount of time broadcast television is watched; just when it is watched. Audiences re-schedule those carefully worked-out sequences so exactly put together to tempt them to stay tuned.

Other than their use of video recorders, audiences' own watching schedules depend on further factors: a prerequisite is that people are at home and wish to watch television, for example. Evidence suggests this is around the early evening, as schedulers assume. But it is also clear that few people have much more than a hazy idea of what might be on at any time, other than for a few 'punctuation' points like the news.

Most important for programme-makers, who are these people who may, as we have seen, not be really 'watching' television much at all? Many programme-makers assume that the audience for their programme is of a particular kind. Thus the producers of *Panorama* on BBC1 have for years believed that their audience is more middle class than that for *Minder*, on Thames. This is not the case. To take *Panorama*: in a six-week period in 1985, when the average audience size was 4.5m, the proportion of those watching who were working class was 65 per cent; this compares with 64 per cent of working-class people in Britain as a whole. This tendency is true of *all* television programmes (although not of radio, where the choices made *are* different).

Mills also looked at choice of programmes. She pointed out that little was known about how programmes are selected and – as is still the case – little about how they are viewed. These questions are important if more understanding is to be brought to the question of what it is that audiences gain from particular programme strands. This affects the debate about sex and violence, for example. Gunter (1985) has shown that perceptions of violence vary depending on who an audience is; the tender-minded see more violence than the tough-minded, for instance. Audience definitions of what violence *is* also fluctuate. So, clearly, do their definitions of what they like. In the sixty years of broadcasting so far, our concepts of what constitutes an 'audience' has changed radically. The increasing sophistication of members of that once-perceived homeogeneous mass-audience would have determined one change. But others have come from the central points about the uses made of the mass media by audiences and their heterogeneity; their differences not their similarities.

AT THE SHARP END: WHAT DO AUDIENCES THINK?

In the time broadcasting has been available as a mass medium, and in part, undoubtedly, because of broadcasting, attitudes which once seemed certain have undergone great change. Radio was put before people as a pre-selected diet by broadcasters who 'knew' what was correct and what was not. Television, when it began in earnest as a mass medium in the 1950s, also had a strong sense of the correct way of approach. It operated in a self-imposed strait-jacket of conventions, many determined by an attitude of deference to authority.

The result was that audiences responded to its factual output, in comparison with the clear-cut partisan Press, as if broadcast news *was* the truth. It has taken a more cynical if more realistic age to come to terms with the techniques by which current events are brought to the video screen or microphone, the selection of images, the editing, the words that are placed over those fleeting pictures to frame them with meaning. It used to be axiomatic that broadcasting was the most trusted medium for news, for instance. As television became the dominant medium in the 1960s it also became the case that television news was where the overwhelming majority of the national audience took its first intelligence in any day. News coverage and its impact on audiences has dominated much media research in universities and polytechnics over the past 15 years; although the initial furore, over research like the Glasgow Media Group's *Bad News* on television news bias, has mostly died down, the result has been that broadcasters have begun to worry somewhat more than they did before about what it is they are doing, and how the audience may perceive it.

A study undertaken for the BBC in 1983 (published the following year) had disturbing things to tell broadcasters about news coverage and perceptions of it. Looking at the coverage in television news of three issues (the Common Market, Unemployment and the Police) the study found that although audiences still considered television to be the most accurate and detailed (41 per cent; only 17 per cent thought the Press most accurate), a third thought television omitted important facts. Between a quarter and a half thought television should have shown more on each of these issues. Up to 46 per cent thought television sometimes *deliberately* misleading, compared with 38 per cent who thought it generally honest. This finding is in marked contrast to earlier research on audience perceptions of the integrity of broadcasting, but it reflects a slow trend by audiences to hold broadcasters more and more at arms length, even suspiciously, a problem which programme-makers increasingly find when they approach the public. In this survey BBC1 emerged as the channel with most audience credibility for accuracy and interest; audiences claimed they were able to distinguish where bias had occurred and to discount it. Research on the Press has shown audiences believe the Press to be more biased.

Another 1980s study of audience comprehension of television news (a BBC internal report) somewhat tentatively suggests that audiences do have difficulty in taking in the wealth of information that news bulletins throw at them. Perhaps most intriguingly the research found that what was said by television newscasters was much more important than what was seen. The report recommended repetition of important items; better ordering of items to indicate which were the most important; the use of graphics wherever possible. It also said broadcasters should be given more incentive to improve comprehensibility. In twenty News and Current Affairs meetings attended by the principal author of the report the audience was mentioned just twice. It is worth emphasising that my own experience is the same as Professor Robinson's. Over a much wider span of types of meeting audiences were rarely discussed, or even mentioned, except as an abstract concept.

Equally, audience members may have very hazy ideas of the broadcasters who make programmes, or of their organisations. While they may have the most clear-cut views (and factual information) on the nature of the family structure in, say, *Dallas* they may have hardly any idea who brings it weekly before them. This is borne out by IBA research which showed that about 40 per cent of viewers thought 'Jewel in the Crown' was a BBC production, rather than a Granada one; the BBC on the whole, is believed to be the originator of fine classic drama. The BBC suffers here as well as gains, possibly because it is so large. ITV companies may gain by being generally small and relatively regional, although when franchise changes result in new programme companies for an area, local viewers often take some time to appreciate what has happened.

But it is true that the BBC is perceived more as an absence than a presence, or as a series of separate bits, radio and television, perhaps a local radio station, or a regional television one. Small group research conducted for this study in May 1985 suggested that for some of the audience at least the image of 'BBC' is simply non-existent. It may be that, with the slow but accelerating proliferation of broadcasting outlets, to expect audiences at large to identify individual 'owners' of programmes is to expect the casual book reader to be able to identify the publisher, or the newspaper and magazine reader to do likewise.

If this is true it will be a much bigger problem for the BBC than for any other broadcasting organisation, given the organisation's belief that it is only by identifying the BBC directly as provider through its programmes that people at least accept the principal of paying for the licence. One of the last major studies undertaken for the BBC on audience attitudes (the AMBO study, 1980) did indeed discover a number of disturbing things. Although nearly three-quarters of the audience had a favourable impression of the BBC, the number who did not had doubled from seven per cent in a previous study to 15 per cent (i.e. to about a sixth). The report also found that for many people the BBC did not exist: the implication here was that the whole range of its activities did not come easily to mind.

Unsurprisingly perhaps, in this AMBO study, where BBC political bias was detected by 20 per cent of the audience, three-quarters thought it was right-wing; about 15 per cent left-wing. The most favourable impressions of the BBC were in the south, the least favourable in the north and in Scotland. On finance three-quarters knew the BBC was financed by licence fee but a surprising 17 per cent believed the money to come directly from Government, a figure to be set against the 30 per cent who thought the BBC to be *controlled* by Government. In fact 20 per cent favoured direct government financing anyway, 49 per cent thought the BBC should take advertising (compare this with some of the most recent data from surveys which suggest that a majority by late 1985 favoured the BBC taking advertising if it meant the licence fee could be held steady). Thirty-one per cent thought the BBC managed its financial affairs badly (perhaps reflecting a comparison with other nationalised industries); forty-three per cent thought it could save money without affecting programme standards.

What this all means (or meant) to the BBC, struggling to keep the public on its side over the licence fee and its future, is hard to decide. Taken with other research (see 'The Image Problem', below), what it seems to amount to is that the public is inconsistent, if not perverse, in its attitudes and, more significantly, its knowledge of broadcasting and how it is put together. The biggest problem remains public indifference to the relationship between good broadcasting and the need for them to pay for it; and in the frequent misunderstanding of broadcast finance. On this latter point, however, few broadcasters would claim more than a working understanding of the exact sums involved and, certainly, the means of holding costs down. But the public believe firmly that BBC 'stars' get very large sums indeed to do various shows and this appears to annoy and irritate.

THE IMAGE PROBLEM

Part of the BBC's overall image problem has been to 'explain' its programme costs, not just its proportionately smaller administrative costs. To a Britain battered by years of public-spending cuts it all looks like too much being spent on too privileged a few. This is borne out by the research commissioned for the BBC to put its case for a continued licence fee system of finance to the Peacock Committee. Broadcasters have been hoist by their own petard: the distorting mirror of news was being applied to them. Suddenly they were thrown up against a public whose perceptions could not easily be shifted.

Ever since the Peacock Committee's brief had been announced various newspapers had commissioned polls which apparently showed that a majority of the British public were in favour of the BBC taking advertising. The BBC research showed exactly the same, although great effort had gone into asking the question in context. Only two groups did not (as a majority). These were members of the top social scale, ABs, who make up 15 per cent of the population; the other group were those who said they disapproved of advertising (20 per cent of the population) but even here 37 per cent said they would support advertising on the BBC.

But the research did find that the public had no clearly defined view of the consequences of different kinds of finance for programme output or scheduling and that, in particular, their knowledge of and attitude to the licence fee was 'complex' – a conundrum, said the report. The public also appeared to see the output of BBC1 similarly to that of ITV; that of BBC2 to that of Channel Four. They had little idea of how ITV was funded (along with many professionals who know but vaguely).

Research in the area of attitudes is notorious for showing what the researcher wants. The arguments much deployed in the Press in the autumn and winter of 1985 consistently suggested that about two-thirds of the public would not be unhappy at the BBC taking some advertisements to raise extra money. The Broadcasting Research Unit, in part funded by the BBC, produced further research which said the opposite. Their questions were, however, as loaded as everyone elses, insisting with respondents that they 'understood' what the implications of advertising on the BBC might be.

It was a further irony of the public debate surrounding the Peacock Committee (see Chapter 12) that the BBC's own research backed that being espoused in the newspapers. The BMRB research for the BBC found, as with AMBO, that most people knew the BBC was funded from the licence fee, but a large minority (17 per cent) said the Government paid. Although around 90 per cent assumed that this fee paid for television only around half realised it also paid for network radio and less than 40 per cent knew that it paid for BBC local radio. This is an illustration of why most people do not know how ITV is funded (the 'its free' belief) and why if there is not a directly related payment (as there is no longer for radio) the public will simply forget, if they ever knew, who pays for a service. Most of those asked (28 per cent) had little idea of how much the current licence was, the average guess putting it lower than the current fee. Even fewer knew by how much it had gone up in 1985.

On value for money, the percentage agreeing it was excellent rose as the sums presented to them were given in shorter time spans. That is, only 11 per cent agreed it was good value at £58 a year but 21 per cent thought so at 15p per day. The bulk of the public appears to believe the licence fee is 'reasonable' value rather than good value. Overall the BMRB report found:

> people's feelings about the licence fee present us with something of conundrum. The majority believe the licence represents value for money and would not wish to give up BBC1/2 in return for paying no licence fee and would be prepared to pay more than the current level to retain BBC1/2; but large numbers have difficulty in finding the money to pay it, many have to save up and a substantial minority would prefer to pay in smaller, more frequent instalments.

All this, the report concludes, is a puzzle which puts the public in the position of understanding at least part of the licence fee system rationally although disliking it. In that respect the BBC may do better than local authorities trying to get their customers to understand the rates and, soon, the community charge. Unfortunately for the BBC broadcasting intrudes on the customer every day, not once or twice a year. Furthermore, parts of the public have begun to insist that they have more than consumer rights: that because broadcasting is the animal it is, they (we) should have a much broader range of general rights. As we have seen these include access.

Again a paradox arises. It sometimes seems that the voices clamouring for more access – and those, sometimes in parallel, sometimes not, clamouring for more 'control' – follow a will-o'-the-wisp of uncertainty of purpose. So many debates overlap here. There are those who seek pure access because they believe they are not 'represented' enough by broadcasting. Minority groups of all kinds are in this group. Then there is a political argument for more access: broadcasting has to express more clearly the aspirations of democracy. Sometimes this gets confused with the minority groups arguments.

Then there are those who believe broadcasting is out of control. Mrs Whitehouse and her own stage army of moral majoritists abide here. But there are many other people who, disagreeing with the implications of the Mrs Whitehouses, are nonetheless perturbed at broadcasting's intrusions and lapses. We know more and more about audiences and audience attitudes; hardly anything about those of producers, especially their images of the audience.

Central to this continuing debate (which is often simply a messy argument) is the question of the portrayal of sex and violence on television, brought back into prominence by the Conservative Government in 1985 groping for a 'Falklands Factor' topic to use in a future General Election campaign. In the context of the mid-1980s a book about broadcasters and their audiences has to examine, however briefly, this crown of thorns, not least now because, for the first time, a formal body is about to begin work on deciding where public taste lies in this most delicate of arenas.

SEX AND DRUGS AND ROCK AND ROLL

The BBC receives most complaints about scheduling; next come complaints about bad language, and of this category a considerable proportion of complainers are unhappy about blasphemy. On-screen nudity is another source of many complaints; violence rates rather less highly. None of this is new: in the 1950s when television was young a similar concern was expressed – as forcibly – about violence and sex in children's comics and in the cinema. Just as it is now, some of that concern was directed at US imports.

The attitude of broadcasters – and this applies to radio drama, for instance – in this area of public concern has not endeared them to audiences. Although there are guidelines, and these are revised from time to time, read aloud they sound arbitrary and even cynical. The standard reply from broadcasters is that they are (a) reflecting 'reality'; (b) the actual number of incidents of violence, or explicit

sexual activity, are low; (c) programmes showing this material only
go out after 9 pm; (d) audiences like 'action'; and finally (e) few
people complain anyway. This last point was the splash headline in
the BBC's own publication *Ariel* in December 1985, when it became
obvious that a campaign on reducing levels of violence on television
was gathering pace. The headline prefaced a story announcing that
the then Director-General, Alasdair Milne, was setting up yet
another internal enquiry which would look, yet again, at the evidence
– and commission further research!

As with the newspaper Press, broadcasters use both sex and
violence to sell – in this case programmes. Audiences tuning to
late-night horror movies, or to *The Sweeney* or *Kojak* know exactly
what they are going to get. Violence is excitement; sex is titillation or
arousing or sometimes amusing. Techniques like these have been a
part of theatre since ancient Greece and always will be. To argue
'reality' or to try to give other reasons for incorporating explicit
scenes of mayhem, bloodshed or the intimacy of intercourse is to fly
in the face of what everyone privately knows and frequently relishes.

Having said that, where are we left? Times have changed. It no
longer applies, as Mrs Whitehouse would have it, that novelists like
Dickens did not have to resort to explicit sex scenes to sell books; in
any case, go back a hundred years to the 18th century and we have
Fanny Hill; go back three hundred and we have the appalling and
explicit violence of the 17th century dramatist, Webster. The central
question about the portrayal – and degree – of sex and violence on
television, or the use of 'bad' language in radio plays is about the
relationship between broadcaster and audience.

To the extent that Mrs Whitehouse makes plain the arrogance
implied by drama programme-makers (and the rest where the cap
fits) when they dismiss public unhappiness at some of what they
produce she does a great service. There is a hypocrisy at work here
which denies while busily doing what it denies. In the weeks after it
had self-righteously denounced BBC television for the degree of
explicit general nastiness in the soap opera *EastEnders*, the *Daily
Mirror* ran for a week the tape transcripts of the moors murderers,
Ian Brady and Myra Hindley. They spared their readers (presumably
including children) nothing of the truly disgusting details. The
separation between the avowed intent of 'public interest' and the
'reflecting reality' of programme-makers is questionable. The *Daily
Mirror* can argue at length, no doubt, that fiction is not the same as
fact; but news coverage has become much more explicit and as the

competition hots up the mistakes multiply, to a point where footage of a public execution can be shown in the early evening news bulletins (normally the 'hard stuff' is kept back until the later news).

All this can be deeply disturbing to many members of the public. The trigger level – the moment most people, or even quite a sizeable minority – get up and publicly protest is probably still some way away. As we have seen, the mechanisms for access, although in theory many, are in practice limited in scope. Part of the BARRTA study, in collaboration with the BBC Broadcasting Research Department Special Projects, polled a national sample to find out how many had thought of complaining; especially, we were interested in why, as we suspected, so many had in fact *not* complained. About a third of those interviewed (in August 1984) said they had felt like complaining either very or fairly often. Around half said they had never felt like complaining. The level of feeling like complaining applied more or less evenly to all groups, although there was a slight correlation between a desire to complain and heavy listening and viewing.

But only two per cent of the one third who wished to complain had ever bothered to do so. The commonest reason given was that it was too much trouble (34 per cent) or that it would make no difference (40 per cent). On both counts it is clear that broadcasters have failed to make those existing mechanisms of accountability sufficiently clear-cut and easily accessible, and that they have, even by their own lights, failed to convince that a complaint will be taken seriously. On the second point we shall later see that complaints are examined with some care by managements, although their estimation of the relevance or significance of any one complaint may be erratic, if not downright eccentric.

The sample was also asked what influences they thought did affect programme-makers. Only a third of the total interviewed thought it fairly likely that complaints from ordinary viewers and listeners would have an impact. Bad press reviews, pressure groups like Mrs Whitehouse's National Viewers and Listeners Association (NVALA) and possible criticism from Government, were thought by half to be important. The most important influence, however, was seen to be ratings and pressure from advertisers – 75 per cent believed that either of these would affect programme-makers' decisions.

Leaving aside the question of advertising, it is demonstrably true that ratings do affect *management* thinking on programmes, probably too much. This obviously can affect programme-makers either fairly quickly, when a series is running, or more slowly, for future planning. It might affect careers if a disaster were signalled, although this is less likely. What the survey also showed is an audience which has a shrewder idea of the mechanisms of broadcasting than many broadcasters might either allow or particularly like. But sixty years after continuous broadcasting began in Britain, with a television generation behind us, and knowing the average time spent listening to radios or watching television, it should not surprise that many people have a sophisticated knowledge of the broadcasting process. (As a footnote to this, a BBC special project study on drama output found that many of the sample audience believed that, in one of the plays viewed, the sex scenes were added purely for titillation.)

At the same time misinformation is rife, as is borne out by the study for the BBC about the licence fee. The public, then, probably has in general a fairly good idea of the general operating principles of broadcasting. They may well have a stunningly good idea of the precise details of plot lines, of the public and private, screen and home lives, of many broadcasters. They have very poor knowledge in general of the details of broadcasting operations or its finances. Although two thirds of the sample knew of broadcast 'feedback' programmes, this has to be compared with the one-third who had heard of open meetings or of the advisory councils.

There is a cogent set of arguments which says this is acceptable: do the public know about the management of British Rail, or how consumer products at large are manufactured? But these arguments mislead. Broadcasters do not believe they are producing the equivalent of moving wallpaper and argue continuously to be treated in a way consistent with the important – and material and spiritual – difference of what they make. And it is true that broadcasting impacts every day in the home, the place where people are most vulnerable because most relaxed.

If that is the case broadcasting must be treated – and be prepared to treat of itself – more like parts of the political system: local government for instance; or like the Health Service, where the desire for accountability in the stricter definition, has grown apace. It has been part of the cross broadcasters have had to bear that their early reluctance to treat more directly with their audiences led at first to groups like the National Viewers and Listeners Association and the redoubtable Mrs Whitehouse. That lady was early on treated disgracefully by the BBC, who refused to allow her any legitimacy – and to its long-term cost. Their argument was she represented no one but herself, words which a number of current senior BBC staff must now be chewing on painfully. In a curious way Mrs Whitehouse did slow down the debate; few of the more thoughtful inside or outside broadcasting wished to be associated with NVALA and the moral majority close behind.

But while the Right mobilised slowly the Left too began to question the rights of broadcasters. This too is a large debate, which grew all through the 1970s. Broadcasters in part have been more sensitive to, and sensitised by, the Left largely because at programme-making level many are of liberal if not left persuasion. Out of such sentiment originally came the 'Open Door' programmes of the BBC (and the subsequent constant pressure from management on the Community Programme Unit). Pluralism in broadcasting has grown because of these pressures. Books have been written, notably MacShane's *Using the Media* (1979) and more recently the excellent *Getting It On* by Jane Drinkwater.

The Media Project, based at The Volunteer Centre in Hertfordshire has helped in social-action broadcasting, whilst many other organisations have become much more aware that the mass media (not just broadcasting) offer a means to approach the public on a range of issues. Interest of a more specialist kind has been aroused through partial studies, like the Glasgow Media Group's *Bad News* books. It is noticeable that all this activity still resides above the level of the individual. The arrogance of remote broadcasters has given way to earnest discussions with the public – but only as represented by pressure groups of one kind or another. In that sense the older methods – letters, phone calls, public meetings – do provide the only way broadcasters normally get to hear or see the man on the Clapham omnibus; that and the woman in the pub, of course.

One criticism of broadcast managements is that they, like politicians, do not behave like the rest of us. They watch television, if at all, under artificial conditions; they inhabit a narrowly focused world of high finance and – in the BBC – west or south-west London social life. They have friends from a similar background or at least from the professionally successful. Meeting the great unwashed at the BBC public meetings at least gives them a chance to mix, however painfully, with the vulgar but all too real mass, to understand its strange compulsions.

ON THE BORDER: DEVELOPING A COMMON CAUSE

Broadcasters might at this point begin to remonstrate that if they are ever to make programmes they have to turn their backs on these very interesting but potentially interfering facts. Part, a large part, of the BBC structure of central management is there to act as a defensive wall behind which creative genius can evolve, untroubled by the mad, the bad and the sad. There is an element of truth in that.

But broadcasters have to have audiences; those audiences are no longer willing to be passive recipients of the largesse of the professional and remote, be it in television, radio or Government. Problems and uncertainty naturally grow from this. As well, technology upsets previously safe positions, creates opportunities and challenges for everyone. As it happens this has come together in Britain to create in broadcasting a 'turbulent field'.

To overcome the immediate uncertainties it is tempting for organisations like the BBC to retreat into secluded if besieged isolation. That attitude still persists, and to a greater degree than is healthy for the BBC. The alternative is on the surface much less appetising: it is to engage in a *praxis* with the public, to immerse itself in the debate it has, admittedly, frequently called for but which it has appeared to use as a smoke-screen to cover its rapid and at times undignified scramble for the fortress walls.

Part II
Standing Alone: the BBC in the 1980s

6 Hide and Seek: Broadcasters and Audience Research

There is a view that says that above all else broadcasters have become obsessed by the ratings, the weekly, quarterly and annual sets of figures which show which channel has had what share of the total viewing and listening audience in any given period. The impression that this is true is easy enough to understand. Broadcasters have frequently given it in the way they react in public to programmes and how they are described.

But broadcasting exists in a semi-vacuum. Its products disappear at the moment of realisation. The figures provided by an increasingly sophisticated audience research survey are the stuff of one kind of reality. What else can be measured? As time has passed, and the dual system of British broadcasting has become more embedded so the 'ratings battle' itself has taken on a ritual meaning.

Changes are now taking place, where challenges to the meaning of ratings as well as to their statistical validity, are part of the challenge being made to the structure of broadcasting. We have not yet reached a point where those challenges are so obvious to most broadcasters. But, slowly, it is penetrating the minds of all broadcasters that knowledge of the audience well beyond raw viewing or listening figures is desirable and available. The techniques of social and market research can be used to assist the creative process; not everything can be settled by having the biggest audience at any one time.

As competition between BBC television and ITV hotted up in the 1960s so the ratings, and winning and losing audience shares, became more and more critical to broadcasting. In this 'war' there is no doubt that the more aggressive protagonist was the BBC. The reasons for this are not hard to find. For thirty years it was a monopoly; other than turning to foreign radio stations like Radio Normandie in the 1930s and Radio Luxembourg in the 1940s and 1950s audiences had no choice but to listen to the BBC. When television opened again after the Second World War it began with a small audience. Television did not become a national medium until well into the 1950s – arguably after the arrival of commercial television when people had a choice.

From that point on BBC television lost heavily in the ratings war, reduced at one moment in the late 1950s to a share below 30 per cent of total audience. It was at this low ebb in its fortunes that BBC management realised there might be a reaction from the audience at large to reject payment of the licence fee. In hitting back with programmes that a mass audience would tune to, the BBC began a long hard haul to keep the balance of audience share at around 50 per cent. To its credit it has often managed to do better than that but older ideas about what was public service broadcasting kept (and keeps) BBC television at a potential disadvantage. It still puts out less entertainment at peak times than does ITV.

The battle lines are now confused by the addition of both BBC2 and Channel Four. But audience weekly shares by the mid-eighties were roughly settled such that BBC1 gets about 35 per cent; ITV about 45 per cent; BBC2 and Channel Four about 10 per cent each. Much can be made – probably irrelevantly – of why this is so. The key to success in the settled system of the duopoly is that the balance does not, over a year, alter much from a ratio of about 55:45 – to *either* BBC or ITV.

There is a strange ambivalence about winning the ratings battle in the BBC. Although the BBC has to demonstrate it is able to retain the very largest audiences available it also has, as a vital part of its function, what Peter Jay once called a 'mission to explain'. There is no immorality in being too popular, but there are associated dangers. To be equal, occasionally ahead, but not to be obviously, consistently beating commercial television (and radio, although the battle here is unequal), is all the Corporation desires. This makes the BBC the more aggressive partner in the ratings game because it actively seeks a precise place in the total ratings, whereas ITV can go for maximum size at all times. It also means, *pace* BBC television schedulers, that they have often in the past been more defensive in their scheduling. Finally, there is just an element of guilt in the Corporation about ratings at all.

The defensiveness of the BBC has another root. When it was decided to re-schedule 'Panorama' from its long-held Monday evening place before the 'Nine O'Clock News' a 'public' outcry could be heard from some quarters denouncing the abandonment of public service virtues. The BBC is peculiarly prone to these pressures, which can be considerable, because it is after all a public body. The public service element in ITV (and ILR) is there by secondary consideration, whatever the IBA may argue. No one is surprised if ITV wishes to maximise its audiences through popular programming. The BBC, by contrast, is expected to succeed but not too well, as if mere success (as judged by audience size) is a vulgar beginning of a slide away from public service. The 'public' who make this an issue tend to be the powerful and articulate. Often media trade unions are among the more vociferous in making their point on these grounds. The most notorious parts of this lobby wheel into action for Radio Four and Radio Three; their existence is a mixed blessing for network controllers and BBC broadcast managers.

The arrival of Channel Four in the autumn of 1982 upset some of the old certainties, but not that much. Channel Four has now settled into a slot which may mean the permanent reduction of the total BBC share to well below 50 per cent, while previously it had taken in total about 50 per cent. Thus Channel Four has reversed the system 'balance'. The alarms ringing in the period between 1983 and 1986 about the BBC's decline may now be put into context. Indeed at least one senior BBC official had accurately predicted the medium term impact that Channel Four would have on BBC total audience share. We still had, in 1988, a rough balance, now maintained over 20 years of television. This is much more remarkable than it seems at first sight. British television appears to have worked inside a very powerful consensus of broad agreement about public service and public taste; a consensus now largely missing. Until now this has been largely defined within the traditions of the BBC, not just as premier programme-maker but as the supreme arbiter of the meaning of public service broadcasting. The challenge to that position has begun and audience research is part of the weaponry deployed on both sides. It has, in a final analysis, the weight of numbers to reinforce its validity, whatever they might be taken to mean.

MEASURING WHAT?

An audience research department began in the BBC in 1939 although audiences had been measured on an ad hoc basis during the 1930s. The department was set up to measure reaction to programmes rather than audience size. The onset of competition changed that drastically. When ITV started advertisers had to know how many people were watching at any given time, rather than their reactions to a programme. ITV (commercial broadcasting in general) is designed to deliver audiences to advertisers in particular packages; that is how it collects its revenue and why advertisers pay. It is a neat inversion of the duty of the BBC which is, roughly, to deliver programmes to audiences.

The problem for ITV in 1955 was that it had to introduce a system of audience measurement which advertisers would accept: the result was the installation at great expense of Television Audience Measurement (TAM) meters in selected homes, all over the country as the commercial system spread. These registered which channel the television set was tuned to. The measurement system was eventually taken over by JICTAR (Joint Industry Committee for Television Audience Research), whose partners were the Independent Television Companies Association; the Incorporated Society of British Advertisers and the Institute of Practitioners in Advertising.

JICTAR research was aimed at reach and frequency; that is it was a longitudinal study, made up of the panel of metered homes. To select the panel it conducted an annual establishment survey, a high quality random survey of homes taken from the electoral register. Interviewers were then dispatched to ensure that those homes picked out for metering did contain within their household the right characteristics for inclusion. But of the 2400 homes on the panel there was constant attrition; some householders refused to co-operate or withdrew early; replacement was a continuing requirement along with strict controls to keep the whole sample representative. Also there were continuous problems in the operation of the panel itself. Apart from the meter attached to the television set, families were asked to keep a weekly diary of viewing and each week the householder posted back the tape from the meter along with the diary. Both were fed into a computer and the diary and tape married to programme output.

A difficulty of this system is that the tape data and the diary information may not match. The system was designed to edit out a diary entry when the meter tape showed the set was not on; but there were many times when the opposite was true: that is, the set was on but no one was watching it. Finally under the JICTAR system there was the fundamental question unanswered as to what 'viewing' meant. The fact that the television set was on, that there was someone in the room (and recorded as such) did not indicate attention or interest.

The BBC started from a very different position. When the Daily Survey started in 1939, a fundamental issue was public accountability – was the service adequate in return for the licence fee? To find out BBC interviewers went into the streets and asked. Approximately 2000 people, aged five and over, were stopped every day at around 150 points selected to be representative of the UK. By 1968 interviewers had to cover all three television networks, four national radio networks and the beginnings of BBC local radio. By 1982, just before the system changed under BARB (see page 92) there were over 80 local radio stations – although obviously only a maximum of three or four in any one area – as well as the four television networks and, in some places, cable services.

For both broadcasters and public the published differences between audience sizes which these two systems produced created a much misunderstood climate of opinion about what the ratings meant. The public, after all, could hardly be expected to understand an arcane debate couched in the language of statistical method. It was this point, among others, that the Annan Committee picked upon. In practice, programme-makers would choose those figures which most suited. Alternatively the whole exercise could, on occasion be dismissed as lies, damned lies and statistics.

The BBC undertook research additionally into the appreciation of programmes, both radio and television. It did this by sending out questionnaires to volunteer panels asking for reactions to programmes. Reaction Indices (RIs) were used for television, General Evaluations (GEs) for radio. A major criticism of the radio panel was that it was recruited via on-air appeals thereby only getting 'supporters' as panel members. The BBC also conducted a small series of special projects. A selection from these were published each year in an Annual Review of Research Findings from the 1970s onward. Finally, there were bigger enquiries of a much more general nature conducted from time to time, as with 'The Peoples' Activities and Use of Time' and 'Daily Life in the Eighties'.

Although the IBA did not itself conduct audience-size measurement research it too had had a long-standing research project into audience appreciation, based on all ITV regions as well as London, resulting in ITV programme Appreciation Indices. The IBA also paid for limited research on particular topics at any time. In 1974–75 these additional surveys cost £33 000, 36 per cent of its research budget.

RINGING IN CHANGE

When the Annan Committee came to look at the problem of audience research one of the items on the agenda was the discrepancies between the two systems of measurement. The other was the cost of audience research. Annan said that audience research was too piecemeal, too narrow, too superficial. The Report suggested further, and damningly, that despite all the apparent activity in the BBC's Broadcasting Research Department, it was swamped by too many facts and figures. Those running it, said the Report, were unable to evaluate what they had, to detect trends. They did not appear to have a coherent research strategy.

Producers had told Annan they did not find the work of the audience researchers from any side of much use; from others the Committee heard that where they had wanted research to be done to help programme-planning the researchers had said they had no time to do it. A number of bodies giving evidence did suggest there ought to be much more co-operation between the two principal systems. Annan went further saying that a common system was an essential requirement. Out of this recommendation the Broadcasters' Audience Research Board was born of an agreement reached in 1978 between the BBC and the ITCA (the Independent Television Companies Association) – now the Television Companies Association (TVCA).

During this time and in the early part of the 1980s, the BBC Broadcasting Research Department underwent fundamental changes, bringing it into much greater prominence within the BBC, and establishing a new set of bona fides within which credibility with programme-makers, and availability to them for special one-off research, were priorities.

The formation of BARB (Broadcasters' Audience Research Board), which began operating the measurement service in August 1981, was not at all easy. It is a limited company originally jointly owned by the BBC and the TVCA. Subsequently Channel Four, S4C and TV-am joined. The BBC and the TVCA are sole shareholders in BARB, whose Board contains equal representatives of both organisations. On the management and technical sub-committees sit representatives of other bodies: ISBA (Incorporated Society of British Advertisers), the IPA (Institute of Practitioners in Advertising), and the IBA, along with Channel Four, S4C and TV-am.

BARB was set up to do two principal things: to provide an audience measurement service; and to provide an audience reaction service. Lengthy discussions had to take place after the company was formed to solve technical problems. BARB appointed AGB Research Ltd to continue to conduct the measurement service, and the BBC Broadcasting Research Department to undertake the reaction service. For the BBC the adoption of the basic JICTAR system for measurement had profound implications. Among other worries by programme staffs were the changes in audience sizes the new system showed. In fact these were now more accurately measured; few programme makers appreciated this at the time, nor wanted to. For them it seemed to suggest confusion. Little effort had gone into explaining in advance the new system and its likely impact on measurement. The impression given is that BBC management had little foreknowledge of the effect the new system would have. The measurement system is based on about 3000 households representative of the UK television-owning homes. Meters are fitted as they used to be with JICTAR; household members and guests use a keypad to indicate who is watching at any time, including guests, in the television room for every minute that the set is on. As before AGB is required to maintain an annual establishment survey of 25 000 households. A large range of variables is measured: television reception, family size, presence of children, socio-economic group, weight of television viewing.

The BBC requested, and were given, improvements to the old JICTAR system: a doubling of the sample size for Wales, full monitoring of all television sets in the metered homes, and addition of weight-of-viewing panel controls. The data are analysed weekly; in the BBC a weekly report is issued showing day by day the amount of viewing of each channel, patterns of viewing, estimates of programme audiences, overall share, etc.

Each week BARB publishes a Top Ten within channels, along with the share of viewing between the channels. Each month it produces a composite Top 50. The data are susceptible to analysis in a number of ways: checking audience flow between programmes, looking at the amount of television children watch, or testing the demographic characteristics of audiences for particular programmes, for example.

MAKING WAVES

All changes are uncomfortable: those which challenge previous positions or force a revaluation of existing prejudices are the most difficult to come to terms with. The problem of audience measurement and appreciation indices was that they had always been used as ammunition by broadcasters, both externally as a defence and an attack on other channels' output; and internally to 'prove' that a particular programme or scheduling decision had been the correct one to make. With the coming of BARB many of these assumptions were thrown violently into relief. Where people believed they had been winning they now found that, according to BARB, they had in fact been losing; or, that they were suddenly losing was how many interpreted it. The immediate result in the BBC was that BARB was blamed for the apparent change, especially (and perhaps inevitably) by those who had been least enthusiastic about setting up a joint system.

So strong was this feeling that Alasdair Milne, then Director-General, ordered an enquiry into BARB, to be conducted by an adviser to the BBC, in the spring of 1983: the strongest hints were given at the time to the adviser that the report should find the arrangements with BARB wanting. Advisers, however, are employed to give advice, however unpalatable. The report said there were five internal BBC criticisms of BARB, that it

(1) was cumbersome and slow;
(2) produced useless and irrelevant information;
(3) used the wrong methods;
(4) produced inaccurate results;
(5) was too expensive.

Discussion of these points demonstrates precisely the ambivalence that programme-makers feel about this kind of quantitative research: that they long for its confirmations while fearing its denials. Much comment about what was felt to be wrong with BARB did not of course emerge in this way.

Producers in the radio services, for instance, felt that the monthly data sheets (these were not in fact from BARB) that they received were adequate; at the same time they wished for more daily data; but their television colleagues were lamenting that they had no time to examine and understand the data they already had even though this, logically, could have only taken about 15 minutes a day. More critically the report pointed to the continuing need for all statistical data to be given in a form sufficient in detail but not overly so and presented so that the recipient would not feel inadequately equipped to understand it. Weekly Programme Review Boards, staffed by mainly senior personnel, do spend too much time worrying over the graphs and tables and re-describing their contents, not enough asking what they mean.

The report further pointed out that the argument against BARB on the grounds of expense was also probably based on a false idea of what audience research had previously cost the BBC. In fact the BBC spent about 0.4 per cent of its total expenditure on research, a figure which compared favourably with the costs to other large organisations that needed to undertake market research.

Presented to a 1983 Television Programme Review Board, the report received a generally hostile reception, not least because there has been a continuing hostility to audience research at Review Boards. BBC executives retain a high level of scepticism about audience research and on occasion are happy to state even at BBC public meetings that it is not worth the paper it is written on, nor can it tell as much about the listening and viewing audience as a single letter or phone call or 'gut reaction'. In the 1980s, with sophisticated (and expensive: in 1983 BARB alone was costing the broadcasters £2.8m a year to run) means at their disposal broadcasters needed a fairly brutal lesson in growing up. Audience research is able to delineate to a considerable extent who audiences are; what they want; how they behave; what they think of what they see and hear. Much is uncomfortable to read, which is why broadcasters, who believe so firmly that theirs is a creative business, find it so hard to take what quantitative (as well as qualitative) research appears very often to be saying. There is a problem as well about interpretation of the figures.

DEVELOPING THE 'SPECIAL PROJECT'

Where audience research has begun to penetrate most into programme-making is through special projects: research which *inter alia* is designed to help programme-makers evaluate programme ideas and, subsequently, the response to a programme or a series. But here too both programme-makers and broadcasting management have sometimes found it hard to swallow what has been uncovered. There have been special reports (one-off studies) done by BBC Broadcasting Research since the setting up of the department. The reports have normally been confidential to the BBC but recently an increasing number have been made available; the results of others have been published, since the 1970s, in an annual review.

Among the first special projects, before 1939, was one on 'Living Habits' – set up to discover facts about people's availability to listen. The war stopped this kind of research dead in its tracks but after 1946 there were a growing number of such *ad hoc* reports. In the early

1950s research was undertaken into who were the burgeoning television-set owners; the effects of crime series – and Dick Barton especially – on juvenile delinquency (an early example of what was to become and remain a media research favourite); and the presentation of ideas and information by television.

The *ad hoc* studies reflect organisational priorities in interesting ways. Television pre-programme studies began to figure more and more as did studies on what television was doing to people. Thus, by the mid-fifties studies had been done on the comprehensibility of statistics on television; on viewer attitudes to quiz games; on afternoon programmes for women. In the 1960s we find studies on channel choice (recognising the impact of ITV at a time when the BBC was suffering most); on audience attentiveness; and, significantly as it came to more and more prominence, audience reaction to General Election coverage.

The first of the BBC's large scale post-war 'time budget' studies, *The Peoples' Activities*, looking at what the national audience were doing every half hour, day by day, was published in 1965. This study has been twice replicated: in 1974–5 and in 1984 (*Daily Life in the 1980s*). The studies are a monumental testament to a fascinating subject; curiously none of the data have been much exploited in programmes. The data are mostly used by outsiders, although *Breakfast Time*, the BBC's early-morning show, used the latest data before it went on-air to check on the habits of its likely audiences.

Only 83 studies were started (and not all finished) between 1939 and 1969; a further 67 were started in the next ten years, mostly completed; in March 1985, special projects were running no less than 73 studies, most of them short term. The turnover was very high, as was the profile of this part of BRD. A much more aggressive 'marketing' policy within the BBC was evident as was a willingness to co-operate with outside agencies (including no less than three separate exercises in collaboration with this study).

Projects undertaken in mid-1984 included for television: an investigation into the appeal of television plays; an evaluation of the audience for *Pebble Mill at One*; an in-depth survey of viewers to *Songs of Praise*; opinions of television output; what were the viewing patterns of the unemployed? In radio (including local radio) a report was being prepared on 'overlap' listening and weekly patterns of listening; listener awareness of changes to VHF and its implications; reactions to the Radio 4 programme, 'Rollercoaster'.

For local radio, studies were under way to survey local loyalties in the vicinity of the planned Radio Shropshire; to establish levels of listening to and support for 'community' radio in areas around Manchester; and an evaluation of the usefulness of motorway signs telling motorists how to tune to their nearest local radio for traffic information.

There is no doubt that, uniquely, the BBC has built up, almost by accident in the past, a huge potential for in-house research, a potential only now being used. There is a long way to go. As well, with the continuous run of cuts (with more in the pipeline), the Broadcasting Research Department is always vulnerable to the much-voiced internal criticism that it does not make programmes. What these critics fail to see is that to make programmes – and ones which viewers will want to hear or see in a much fiercer competitive environment – requires more and more intelligence-gathering at earlier and earlier stages.

This leaves the problem of programme-makers' 'gut-feelings'. These could be dismissed as irrelevant in this environment because the mistakes they lead to are going to be too expensive to contemplate. But there will always be a need for 'feelings', informed as they may be by long experience in programme-making (or scheduling). The art of programme-making undoubtedly needs the 'science' of market research; it will always need confidence in its own less measurable intuitions.

Good audience research, both quantitative and qualitative; audience measurement; audience appreciation; and audience attitudes, all have much to say to the programme-maker prepared to listen. The key area which demonstrates this is educational broadcasting where it has long been recognised and built into the programme-making process.

Research into audiences (and much of the rest of a massive and constantly growing body of knowledge) shows that audiences maintain a close and often highly informed interest in the works of the broadcasters. This knowledge may have been enhanced of late by the BBC's own efforts to explain itself to its 'shareholders'. It also shows that this immense interest is two-edged. The public like broadcasting; they use it a great deal. They are clearly prepared to pay for it, although other evidence suggests that they do not often relate the licence fee to their own use of the output in any way. But they are not sufficiently consulted at nodal points in broadcasting's own debates; if broadcasters need audiences then the relationship has yet to be hammered out; it remains the case that audiences are bought and sold on the market – even by the BBC in its own politicking. Audiences are growing increasingly aware that this might be so.

Audience research is one of the more valuable and tested means of establishing greater and lesser detailed facts about the people who pay for broadcasting (if only through increased prices of consumer goods). That it has been less well used overall by broadcasters is a problem for the future. More and more producers are finding that pre-programme research, for instance, can help planning, but it may well be that programme-makers in particular will always deny themselves the full extent of audience research findings because they need to retain the creative mystique which will allow a programme to be made which apparently goes against the grain of audience acceptance.

7 The People Machine

The Annan Committee was disparaging about broadcasting advisory bodies, reporting that one member of such a body had described it as 'middle-class, middle-aged and middle-brow'. Ten years after the report was published this observation was still accurate. Although the BBC has made strenuous efforts to alter the composition of a number of its advisory bodies, they remain stubbornly white collar.

At the BBC – in the centre, in the regions, and in the local radio stations – advisory councils have been perceived in general as useful means to gauge the public temperature on a range of broadcasting issues. The BBC is not alone in having such bodies; the IBA and a number of the ITV programme companies also have advisory bodies although Channel Four does not. The BBC has developed the most extensive network: over 60 advisory bodies exist, bringing in 1000 or so members of the public – although not representative, useful for what they can do. The overall pattern of the advisory structure may be divided into three parts. First and with most real power are the National Broadcasting Councils of Scotland, Wales and Northern Ireland. Second there are the specialist committees. Most notable among these are the education committees which have *de facto* veto powers over programmes.

Then there is the agricultural committee, science, engineering, the industry and business consultative group, music, Asian, and the joint (with the IBA) religious committee, CRAC. Many of the central specialist committees are 'shadowed' by national regional ones, on agriculture, music, religion, appeals, education. Finally, there are the regional advisory councils for English regional television areas, reduced in 1986 from eight to five, and the dozens of local radio councils.

Sitting awkwardly among all these committees is the General Advisory Council (GAC) which, although London-based, may best be thought of as part of the lowest level of advice giving, despite vehement denial of this by the BBC, and the long survival of the GAC. Although many influential people are invited to be among its members its ponderous nature and diffuse operation mean it is less effective than it might be.

The committees arose early on. Reith, almost as soon as he became General Manager of the old Company, appointed a religious advisory committee, following that with one for education. Others were formed, notably the committee on the spoken word, and the General Advisory Council began its life in 1935. The driving force behind these committees and councils has always been with the BBC at the centre; they remain part of the paternal 'old' BBC, with an understanding that in some fashion or other the 'great and the good' be they national or local figures, will be asked for advice.

Although the BBC sets great store by them, many of the members complain that their purpose is unclear to them. This complaint is a common one made by 'advisers', wherever they operate and whoever appoints them. BBC programme-makers, outside specialist areas, also say they have little idea of what these committees are for; certainly not, they opine, to give 'professionals' advice. The committees are formally accountable within the BBC to the Directorate of Public Affairs and its many parts. Regional Television and Local Radio committees, while clearly reporting up in this formal way, do give much valuable ground-level advice directly to the relevant television or radio station.

Programme-makers in specialist areas (like science) tend to have a clearer view of what their own advisory group does for them and how it fits in with other forms of advice. The clearest distinction can be made, when discussing the usefulness of the advisory councils, between education and the rest of programme-making. The educational broadcasters have a much closer relationship with the councils which serve them; a relationship which approaches veto powers. Of the other specialist areas agriculture exerts a strong pull, as does science and of course religion, where the unique joint committee, CRAC, operates.

The breakdown of the advisory groups can be made in different ways from the one given here: for instance, constitutionally the GAC is in a quite different set of circumstances from the national broadcasting councils; nevertheless it is in the same category of informal relationship, its lack of formal power balanced by its proximity to the centre of the BBC and by its ability to pull in, how ever on occasion reluctantly, all senior BBC managers four times a year for some kind of general discussion on output.

NATIONAL BROADCASTING COUNCILS

The National Broadcasting Councils meet once a month, normally in the national regions; once a year in London. They can meet where they wish and some creative tensions are evident when a council decides it wants to meet outside the normally accepted geographical pattern. One option the National Councils have not taken up is to meet once in a while in a television studio when the cameras are switched on, or in a radio suite similarly switched on in order to broadcast. (In fact the BBC has broadcast parts of a public meeting on air – see p. 117 – but says, justifiably no doubt, that to listen to such meetings is very dull. Advisory Committee meetings – but not necessarily National Broadcasting Councils – might also be rather boring.)

The SBC, BCW and BCNI (to give them their BBC titles) are fairly powerful bodies. They do have executive powers, they do receive quite detailed financial and personnel information. None of the individual members perhaps quite realises how strong in constitutional terms they are; BBC senior staff in the regions are not particularly anxious to tell them. *Vis-à-vis* the centre they are additionally powerful because their meetings are chaired, respectively, by the national governors of Scotland, Wales and Northern Ireland. This enables local managers to feed messages directly back to Board of Governor (BoG) meetings in London. This facility has led to accusations that England is under-represented against the demands of the powerful Celtic fringe as it has no 'region' and no regional governor. The 'new' regional structure, agreed and rushed through in the post-1985 licence fee financial crisis, will go some way to remedy this but not all that far. For instance, the South East remains a big problem in terms of regional identity, as does the concept of 'England' overall.

The National Broadcasting Councils have similar problems of composition along with the English regional television and local radio councils. At the same time there are 'balances' in terms of geography and background if not in many other senses. All this has eventually to be agreed by London and the Board of Governors. As the National Councils have executive power this agreement by London is no rubber stamp: who they are can make a big difference to relations between the national regions and the centre.

The National Councils vary in the use of their executive powers – and knowledge of them. On the whole members do not appreciate – nor apparently ask, much – what they could in fact do should they so choose. The BBC treats its National Councils with circumspection but, in its own interests, with a degree of absentmindedness. That is, a strong impression can be given that were members to enquire too deeply how far they might go in exercising their rights, the BBC might find it difficult to articulate what those rights were. This is understandable. Regional senior staff stress they are well aware of the powers of the National Councils. At the same time they take some care to lead their Councils along particular roads.

What, then are those powers? The National Councils are told in the Royal Charter that their 'function' is:

(1)   controlling the policy and *content* [emphasis added] of the programmes for reception in that region;
(2)   such other functions as the BBC may devolve [i.e. staff appointments at senior levels];
(3)   tendering advice.

It is with the last function that the BBC is most happy, of course, and the Broadcasting Councils were given their draconian brief in the floodtide of the devolution debate of the 1970s. They can function usefully for the regions in acting as a lobby, partly through their governor/chairman, partly through the exercise of the Celtic lobby of three governors, collectively.

Of the three councils the most obviously established is the Scottish. The Welsh Council seems curiously uncertain, possibly because, despite the noises made by Welsh nationalists, Wales remains several places not very connected. The newest council, in Northern Ireland, has yet to flex its muscles. It is weakened by the same divisions, potentially, as the community it represents and serves. Not even 60 years of BBC consensus can change *that* overnight.

The National Councils reflect their region (or nation). They are able to exert a more powerful moral pressure on the BBC centrally than could the old English regional television councils. (The five new ones may well turn out to be more powerful.) At the same time they are welcomed locally by broadcasters who see in their existence a defence against encroachments of either London-based policies or London-launched cuts. The policies are worked out locally by the broadcasters, not, in general, by the Councils.

THE SPECIALIST COMMITTEES

There were in 1986 twenty-four specialist committees, including all the national regional versions of the religious, agricultural, appeals and schools councils. Centrally the councils are:

Central Religious Advisory Committee (CRAC), joint with the IBA, as is the Appeals Committee;

Schools Broadcasting Council of the UK (see Chapter 11);

Continuing Education Advisory Council (see Chapter 11);

Agricultural Advisory Committee;

Central Music Advisory Committee

Central Appeals Advisory Committee;

Engineering Advisory Committee;

Science Consultative Group;

Industrial and Business Affairs Consultative Group;

Asian Programme Advisory Committee.

Regionally:

Scotland had its own religious, education, agriculture, music, appeals and Gaelic committees;

Wales had its own religious, education, agriculture and appeals committees;

Northern Ireland had its own religious (mixed denomination, it should be noted), education, agriculture and appeals committees.

These bodies meet on average three times a year. They are able to bring specific advice. Agriculture, science, engineering, business and the Asian councils all work closely with programme-makers. The view of programme-makers is that they are reasonably effective and that they are welcome. This is one area of the advisory system where both advisers and the advised combine to agree that there is a mutual value.

This is not to suggest that tensions do not arise. Professional farmers, scientists or businessmen frequently feel that broadcasting is not accurately reflecting their constituencies at any one time. It would be wrong to suggest, in saying this, that members of these bodies are unified in their views over any one issue. Frequent divisions of opinion occur between advisers and quite often some advisers will side with broadcasters against other advisers or broadcasters. Sometimes all will unite against a management position – usually when budget cuts are on the agenda.

The biggest tensions arise not so much from the specialist output but from general news and current affairs programmes. The BBC needs these bodies badly, however, if it is to keep its place as a perceptive interpreter of British culture.

The Asian Committee is part of that desire. The BBC has been well aware in recent years that, like many other British institutions, it has not kept pace with ethnic changes in the way it has recruited. The Corporation has tried belatedly (many Asians believe it is *too* late) to recruit more young Asians to its ranks. The Asian council is another attempt at bridge-building. Asian community leaders were happy to agree to having a council; West Indian community leaders were opposed to having one on the grounds that they did not wish to bring attention to any differences between them and the majority culture (this was in the late 1960s). The Asian Council has its own peculiar problems (not dissimilar to the Northern Ireland religious council). Complaints against the BBC often revolve around perceptions of the output being far too culturally insensitive to, for example, Asian attitudes to sexual behaviour.

The Asian Programme Advisory Committee is enjoined to discuss Asian programmes. But, inevitably, its interests continually spill into general programme areas. This is a dilemma for the BBC with respect to all specialist councils. Yet it would be generally true to say that some of the most fruitful advice emerges from the more general discussions, not the particular. On specialist councils additional value is obtained because producers come and listen.

The BBC decision to set up a consultative group (a first-stage advisory body, though in practice its deliberations are the same as those of full councils) on business and industry was motivated internally by the desire to deny the complaint that the whole country, including the BBC, was anti-industry. The immediate problem in setting up the group was arranging for both management and trade union members to be part of one body. There were fears that the meetings would turn into slanging matches between the two sides of industry with the BBC holding the ring. If anything the attacks have been from both sides against the BBC.

Membership of all these councils remains less problematic than for the general councils. The BBC has many antennae pushed out into the various communities of interest, not least through the programme contacts it makes. Many of those invited on to advisory councils have previously been involved with broadcasting, either as contributors to programmes or, in one form or another, as complainants. As with many other institutions the BBC could not get as many useful people on to its councils as it does if they had not first raised their own profile by complaining (seldom by praising).

THE GAC AND THE REGIONAL AND LOCAL RADIO ADVISORY COUNCILS

The General Advisory Council is itself unusual in that 'representatives' from all major areas of British life sit on this Council. It normally meets four times a year, and for some time its agenda was dominated by discussion of papers previously prepared by the BBC Secretariat (see chapter 8).

The GAC is attended by the Governors who by convention do not normally speak, just listen; the chairman of the Board sits alongside the chairman of the GAC with the Director-General on the other side. The meeting is attended by many senior BBC staff (e.g. Board of Management members, Controllers, regional staff, etc.) and beset by dozens of other BBC officials. As it has about 60 members, the atmosphere in the BBC Council Chamber at Broadcasting House where it normally meets is frequently airless. This physical oppression can sometimes spill into the meeting, insofar as there is sometimes a 'stuffy' atmosphere among the assembly.

The Director-General will give a report, which may take some time if the BBC has been involved in any public or internal controversy – more and more common. Discussion of the main paper follows with a degree of domination from BBC staff who may be called upon constantly to answer a specific point. The size of the GAC inhibits sensible debate, the top table being the only group clearly able to see who is who – and often who exactly is speaking. The GAC is dominated by interest groups, or by noisy individuals who tend to push their point of view, knowing they may only have one chance to say something. It has by its current constitution to include all five regional advisory council chairmen and the chairman of the chairmen of the local councils (15 per cent of the radio total); MPs make up another, smaller but significant, pressure group (for time and attention).

There are few 'ordinary' people in any sense of the word; the BBC defends this by saying that the Council ought to be (effectively) a version of the great and the good. The Council, by asking for papers, does invite broadcasters to think about what they do and in that sense it is useful, but published papers take time to emerge. A recent suggestion (during a discussion on accountability) that the Council ought to be open to the Press if not to the public drew gasps of disbelief from the BBC side.

BBC advisory councils are not encouraged to vote. The potential for divisiveness, the constitutional (and real) question of what any vote would mean, all lend weight to this argument. But, again note, not voting suggests a high level of consensus, now increasingly missing from all public or semi-public deliberations outside the BBC. In fact the GAC would not sink or swim on the issue of voting. It is already outmoded and by and large the least useful part of the BBC advisory structure, perpetuating as it does three abiding but dangerous cultural myths – of centralism, secrecy, and élitism. In fact the GAC represents a classic paternal model of what constitutes both advice and accountability. And although the above-the-line costs are relatively small (in 1984–85 they were just short of £22 000 of which £12 000 were members' expenses), the hidden costs must be considerable. These include a large amount of staff time and effort throughout parts of the BBC, and often at senior levels, to prepare for meetings and to attend them.

The GAC exerts some weight – the attendance of governors ensures that. It has also performed a useful function in often getting the Corporation to produce published papers on particular topics – news values, or industrial coverage. But continuity of interest is a continuous irritant to both sides, broadcast staff and members. The Council does take up a lot of time, does expend a lot of hot air (and eat a quantity of good food).

Throughout the recent troubles of the BBC, especially with the attack on its integrity from the Conservative Central Office, BBC management staff have stressed the importance of a body like the GAC, saying it is a forum where exactly that kind of consensus the BBC needs to keep its central purpose alive is still able to surface. While there is good reason to suppose that the GAC functions in this way as a morale-booster its lamentable failure is in its external public face, which is more or less missing. Even internally one might doubt how far its pronouncements carry any real weight, however pro-BBC they might be. The fact remains that in the kind of public rows the BBC seemed increasingly in 1985–86 to be engaged in, only the Board of Governors could carry the weight needed. And it has only been since the autumn of 1986 that both the chairman and the vice-chairman, Duke Hussey and Joel Barnett, respectively, have themselves been of sufficient 'weight' to be of any help.

There were five regional advisory councils, one for each English television region from November 1986; previously there were eight smaller regions. There is also an advisory council for each BBC local radio station. About 135 people are members of the RACs, some 400 members of the local radio councils. The RAC members were recruited by the eight regional television managers; the local radio members by station managers. Now the RAC members will be recruited by the five Heads of Broadcasting. A sub-committee of the Board of Governors makes final the choices, based on often quite complicated pre-set 'requirements', details of some of which would have already been passed to local managers.

Members sit for three years and a third retire each year. The load on the local managers involved in the initial picking, the sifting and final decision-taking is high. The load is increased at the bottom end by extension of the demands made over the years by the centre, both from Governors and bureaucracy, as to who is required. Great efforts have been made to ensure that the Regional Television Managers and the station managers are putting forward the best people for consideration. The system will now bring Heads of Broadcasting into the same role that the Regional Television Managers had before. What follows describes the situation before November 1986, but we may assume similar rules will apply and similar problems develop. Two major changes there have been. First the new Regional Councils will be larger; second they will have, as a matter of course, all local radio advisory council chairmen as members.

Although the RTMs and the station managers tried to fulfil the norms required of them, they were under local pressures as well. The managers, naturally enough, suggested that they were trying to pick the 'bloody-minded' to sit on their council. Up to a point this may be true but few would wish to pack a council with people who spent all their time arguing over how badly you had done your job. This is borne out by central BBC officials who will refer to individual members of these councils as 'unfortunate choices', or 'not quite right', largely where the individual concerned has transgressed the finely drawn line between polite but heated discussion, and what is perceived to be premeditated and unwarranted attack.

In short the BBC wants and asks for advice, but the terms of the debate are couched in terms of classic liberal philosophy where the advisers have to know the rules. These are unwritten and, inevitably, middle-class and professional in outlook. Thus, the paradox at the heart of the general advisory council system outside the specialist committees or the GAC is that the BBC seeks a 'type' of member who may be difficult to find even among the middle class.

There is a continuous assumption of that same consensus, a

presumption less and less easy to establish in advisory council members, who are acutely aware of their own shortcomings in this respect. In a survey carried out for the BARRTA study, the first formal study ever undertaken, comments about middle-classness and middle-groundedness abounded.

At the same time advisory council members complained they were largely uncertain as to their role within broadcasting. Regional advisory councils felt particularly aggrieved over various decisions taken in the early 1980s by television management over the early evening news and current affairs programme 'Sixty Minutes' and its predecessor, 'Nationwide', and about regional television output generally.

The tension evinced here lies across quite different views of the roles of this part of the advisory council structure. There was evidence that central television management were convinced in the early 1980s that regional television management (under the control of what eventually mutated into the Public Affairs Directorate) were using the RACs to push for more resources. This was possible partly because the RAC chairmen had the ear of the chairman of BoG in a meeting which took place immediately before the GAC. (This meeting has now been ended, to be replaced by one chaired by the Governor who chairs the BoG panel on membership of Advisory Bodies and Councils. Previously, it was chaired by one of the RAC chairman and was therefore a much less controllable meeting, apart from being anomalously placed in the advisory system.) The chairmen met privately the night before to arrange the agenda for this subsequent discussion with the chairman of the Board of Governors.

Central television management took the view that they had to manage the whole output, especially the vital battles being fought over schedules; to concede that the regions had a special place in this system would be to build a nightmarish barrier across strategic planning. In any case, the argument went, lack of finance precluded many regional plans. The solution to this overarching dilemma eventually encompassed the network production centres and it was in an attempt to begin to resolve the financial side that the decision was taken in July 1985, to concentrate more output for the network in the regions, and to restructure those regions that existed into a new system. But this decision was not taken for the benefit of the regions or their RACs. In fact the decision immediately meant the whole regional advisory council structure was put in some doubt.

Local radio councils have had, on the whole, an easier time.

They gain from the relatively small catchment area from which members can be chosen. As with the RACs they are much concerned to establish a definite role. Some succeed better than others; much depends on their relationship with the local senior station staff and the willingness of broadcasters to tell them things as well as use their advice. One station invited its members to man the telephones on a Saturday; this may be compared with the Regional Television Manager who invited his RAC members to attend the regional programme review board.

Fears that the professional broadcasters would find this threatening were rapidly replaced with surprise that RAC members were able to grasp the issues and to contribute positively to such meetings. Both examples demonstrate the desire of this group of advisory body members to do something – anything – to make them feel more useful than just as part of a talking shop – this being the age of the doer. Secondly, it shows once again that over-defensiveness in professional broadcasting is so often misplaced. But it also highlights a constant theme. That is, where an adviser can most be useful is at the grass roots, at the point of closest contact with the professional.

A major problem with advisory councils in the BBC is that they often have split purposes. The most useful, the 'professional' or interest group committees can play a vital part in helping programme-makers although even this relationship can go sour; the music committee, in the past, has been accused of being a forum for bargaining over who got what work on a particular network. The 'lay' committees, like the local radio or regional television committees, can have local influence. But central management have begun to take over more and more these intrinsically small-scale localised functions, in order to feed intelligence back to the centre. The most fruitful part of the lay council structure has been undermined by this process for although the RAC members in particular feel flattered that 'London' visits their meetings, many also feel that 'London' is fobbing them off when awkward questions are asked.

The RACs, much more than the local radio committees, were used locally by the RTMs to try to place resource-based requests in the centre. In this way they are similar to the use made of the National Broadcasting Councils by national region controllers. Advisers on these councils most frequently complain that they have little, if any, understanding of their roles. This, as has already been remarked, is true of most 'advisory' bodies. In the case of the BBC it becomes fairly evident that what was a loosely defined field of operation in the past now needs considered thought. The BBC does not know quite what its lay councils are for. Intelligence for the centre or more directly for local broadcasters? Public relations or a means for programme-makers to meet the people? An expression of the central philosophy of 'It's Your BBC'? or a means of keeping the local or regional establishments and interest groups happy – or quiet?

Equally, the use of lay members is attenuated because they have little idea of their more valuable input. All these people are flattered that the BBC should pick them; nearly all are willing to put work into making their contribution that little bit more significant. Part of the problem, from their side, is that the BBC does not take them sufficiently into its corporate confidence.

This complaint arises with local radio committee chairmen, a collection of a few dozen individuals with a common cause in the maintenance and further development of BBC local radio. They too have bitterly complained that the BBC at the centre does not in practice take them into its confidence. Centrally, the BBC worries that such confidences will leak, and leak extensively, eventually to return in the national Press. Sensitivity to Press comment has increased in the BBC as time has passed, although it has always in one sense had a bad Press. But advisers do stand in an uncomfortable relationship with professional broadcasting.

There is a genuine concern lest information is passed to 'outsiders' before it is common knowledge among staff. Again, this latter point might be held to be the result of not explaining sufficiently inside the organisation what the advisory council structure is and what it can do for the BBC.

In an effort to retain a degree of company loyalty the BBC has stressed, in the past, the 'honour' of being asked to be an adviser; again, to some extent, the mystery surrounding appointments reinforces this sense of being in a state of grace. But those ties of loyalty have weakened across the UK: more and more 'advisers' are taking literally the unfortunate slogan 'It's Your BBC' and demanding answers. The old reply, of professionals being left to make the final judgement, sounds weaker especially when it is publicly plain that those same 'professionals' make large scale and often costly errors.

Although advisory council members of the RACs and the local radio councils are not chosen to represent constituencies of interest many members feel they do so – and that that is why they are chosen. In choosing them in the first place the BBC managers locally are aware that they ought to find people from the widest geographical spread; the widest range of ages. There were obvious 'instructions' to balance the sexes, and to reflect the geography of the region or the radio station editorial area. It means two-fers and three-fers abound (such as fully employed working-class women from Worcester etc.).

In practice the councils are heavily dominated by middle-class, middle-brow and middle-aged people, those with time on their hands and a (middle-class) desire to do something useful. There is a chronic shortage of young people, although some local radio stations have young peoples' panels attached to the councils; others try to get out to discover what young people and other interest groups want. The councils universally believe the BBC does not give them enough publicity (or help in general). To counter this BBC English Regional Television management started two pilot schemes to publicise RAC work in the south-west and, in June 1985, in the eastern regions.

For the BARRTA study a survey of RAC and local radio membership was conducted by mailed-out questionnaire, using the BBC's own address list. The BBC keeps background information on its advisory council members but had not previously attempted to collect data on the total membership. Questions were asked about when members had joined their councils, whether they had known about their existence previously, why they thought they had been asked to join. Data were also collected about attitudes to the councils' work, and a set of questions, matched with the BBC's own Broadcasting Research Department's standard question form on listening and viewing patterns, was added in an effort to discover how far advisory council members varied in the pattern of their listening and viewing, and which services they used. These data also gave a clue to the attitudes of members (although no specific attitude questions were asked). Finally, basic demographic data were collected.

The overall response rate was surprisingly low; subsequently it emerged that a number of members thought the survey to be tied to the BBC; that is, they were unhappy about whether the data might be used to identify them in some way, although the independence of the survey and the confidentiality of its results were stressed both in the questionnaire and in meetings with councils. There was, in some cases, a surprisingly negative response to the whole concept of surveys to discover information of this or any kind. In what follows the figures in brackets refer to (a) RAC members; (b) local radio advisory council members. Data from the two groups differed both in form and in content – there were sharp contrasts in the ways the two groups answered questions.

About half the members had heard of the work of the advisory councils before joining (48.5 per cent; 54 per cent). Four-fifths had been invited to become members (82 per cent; 59 per cent). This in fact applied to all the RAC members; but a number of local radio council members were sitting on RACs by the time the survey was undertaken, accounting for the remainder who said they were volunteers. About one fifth (16 per cent; 19 per cent) were members of similar bodies; again, about half (53 per cent; 59 per cent) thought they *were* representative of an interest group although only (35 per cent; 59 per cent) thought that that was why they had been invited to become a member. Slightly under half (46 per cent; 66 per cent) thought their council representative of its area.

Two-fifths thought they had been able to influence events in ways their council had wanted (but a quarter thought not and a further quarter were unsure). More interestingly, around half thought that belonging to a council had influenced their attitude to both broadcasting and broadcasters (we did not ask whether this influence was negative or positive). About three-fifths (63 per cent; 65 per cent) thought the BBC benefited from their council's work and about the same number thought the BBC generally helped the council in its work (only half LRAC members thought this). But four-fifths did not believe the BBC did enough to make the work of the councils known to audiences (81 per cent; 76 per cent). Consistent with this question, nearly everyone (98.5 per cent; 90.5 per cent) thought their councils were not very well known about, or not known about at all locally.

There is, it has to be said, a schizophrenic attitude among members manifest in this. Although many wanted to be identified more positively locally, many did not, believing, with some justification, that were their telephone numbers to become publicly available they would be the instant target for cranks and lunatics. There was a tension between being involved with the glamorous aspects of broadcasting, and the down-side of being a (semi-) public figure. As a footnote to the identification problem, the most extreme example came from one member of a council who said he was quite sure that were it to be known locally that he was a member, he would be expected to resolve all kinds of local social problems. He was very much a token working-class member (and, he said, he knew it) and the BBC was seen by his 'constituents' as part of the authorities. This belief may be compared with the BBC's experiences when first they held a public meeting in Moss Side – the ethnically-mixed and very poor area of Manchester where riots occurred in 1981 (see page 119).

The data provided by the survey on viewing and listening demonstrate clearly that advisory council members are not representative of the general audience. Two-thirds of the RAC respondents said they mostly listened to Radio Four (27 per cent of LRAC members); this compared with 12 per cent nationally. Nearly two-fifths listened to local radio (a third to BBC local radio) compared with nine per cent nationally. Of LRAC respondents, unsurprisingly 89 per cent were listening to BBC and ILR local radio (BBC, 85 per cent) while a quarter (27 per cent) listened to Radio Four. Radio Three was listened to by 15 per cent of RAC members compared with 2 per cent nationally. Radio One, nationally the most popular with 30 per cent of the national audience (BBC audience research figures of 1984) was listened to by only 16 per cent (5 per cent of LRAC members).

Similarly for television, for although nationally BBC1 was getting only 36 per cent of the national audience RAC members were watching it for a staggering 86 per cent of the time (LRAC members 57 per cent); BBC2 was getting 19 per cent (16 per cent) compared with 10 per cent nationally (even Channel Four was getting around 10 per cent from each compared with six per cent nationally at the time of the survey).

Finally, if further proof were needed, demographically the councils were heavily weighted to the older age-groups. Strenuous efforts have been made by the BBC to balance the books in these respects, largely unsuccessfully. There are still too few women, young people and Blacks, and numerically too many older middle-aged, middle-class, white, males. Overall, 56 per cent were male (61 per cent of LRAC members). Nationally the figures are 49 per cent against 51 per cent. The age skew is much more dramatic. Taking just three adult age-ranges nationally (16–29; 30–59; and over 60) the national percentages are 23, 36 and 20.5 respectively. For council membership the percentage figures are 10 (6.5), 76.5 (81), and 12 (12). That is, the councils are overwhelmingly middle aged.

A familiar pattern is followed in education and in religion. Two-fifths of the survey respondents finished full-time education after the age of 20, that is, most of these went to university. The same percentage claimed they regularly attended a church (about 8 per cent nationally still do so). Around three-quarters to four-fifths were married. Only two members admitted to being unemployed.

It is axiomatic within the BBC that these findings are perfectly consistent with what they know to be the case; that they have tried very hard to break this mould, clearly unsuccessfully. It is equally axiomatic that the commonest outside complaint about the councils is that they are unrepresentative. This leaves two questions: are they in their present form any use to the BBC; are they the best that could be expected?

The answer to the first question is self-evidently yes. But this has to be qualified. The importance of the regional television and local radio councils is that they represent a public presence in the all too often hidden world of professional broadcasting. Their middle-class and middle-age profile is actually an advantage here because council members are articulate enough, and confident enough, to sound off about what they do and do not like in broadcasting. Working-class and younger members, when asked for an opinion, are often stumblingly inadequate, unless they have that other attribute common to many members, a university degree.

The main problem with the councils, identifiable from many comments from members and from observation, is that no one has a clear idea of the best role they could play; currently they wash about in the flotsam and jetsam of muddled discussion and confining agendas. The regional councils meet too infrequently and, incidentally, have few contacts with each other outside these meetings. BBC staff, understandably think they meet as often as the system can sustain, or that professional pride could bear. Listening to the comments made at the meetings about output a casual observer would be most struck by how sensitive broadcasters are to any criticism at all.

The councils' work, centrally, does have some impact. Just how much on any particular question is almost impossible to judge. Central and local management like to know what the councils think, partly at least to be able to counter it later, when they have probably made the decisions they first intended to make. Again, this seems to be a complete waste of everyone's time. But people have changed. Members of councils will say more, and say it more often and more loudly, than they would have done a few years ago. Since the last war, even since the 1960s, a gale has been blowing through the UK. Hugh Greene's idea of letting open a few windows in Broadcasting House was true elsewhere too. By admitting the new breed of advisers into some of the internal workings of broadcasting, broadcasters are having to undo assumptions about their own standing *vis-à-vis* the audience. They should listen harder.

PUBLIC MEETINGS

The advisory councils are changing – slowly. This is more apparent in the regional councils and as more and more local radio councils are formed. The BBC leads these changes from the centre, prompted by the gentlest of council-member pressures.

One recurring issue which has been taken up has been the extent and nature of community knowledge of the existence of either the advisory councils or their members. In an effort to publicise their work one regional council, the south-west, in 1976 put forward the proposal to hold a public meeting. At the time the suggestion was greeted with some dismay by the BBC in London, fearing there would be an unseemly (and uncontrolled) fiasco. The council went ahead and the meeting, in Truro, chaired by Professor Charles Thomas, was a great success. Although there had been other meetings where BBC staff met the public and questions were asked (and answered) the Truro meeting marks the start of what soon became a concerted and continuing campaign by the BBC to bring itself more into the public domain. Since that meeting there have been well over a hundred all over the country. The one hundredth anniversary meeting was held again in Truro, chaired by the then South-West Advisory Council Chairman, Daphne Lawry, just prior to her retirement.

But by then (1983) there had in general been great changes. As the RACs were often unable to attract sufficient people on their own account they turned more and more to London to provide the big names. At the same time a tussle began over who should chair the meetings. Local advisory council chairmen felt it was their job, as they were the host. London began to feel this was a disastrous prerogative, given the lack of expertise often shown.

Thus came Information Division into the picture, the department within the BBC which looks after the central press offices and the house newspaper *Ariel*, and which is now overseen by the Directorate of Public Affairs, after a time under the Assistant Director General's office. The local initiative was by now part of the central corporate image-making trend. Public meetings too became a major part of licence fee campaigns and as such they could not, so the centre argued, be allowed to be seen as 'amateur'.

Part of the centre's solution was to 'offer' a big name as chairman – Esther Rantzen, Angela Rippon, Nick Ross, Sue MacGregor – pointing out as well that locally these were names that would pull the

TABLE 7.1 *A BBC public meetings list*

1976				**1981**		
1	25 May	Truro		66	12 February	Aylesbury
2	14 October	Bath		67	19 February	Carmarthen
3	29 November	Weston-super-Mare		68	5 March	Manchester
1977				69	30 April	Sunderland
4	13 January	Hove		70	19 May	Blackpool
5	28 April	Redcar		71	22 May	Gloucester
6	17 May	Barnstaple		72	1 June	Wolverhampton
7	26 May	Bury St. Edmunds		73	3 June	Leatherhead
8	10 November	Evesham		74	5 June	Maidstone
9	14 December	Hexham		75	8 June	Carlisle
1978				76	25 June	Southampton
10	7 February	Basingstoke		77	24 September	Peterborough
11	5 April	Stoke-on-Trent		78	7 October	Hull
12	9 May	Torbay		79	15 October	Newquay
13	18 May	Bedford		80	29 October	Milton Keynes
14	23 May	Workington		81	5 November	Aberdeen
15	30 May	Hounslow		**1982**		
16	12 June	Motherwell		82	24 May	Eastbourne
17	20 July	Bromley		83	7 June	Basildon
18	6 September	Kensington		84	23 June	Chester
19	29 September	Kingswood (Bristol)		85	6 July	Moss Side (Manchester)
20	25 October	Slough		86	21 July	Leicester
21	2 November	Pontypridd		87	14 September	Shrewsbury
22	13 November	Stirling		88	17 September	Yeovil
1979				89	29 September	Diss
23	10 January	Nottingham		90	5 October	Middlesborough
24	31 January	Gravesend		91	18 October	Newcastle
25	26 February	Hitchin		92	19 October	Lyme Regis
26	15 March	Wrexham		93	4 November	Kelso
27	29 March	Ballymena		**1983**		
28	17 April	Twickenham		94	16 March	Halifax
29	9 May	Doncaster		95	29 March	Lincoln

30	14 May	Plymouth
31	17 May	Portsmouth
32	17 May	Cowley
33	24 May	Ipswich
34	26 June	Chelmsford
35	4 September	Bognor Regis (Butlin's)
36	21 September	Bristol
37	9 October	Concert Hall, Broadcasting House
38	18 October	Cwmbran
39	30 October	Morpeth
40	6 November	Colchester Garrison
41	21 November	All Souls, Langham Place
42	3 December	Manchester City FC
43	11 December	Putney Hospice
44	18 December	Worksop
1980		
45	16 January	Reading
46	19 March	St Albans
47	27 March	Portadown
48	28 March	Pimlico School
49	17 April	Cwmbran
50	22 April	Guildford
51	24 April	Blackburn
52	14 May	Oxford
53	22 May	Coventry
54	22 May	Tunbridge Wells
55	29 May	Poole
56	9 June	Watford
57	26 June	Scunthorpe
58	25 September	Cambridge
59	13 October	Sheffield
60	16 October	Trowbridge
61	21 October	Canterbury
62	30 October	Exeter
63	3 November	Berwick
64	18 November	Brighton
65	19 November	Cambridge (Students' Union)
96	23 June	Newry (N. Ireland)
97	7 September	King's Lynn
98	6 October	Perth (Scotland)
99	12 October	South Norwood
100	17 October	Truro
101	27 October	Salisbury
102	8 December	Moss Side (Manchester)
1984		
103	15 February	High Wycombe
104	23 February	Weston-super-Mare
105	13 March	Hertford
106	28 March	Folkestone
107	12 July	Stone-on-Trent
108	4 September	Northampton
109	12 September	South Shields
110	4 October	Kirkcaldy
111	23 October	Chatham
112	5 December	City of London
1985		
113	8 February	Newtown (Wales)
114	26 February	Leeds
115	25 September	St Helens
116	6 November	Colchester
117	26 November	Winchester
118	3 December	Tavistock
1986		
119	6 February	Crawley
120	27 February	Windsor
121	29 April	Lewisham
122	14 May	Derby
123	11 June	York
124	11 September	Southall
125	9 December	Chippenham

(Courtesy of the British Broadcasting Corporation.)

crowds, unlike a line-up of senior but unknown BBC executives, marshalled by an equally unknown RAC chairman. As the Corporate Publicity office began to exercise more and more sway there was a tendency to bring the platform party on as if a variety show were beginning, using the chairman to crack the appropriate jokes. More sensibly, BBC engineers made sure that the microphones worked and that the audience had plenty of well-placed microphones as well, so that their questions could be well put.

Meetings have been held all over the UK. A map in the Corporate Publicity HQ in London shows where gaps exist and where the team should concentrate next. The national regions may or may not choose to have public meetings. Scotland has had the most; and there is continued concern to cover the whole of England. Wales had early on decided, from the region, not to have any meetings although one was held there during the 1984–85 licence fee campaign, attracting less than 40 people (the average meeting attracts well over 150). The meetings are held in town and village halls, in schools and colleges, or in community centres. Corporate Publicity expends a good deal of effort and energy worrying over the precise location, both to determine the acoustic suitability and the centrality of the location. Towns and cities get the majority of venues merely on a cost-effective basis. Much thought and pre-preparation goes into choosing a place to go.

A joint survey, done for both the BARRTA study and for Corporate Publicity, the latter worried that they might not be getting the kind of people they should, especially during the run-up to the licence fee campaign in 1984, in fact showed attenders of these meetings were a better cross-section of the national audiences than might have been supposed, though predictably there was a skew towards the older age-groups, the more middle class and, in effect, middle brow. This exactly parallels the 'problem' of lay advisory council membership, just as it reflects the high probability that these broad categories will be most interested in turning out to listen to, and ask questions of, the BBC. However, as BBC executives, attending these meetings both as panellists and observers, intuitively recognised the meetings could not tell anyone much about the national audience and its tastes.

Also unrepresentative was these audiences' knowledge of advisory councils and the fact that up to a half had previously contacted the BBC by phone or letter. Most had not come very far; most had come to ask a question or 'meet the BBC'; up to two-thirds felt frustrated at not having got their question asked, often, they felt, because others had asked long-winded or boring questions. The research results here are clear: public meetings are a means for the BBC – particularly senior executives – to meet a self-selected part of the national audience: more middle-class, more articulate, more aware. An audience that at least is not wholly London or south-east in origin, tastes and outlook.

Do BBC executives (and the governor always present at the meetings) take note of what is said? Like the Duty Log (see p. 121), or the 'accidental' or well-argued letter, public meetings do have an impact. Public meetings influence, like those letters, because the audiences will reflect more often than not some of what the middle-class broadcaster wants to hear; not always, but sometimes.

The impact of a well-put question from an angry viewer about the showing of funeral scenes on the main news bulletins will be remembered more than audience research which might suggest that a national audience feels differently. Public meetings can and do change opinions; they may not always change them rationally, and the effect may be short-lived. On the other hand, like advisory councils, there is a danger that their purpose be misconstrued or confused. They are best when they provide an opportunity for senior BBC staff to meet the 'awful' British public – their audience in part – to have to confront the anger that some of their decisions induce. That mere fact is critical because broadcasters, especially senior broadcasters, live in a London-based hothouse in which, more often than not, they do not indulge in 'normal' television viewing.

Public meetings are also held for specialist groups. Efforts to hold meetings in factory canteens have not been successful although those held in schools and old peoples' homes, often in advance of the main evening public meeting, have been. Two meetings have been held in Moss Side, Manchester's black ghetto area.

The first, in July 1982, was described as very necessary but very hostile and frightening by many taking part. It was on this occasion that the BBC staff attending realised they were the target for a general attack on white authority. The only Whites present were BBC staff, a fact which alone is said to have changed attitudes in the BBC. But the sheer size and bureaucratic complexity of the BBC was highlighted when a second, and promised, follow-up meeting was held in December 1983. The BBC had simply not managed to decide exactly how its policies on employing Blacks was to work. Further, one of the panellists could not understand why, in the light of the first meeting (the same people were on the platform), there was black anger at the showing of Tarzan films on BBC2. The meeting was in fact boycotted by many local Blacks, told by a central local community leader that the BBC had failed to deliver.

Public meetings can bring broadcast managements sharply up against public perceptions particularly when they leave the general and concentrate on the particular. The apparent added advantage of a governor attending these meetings, although not on the platform, reporting back to BoG, can be negative, especially if that governor's perceptions of the meeting are in any way affected by incidents. This applies to BBC staff, senior or junior, but as with letters and the Duty Logs, the immediacy and emotional impact of say a very angry questioner can have an undue effect.

Broadcast staff may have a highly-coloured view of a meeting because they are struck by the passions with which audiences hold views. There is an over-defensive reaction by some managers to all questions directed at them. They see a part of the geneal public as not likely to be representative or particularly friendly (again complainers are more likely to turn out than praisers). Busy broadcasters are likely to resent turning out to places far away from their London base. Although all senior BBC staff interviewed on this question tended to start by saying how important the meetings were, a few of the more forthright added that it was often a great burden for no purpose, *all* the questions being predictable, usually tritely put, and all too often hostile.

TELEPHONING THE BBC

The BBC takes thousands of telephone calls from the public every day. As with letters the majority will be requests. All the calls to the larger establishments are logged. In the case of Television Centre, Broadcasting House and some of the large regional centres, calls asking for something, praising or complaining, are put through to the Duty Offices. Here all calls are logged, eventually to become part of daily-distributed documents telling a selected number of senior staff what was said about which programmes broadcast the night before.

The average viewer or listener phoning the BBC and asking to be put through to the programme-maker will almost invariably find himself talking to one of the Duty Officers. If the central BBC

Programme Correspondence Section (the PCS: see Chapter 8) is in the front line, the Duty Officers are the shock troops, the poor bloody infantry who get the audience in person shouting down the telephone. They can individually or collectively do great damage (or equally great good) to the BBC and its reputation. They have to make instant judgements on how to handle a call; assess the seriousness of the complaint; respond at the moment; whether the caller is who he says he is and, therefore, whether to put him through to any higher authority.

As with PCS staff, Duty Office staff are little known about by programme-makers, often held in the kind of contempt only programme-makers can have for 'non-professionals' within broadcasting. Equally, in the management structure they are not recognised for what they are: the physical representatives of the Corporation at many significant times in the day when managers are not in. Perforce they have to explain policy; sometimes they have to guess at what that would be were the BBC to have it, for the BBC is not so infallible that it has a policy lined up on every topic the public decides to raise.

Central Duty Office staff produce a daily log which is circulated to every senior manager by the following morning. It details all calls complaining or praising particular programmes or output in general, summing the remarks made or quoting directly. The system changed in the autumn of 1987 when the new Policy and Planning Unit began work. Now, as well as the daily phone call summaries, a short summary of both phone calls and letters is distributed each week by the PPU. It's conclusions are, everyone admits, not scientific, but give a flavour of the comments made. These logs greet management on their desks each morning where they are read and chewed over. Their immediacy helps to concentrate management minds and, in the current absence of overnight audience research statistics, the Duty Log and the weekly Summary become the only viable and institutionally sanctioned means of assessing audience response. As such they are of course flawed: every senior manager will remind himself of this. But their impact is potentially large. As with letters, managers who heard or saw the same output, and for whom exists similar concern as might be expressed in the Duty Log or Summary, may well act to change output *in the long run*. In the short run they may well express the concerns at Programme Review Board, or to the programme-makers directly, or both.

To anyone wanting to make a protest directly to senior management a simple telephone call can have ten times the impact of a well-argued letter. Certainly, if delivered carefully and cogently to the Duty Office staff, such a call will have a certain place in the log which will be read by the Director-General and his Board of Management on the following morning. Phone callers as a class, like letter writers, are hard to classify. In regional centres, claim regional managers, they do mirror local audiences and therefore opinions quite closely.

The regional centres also point out that more often than not their switchboards will not divert calls to the Duty Offices (or cannot if there is none) but will put them straight through to the programme office. In the case of the nightly BBC regional news programmes this does lead to those who telephone talking directly and swiftly to the journalist, if not the news editor, who has just put out an item. The effect on these journalists can be sudden and forceful. The same regional managers point out, however, that they welcome public comment and feedback of this kind as they have to live in a much smaller community, where they have to be accepted and acceptable. It is the size of the London programme-making centres, they say, which gives BBC broadcasting a bad name, in particular the public perception of its remoteness.

The London Duty Offices tend to get southerners – the calls have to be paid for. The smarter make their calls direct to the programme, like Radio 4's *Today*, for instance. Regular programmes get regular calls, and callers and broadcasters have begun to see the value of this for stimulating output. Many radio programmes now have 'letter pages' where controversy rages. The broadcasters themselves, in the more relaxed atmosphere of the 1980s, are allowed to voice their opinions more, and do. The arguments that used to rule like iron rods within the BBC, that all output was impartial, that news was read and edited by automata, have been blown asunder by the research work on media in universities, and by the growing sophistication of audiences. Needless to say, this has been foreseen within broadcasting; sometimes broadcasters are behind, sometimes ahead.

The growth of consumer programmes like *Watchdog* and *Checkpoint* are witness to this. They continue to create problems, mostly legal. The management view, in television at least, is that consumer strands are best contained within other, more general, programmes. Sceptics within the BBC believe that this is a retreat from the financial implications of having to put aside large libel indemnities, and from the general management dislike of programmes which of their nature are 'oppositional'. In short this is a retreat to the self-conscious self-effacing conservatism of the penurious. Audiences like consumer programmes though, just as they have come to like the more abrasive broadcasting style of the 1980s. Both sides, it seems, have lowered fences to talk more to each other.

8 The Pull of Gravity

LETTERS TO THE BBC

No one can be sure how many letters are received each year although a rough estimate is three million. In truth the figure may be even more, as the annually published figure is based largely on Programme Correspondence Section (PCS) returns and guestimates of regional inputs. Centrally, about half a million letters arrive each year. But producers and their programmes get hundreds or even thousands of letters which are not logged. Well-known programme-makers themselves will get many more, as will the personality presenters who choose to answer some, if not all, of their own letters. One Saturday morning programme series for children recently received in total *five million* request and other letters.

Broadcasting has over the years encouraged this flood: thousands of letters are solicited directly on-air; at other times presenters despairingly ask listeners and viewers not to send any correspondence. In the front line, at PCS, they have seen the results of an unguarded suggestion about communing with a programme or its presenter. Out there, it seems, is a vast army waiting to disprove the adage that letter writing is a dying art.

The British viewing and listening public write a great amount, judging by the weekly, monthly and annual totals produced by PCS. They write in ones and twos, in dozens, in hundreds and often in thousands, an endlessly accumulating mass of words, hand-written on postcards, portentously typed on headed notepaper, scribbled on the backs of envelopes, copper-plated in green ink on vellum. They write demanding, requesting, cajoling and begging. They write from all over Britain and well beyond. The letters come from all social classes as far as one can judge, from all educational levels and from every age group.

About 10000 letters come to the BBC at Broadcasting House in London each week. PCS additionally handles about 150000 a year. The Programme Correspondence Section is an old-fashioned but dedicated department of clerks situated in the mid 80s in Cavendish Square just a hundred yards from Broadcasting House. The PCS produces a weekly log of correspondence – crude statistics along with pertinent, usually critical, extracts for senior managers to read at leisure.

To spend a day in PCS is to spend a day in a world where the meaning of the expression *Aunty BBC* becomes immediately obvious. The people who write often seem to address a relative, just like a faintly distant, somewhat elderly, maiden aunt. They write movingly, simply, asking, asking, asking. Broadcasting raises expectations. It is unclear how often it subsequently fulfils them – we may surmise 'not often'. It raises expectations deliberately, as a showman or a good teacher wishes to grab an audience's interest. But because there are constraints of time it has to let go suddenly, after half an hour, or an hour. We have all felt that let-down, the bump at the end of a good programme when the conversation is beginning to get stimulating, only to be curtailed.

With other media, a newspaper, a magazine, there is the ability to re-read, or to stop, to continue; other sources may lie easily to hand. The activity itself is more quietist. Broadcasting by contrast lives by hype, by emotional temperature-raising. To attend a programme-planning meeting, to watch studio recording, or to see the careful editing of video and film, the dubbing and over-dubbing of music and sound on to a master tape, is to watch this process created, to hear it exhorted by producer and director, to understand the intricacies of its recapture by a skilful editor.

Broadcasting emerges into an environment where, very often, to raise the emotional temperature is to trigger a response inadequate for the recipient to feel satisfied. Appetites are awoken – often, note, when we are relaxed rather than alert – only to have them left unsated, hungry for some kind of action. Letter-writing has become that chief response.

People write to broadcasters for all sorts of reasons: they write to the BBC in vast numbers probably because they can identify it as a place to write to. Unlike the IBA, whose function is publicly less well known, or even local ITV companies whose address may be in a neighbouring city, the BBC has the advantage to the public of being in London (that, at least is where they *know* it has a front office – as do the Post Office). They write mostly to ask something: request letters make up the bulk. The requests are for details of music played as background or introductory, for names and autographs of broadcasters going back twenty, thirty years. Some delight in trying to test the BBC memory to the limit. They are rarely winners in this game. Many, many others write to thank the BBC for programmes, to ask for repeats and to scatter a largesse of goodwill. Only a minority write to complain, to cajole or seriously to exhort. The BBC corporately would be perfectly justified in largely ignoring all these letters, other than to reply on a postcard, perhaps, thanking them for their views.

In many cases there is no time to answer at length all those letters, pro and anti, which pour through the door. But it is BBC policy to take more seriously those letters which criticise, and to circulate more of the comments coming from this source, in a weekly document, than those which praise. This 'Weekly Analysis of Programme Correspondence and Telephone Calls' is a confidential document circulated to BoG, BoM and senior management down to heads of department and editors. It is not seen as a matter of course by producers although its contents may be drawn to their attention, and they may request to see it. The document is now compiled by PU, seeking to highlight more the criticisms than the praise, although praise is mentioned. Totals of letters received for particular programmes are given and where certain programmes attract regular mail running weekly totals are given. Quarterly figures are also collated. Similar data are made available in this document for totals of phone calls and this can be read by management in conjunction with the Duty Logs.

Management do read the 'Weekly Analysis' regularly. They also discuss whatever parts of its contents are relevant at BoM, Programme Review and editors meetings, although such discussion may be truncated by the pressure of the agenda. In particularly controversial cases what goes into this document can result in lengthy argument. How far it affects programme-making and BBC policy is impossible to determine with any accuracy. All senior management will mention it as a source – but only one source – in any decision-taking process to do with either programme-making or general policy. At the same time such managers get other letters, either addressed directly to them (usually not many, except to obvious people like the Director-General); or sent on by PCS for perusal and comment.

A number of senior broadcasters (now nearly all in management) pointed out that they had been much affected by letters which they happened to have read at a time when they were concerned over the same issues and had, maybe, begun to reach the same conclusions as the writer. Letters may be only a part of the process by which broadcasters 'self-research' future possible policies but they can have enormous impact. To outsiders this impact is surprisingly often mentioned: far more, in fact, than mention is made of the more scientific broadcast audience research. The argument against more of the programme-making staff seeing the log is two-fold. First, that programme-makers may react so badly to some criticism that they will send off an abusive letter to the writer, a letter which will then be published as an example of BBC (rather than individual) arrogance. Second, that letters are un-representative and can have an adverse effect on programme-makers who might be discouraged. Neither argument stands up. Some departments discuss letters sent directly to them as a matter of course; others use letters as a vital source of future material (perhaps the most obvious example here being *That's Life*). In any case it is well known, centrally, that many letters do go to the programme-makers who say what they will if they reply at all. The BBC, corporately, is once again a very easy ship to breach; PCS staff know they are only getting some letters because the departments, or programmes concerned, cannot be bothered to answer them.

Programme Correspondence staff will answer most letters sent to them by one route or another. Sensitive ones, or those coming from particular sources like MPs, are sent on to senior management either to be dealt with by their own staff, or to be returned with a draft reply. When an issue emerges, such as controversy over abortion, then PCS may request a general draft reply from management which can be incorporated into the many thousands of 'personal' letters PCS write back. There is an intriguing and significant difference in attitude between the PCS staff and those dealing with letters directly in management. While PCS staff on the whole 'believe in' the authenticity of their correspondents management often do not, a kind of *trahison des clercs* in reverse. One former member of the old Secretariat classified his correspondents as 'geriatric fascists'; another suggested that seen from Secretariat the view of the audience was 'monstrous'. The latter set of attitudes, because it spans a number of related points, is closer to many programme-makers' unguarded comments about the audiences they serve.

But who writes, and what do they write about? Statistics are not kept on the authors. It would be difficult to judge easily the social class, age and education of many correspondents, even if there were time; geographical spread could only be worked out from postmarks. Some topics trigger massive responses. It is clear that out of the *mass* audience only a very few in fact respond in any way by writing or telephoning: possibly two per cent.

On subjects, it is easy to comb through letter files and through the compilations, to see what basic topics upset viewers and listeners.

Unsurprising though the list is, it is worth repeating. In approximate
first rank is scheduling, followed by bad language and violence,
followed by any form of explicit reference to sex, then any form of
perceived violence or cruelty to animals, then any form of perceived
adverse reference to the Royal Family. Perception, as we have seen
in Chapter 5, is all; many of the complaints made by viewers and
listeners turn out not to have been based on what was said or shown.
There is an intractable gap here between audiences and media. The
list continues with repeats, especially of American series (the question usually asked is why are there so many? – another mispercep-
tion). Scheduling – any form of interruption to the viewers' own
programme-preference infuriates them if their choice is not on when
they want it. Sports fans hate it when their programme ends
according to the schedules; sports unfans are equally infuriated when
sports programmes overrun.

It would be easy to become cynical in these circumstances: for the
broadcasters, trying to do their best, trying to balance schedules to
give the maximum enjoyment and enlightenment to the maximum
number for the maximum amount of time, these attitudes must at
times indeed seem to be those of, at least, a monstrously ungrateful
public. But there are other sides to the correspondence which show
an entirely different set of audiences. Broadcasting reaches out and
touches people; it does, albeit for a short time, affect their lives and
their thinking (no one contemplating the Live-Aid concert, or the
earlier newsfilm on Ethiopia before Christmas, 1984, could think
otherwise). Sometimes, perhaps more often than we have studied in
any scientific way, broadcasting changes people or their lives.

The BBC, through PCS, but also through individuals in senior
management where they reply personally, and through producers, does
find time to reply in detail and individually to the letter writers. It is an
impressive operation and one which does the BBC much credit for it
cannot be said to be anything other than an example of a belief in
'pure' accountability which makes them do it. In the recent discussion
of possible cuts PCS was, for a time, a candidate. It would have been
a grave error for, again, although PCS does appear to be far from
programme-making, and incidentally very unglamorous, it does
complete one of the circles between programme-maker and viewer.

This circle was for too long a straight line: the programme-maker
gave the audience an offering and the relationship ended. Gradually
programme-makers have begun to see that listeners and viewers
could provide valuable material: that is, they could become subjects.

We are now moving on from that (still exploitive) relationship into two much more interesting possibilities. The first is that programme-makers can provide facilities for audiences, or small parts of an audience, to make a programme. The Community Programme Unit in the BBC, and access-type programmes in general, take account of this pressure. Second, programme-makers have begun to see what they offer as a resource, rather than as simply a product; a starting-point, not a dead end. Feedback does not have to come through letters and phone calls, as we shall see. It can involve audiences through study material – through, in fact, a much broader emphasis on the educative function – and on social awareness. Events like the annual telethons for children's charities, special programmes on drug abuse and how to deal with it, all are the beginnings of this new and quite different use of television. (The way in which these dynamics are encouraged and engaged through organisations like Broadcasting Support Services is dealt with in Chapter 11.) But it was with the simple letter that it began – and still in many respects it remains – a small but vital link in a chain. One of the proudest files kept by PCS is that of people who have written a second time to thank them for their first reply.

Letters can end up in a variety of places in the BBC. What is clear is that some people may not have written in the past because they were afraid their letter would end up being read on air, for example on *Points of View*, the ten-minute letter programme on BBC1. Programmes like this have been popular with audiences for years. At the same time they reflect part of the earlier idea of broadcasters that audiences were there to be passive and occasionally a source of amusement to themselves, a distorting mirror you held up, if rarely, to show how awful they were.

This attitude remains in a number of quiz shows, in *That's Life* (where it is tempered with more serious purpose) or in *Game for a Laugh* where it is not. Children are quite often targets because their innocence is easy to exploit. Adults do appear to have an almost endless desire to make fools of themselves on television, accepting the role they are placed in by these programmes. Internationally, *Jeux Sans Frontières* is still popular. But television and radio (the latter in advance of the former) have moved on. A close reading of PCS's letters files would bring many programme-makers, wherever they came from, to a sudden halt.

Extracting in any meaningful way from such a wealth of letters written to the BBC is impossible but what follow are samples to show the kind of concerns and the responses. The subjects reflect in good measure the main concerns as outlined above. Thus:

> ... I write to protest in the strongest possible terms about a scene in last night's BBC2 film "The Tree of Wooden Clogs" [*sic*]. The sight of a live screaming pig being disembowelled was not only revolting but totally unnecessary. Why was this scene not cut...

(part reply from PCS):

> You asked why the incident you mention was not cut. I should explain that it is a basic principle of BBC policy not to make cuts in films and programmes bought from outside, except in the most exceptional circumstances as we think the audience has a right to see a film or play as its original writer and director conceived it.

Or, in a letter about the 'Cleopatras' drama, by common consent inside the BBC not a very worthy part of the output:

> Just a few lines to strongly complain of your Cleopatra on BBC2, 10.05 on Wednesday. We found it most disgusting to see ladys' dancing around crudely with nothing covering there [*sic*] breasts. There is no need at all to show this kind of thing on tv. There is far too much nudety [*sic*] on our home tvs these days. It was most uncalled for ...

On the other hand we get this letter on the same subject:

> Thank you for the Cleopatra series – a real pleasure to watch compared to a normal tv output of over-rated personality shows, gory medical details, human-interest sob-stuff and a morbid obsession with minorities, insanity, infirmity, sickness, sorrow and sadness plus sewage and other revolting subjects at meal-time news-readings ... special thanks to the delightful unnamed maidens and their beautiful bosoms ...
>
> (from a 66-year-old man)

Letters about the way animals are used in programmes get very long and detailed replies, carefully explaining how well they are treated and what safeguards are used. Letters to children also are usually very carefully written with particular heed to see that queries are answered. Care in replies is genuine and constant.

The staff of PCS is small but unusually dedicated, a curiously isolated group, well away from programme-making yet in the front-line of its defence. The PCS staff also have to cope with real and sometimes overwhelming emotion. When BBC1 put out a series of programmes on medical ethics, *The Doctors' Dilemma*, many viewers subsequently wrote to praise the programmes. One, about whether to tell a terminally-ill relative that he or she was dying, brought forth an astonishing postbag from viewers who had been in those circumstances. All thanked the BBC for tackling such a difficult subject; many went on to relay their own experience at great length and as to an old and close friend.

Letters are also received by programme-makers: they can choose either to reply or to send their mail on to PCS. The bureaucracy encourages producers to forward any mail which seems to raise contentious points; there is continuing concern centrally that a producer may, in replying, cut right across BBC policy, or simply be rude to a correspondent who has irritated or annoyed. The system does not work well: it is uncoordinated and, worse, it displays no coherence of purpose: it is obvious that producers ought to see many of the letters PCS receive, not least because it would enable them to assess a part of their own audience and the response to their own programmes.

FEEDBACK PROGRAMMES

Feedback programmes range from the mildly critical to the tense and the terse. Channel Four's *Right to Reply* might be thought of as a good example of the latter. The BBC, by contrast, has tended to go for either the mild or the madcap. As examples of the mild, in 1985 there were *Did You See?* on television and *Feedback* on radio; *Points of View*, a puerile remnant of the silly sixties, is the only one of the 'madcap' remaining, now thankfully modified, although still arguably treating the viewer as a butt for amusement.

Programmes of feedback are designed to give substance to the ever-elusive relationship between the programme-maker and the viewer or listener. There is another category of programme, much broader (see Table 8.1) of programmes which at any one time might be said to have an audience-related element. Although, strictly speaking these cannot be called feedback programmes, they do have the edge on the majority of output in that audiences may well feel they have had a fairer chance to express opinions, and not just on broadcasting. In this second category we would have to place all phone-in programmes, of which there have been a growing number.

TABLE 8.1   *BBC feedback and feedback element programmes for Winter 1988 (week ending 18 March)*

1 *Direct feedback programmes – where audiences are asked to comment on broadcasting*

Open Air	BBC1	Mon–Fri	09.00–09.20
Open Space	BBC2	Mon	19.40–20.10
Points of View	BBC1	Wed	20.50–21.00

2 *'Professional' comment programmes on broadcasting*

Review	BBC2	Sun	17.15–17.55	
Critics Forum	R3	Sat	17.45–18.35	
The Radio Programme	R4	Sun	15.30–16.00	(repeat, Tue, 20.00)

3 *Indirect feedback element programmes where audiences may be involved in comments (including letters)*

Going Live!	BBC1	Sat	09.30–12.12	
Network East	BBC2	Sat	14.45–15.25	(repeat, BBC1, Sun, 11.35)
See Hear	BBC1	Sun	12.10–12.35	(repeat BBC2 Mon, 15.00)
Fax	BBC1	Sun	17.05–17.30	
Lifeline	BBC1	Sun	18.15–18.25	(repeat, BBC1, Fri, 15.30)
That's Life!	BBC1	Sun	21.15–22.00	
Kilroy	BBC1	Mon–Fri	09.20–10.00	
Advice Shop	BBC2	Mon	16.00–16.30	
Watchdog	BBC1	Mon	19.40–20.05	
Crimewatch UK	BBC1	Thu	21.40–22.20 + 23.40–23.30	
Question Time	BBC1	Thu	22.40–23.40	
Ask Margo	BBC1	Fri	15.20–15.30	
Today	R4	Mon–Sat	06.30–09.00 (approx)	
Breakaway	R4	Sat	09.30–10.00	
Your Concert Choice	R3	Sun	08.35–10.30	
Gardeners' Question Time	R4	Sun	14.00–14.30	(repeat Wed, 10.00)
Down Your Way	R4	Sun	17.00–17.50	(repeat Mon, 11.00)
You and Yours	R4	Mon–Fri	12.00–12.25	
Woman's Hour	R4	Mon–Fri	14.00–15.00	
Call Nick Ross	R4	Tue	09.05–10.00	
In Touch	R4	Tue	21.15–21.45	
Enquire Within	R4	Wed	11.47–12.00	
Does He Take Sugar?	R4	Thu	21.00–21.30	

NOTE There are other programmes to which category three could be applied; notably a number of DJ-led ones on Radio 1 and Radio 2; they have not been included as the intention is not primarily audience-orientated.

Phone-in programmes create their own problems, notably those which often occur on local radio where the mad and the sad tend to get maximum air-time. Better organised phone-ins, like the BBC Radio Four, 'It's Your World' can provide listeners with a unique opportunity to ask world leaders what they think they are doing.

Behind this second tranche of viewer/listener input programmes lies yet another. These are what could loosely be called consumer-orientated programmes. Perhaps the finest example of these is *Woman's Hour* on Radio Four. A long-standing programme, it has consistently fulfilled its place as a specialist audience-orientated programme which draws in a broader casual listening public. It cares about its listeners; it also listens to them, reacts to their concerns.

Other programmes in this category are specialist as well: *See Hear, Does He Take Sugar?, In Touch, You and Yours.* More broadly still could be included *The Jimmy Young Show, Blue Peter,* and the past programmes *Nationwide* and *Checkpoint.* Many continuing education programmes (see Chapter 11) also would come into this category. This list is by no means arbitrary but it is longer than one might expect. Many programme strands have now built in an awareness of their audience which far transcends traditional ideas. Involvement is the key to many programmes, ensuring that when a programme is off-air its audience continues. To some extent this is good marketing; but in many programmes of this kind there is a genuine programme-maker–audience relationship.

Clearly, programmes like *In Touch*, a Radio 4 programme for the blind, can capitalise more easily on their audiences desire to stay 'in touch' but other programmes have been able to effect a similar and lasting relationship.

PROGRAMMES DEALING DIRECTLY WITH BROADCASTING

Other than inserts into programmes, such as the 'letters pages' which often discuss coverage in, say, the BBC Radio Four *Today* programme, there were in 1986 four regular direct feedback programmes. Of these Channel Four's *Right to Reply* will be dealt with in Chapter 10.

Did You See? on BBC2 television is the most serious attempt to put television output in some form of critical light. It deals with output from all television and normally has a group of invited guests supervised by Ludovic Kennedy in studio discussion. Each week there is an inserted slot by another invited guest looking at, say, news values, or sports coverage. The programme is old-fashioned, safe: the feedback comes from safe middle-class professionals, often with a direct interest in the mass media, if not broadcasting. Their comments can be extraordinarily dull, prosaic, uninformed. The programme lends some weight to the view that to treat most broadcasting as worthy of anything other than moving wallpaper is to give it too much attention.

Feedback, the BBC Radio Four programme (which began life as *Disgusted, Tunbridge Wells*) does direct its attention more at programme-maker and programme-organiser lapses and lacunae. In it, listeners write or telephone to complain about aspects of the radio output. As such it marks a departure in BBC programme terms because it does try to treat its subjects seriously.

The main weakness of programmes like this is that they keep the public at arm's length while allowing the broadcast staff direct air-time. The intermediary is the presenter but as he or she has a contract with the broadcasters under attack it would be a curious inversion of human nature to decide to turn on one's employers in the way one might have to do in order to satisfy the complainant. (Channel Four have managed to get round this with some difficulty and their solution is only partially successful.)

The easy alternative is of course for broadcasters simply to treat audience complaints as a joke. *Points of View* had been doing this for years, using a 'comic' presenter. The programme gets about ten minutes of admittedly peak air-time on BBC1 but it almost certainly does damage to the rest of the BBC's efforts to be accountable. The programme does irritate as many as it amuses. Again, it is an example of a very old-fashioned attitude which says the audience is a strange animal to be kept at arm's length, fobbed off, put in a position where any one member of it is there to be laughed at by the rest. It fits into the *Game for a Laugh*, *Candid Camera* format. By the end of 1985 BBC television management were actively seeking a serious addition, and this emerged as part of the new daytime scheduling from the BBC as a five-day half-hour show called *Open Air*. This astonishing jump in the television broadcast level of accountability was due both to a commitment by former BBC1 chief Michael Grade, and to the need to fill vast areas of the daytime with very cheap programmes, preferably using the audience as bait.

Points of View gets big audiences, largely because of its position immediately before the *Nine O'Clock News*. Feedback programmes should be serious attempts to get answers out of broadcasters or they should not be done at all. Audiences are well aware of the short-comings of broadcasters; laughing off complaints is not a tenable option. Although its position in the daytime means *Open Air* will not get very large audiences, nonetheless its five-day format means that a great deal more audience participation on the fringes of broadcast decision-making is here to stay.

In a very different category, but perhaps best included with 'feedback programmes', is the 'See For Yourself' annual effort by the BBC to present a direct report to licence payers. 'See For Yourself' was first broadcast in 1988. In 1989 it concentrated on how 'Children in Need' was made, on a breakdown of costs for one minute of television drama, and on the changes planned for network radio in the light of Government proposals on enhanced competition. A booklet inserted in *Radio Times*, *The Listener* and the BBC staff newspaper *Ariel* accompanied the programme. Shown in January, it was backed by a week-long series of radio and television phone-ins and regional programmes. It has represented the BBC's recognition, at the top, that its own channels are perhaps the best means of publicising its cause.

9 Managing Creativity, Managing Management

The centre stage in any discussion of accountability in broadcasting in Britain is inevitably held by the BBC. The BBC has increasingly made itself more accountable; but in the 1980s the issue is whether that accountability is sufficient or even of the appropriate kind.

The BBC, through the evolution of its founding document, the Royal Charter, has moved towards its audiences and towards the public, for there is a difference. That is, all television-owning households have to pay the licence fee; the percentage of those households who can claim hardly ever or never to watch BBC television is minute. None the less there is a philosophical point to be made here between the act of paying a licence fee for (in fact) the right to receive *all* UK television services, and watching BBC television.

The BBC is caught in this philosophical cleft stick. If it more publicly acknowledged, or encouraged everyone else to acknowledge, that the licence fee applies to all broadcasting it might thereby take some of the heat off the idea that it is the BBC that keeps asking for more money. At the same time it would draw attention to the possibility of part of that licence fee being used to subsidise other services (not inconceivably Channel Four).

For all its faults, many of which are under scrutiny here, the BBC, corporately, does hold a firm belief that it has to be accountable to its public as characterised by the term 'audience' (to the BBC they are synonymous) as well as to government and the State. Although the terms of this vital debate have changed over time – and are changing still – that one fact has to be borne in mind.

But the problem is that the BBC is not one place, does not have one voice, cannot agree internally at any one time what the issue of accountability is: definitions fly up in all directions. As well, the BBC has suffered and continues to suffer more than many organisations of its type from a truly staggering secretiveness – this among people who ostensibly eschew secrecy in favour of creative development. Party lines exist – some more strongly flagged than others. One internal metaphor for the Corporation is to compare it with the Kremlin. But with broadcasters leaking secrets is endemic; with an ostensible climate of creative freedom, and with many freelance employees, hard 'party' loyalties often do not apply. Neither, increasingly, do more obvious organisational ones. Older BBC staff rue the day that events surrounding the *Real Lives* controversy could become so public so quickly, as we shall see.

In part this is a reflection of the interest in broadcasting by the other media. The Press, in particular the national popular Press, have come more and more to use broadcasting (mostly television) as a vehicle for entertainment news. Taylor and Mullan (1986) suggest that up to 60 journalists may be covering broadcasting daily. Even if BBC staff wanted to keep a discreet silence they would find it hard to do so. As finances have tightened, and anguish over programme decisions have concomitantly grown, so has public hand-wringing.

There is too a firm belief at producer level in the BBC that management in general is not serving them well. The truth is more prosaic. Hard decisions are never easy to take. Given the BBC's failure to develop a strong management at all levels and especially, at least until the mid 1980s, to train it well to deal with staff communications, the number of flashpoints in such a large and actively creative organisation have been inevitably increasing.

Burns (1977) wrote at the end of his remarkable study of BBC personnel, undertaken in the 1960s, that:

> Even now, a good fifty years after its foundation, the BBC is still at some stage anterior to full social acceptance and identity, still short of the completely institutionalised form in which it can lapse into unselfconscious performance of a familiar role.

He says that the BBC is immature and unformed and he casts back a philosophical net to gather in Reith's vision as the only one possible for the BBC to grasp, given the plethora of different attitudes and commitments it has gathered to itself. This is especially true if it is to free itself from the trammels of Government.

The problems may remain visible at this level; they also lie deep inside the BBC and its management structures. The relationship which continues to cause the most difficulty is that between the Board of Governors and the Board of Management. In the summer of 1985 it was the growth of these uncertainties that led to yet another set of problems for BBC management, the banning of *Real Lives*.

The immediate issue at the end of July 1985 was the discovery by the Board of Governors, through the newspapers, of all places, that the BBC was about to screen a programme on Northern Irish

extremism. Programmes on Northern Ireland have been for fifty
years a source of tension within the BBC. Before 1969 much of this
tension was contained (see Rex Cathcart's somewhat bland *Most
Contrary Region*, 1985). After the new 'troubles' began television
brought vividly into mainland homes what those seemingly far away
problems were. Once the bombs began exploding on mainland soil in
the 1970s things were never going to be the same again for British
broadcasters.

The BBC has maintained it has a particular and unique problem
when screening television programmes relating to the province. It
goes like this: given we (the BBC) are a national instrument of
broadcasting, and given we seek to bring programmes before all the
people of the UK, we have to ensure that any programme may be
transmitted simultaneously, anywhere. ITV companies can opt out of
the network; BBC regions can, of course, but must not have to make
a forced choice over any one programme, especially because that
choice may be informed by the potential threat to people's lives in
that region were the programme to be screened.

The dilemma, and it is a real one, not just invented by censors, is a
growing one for broadcasters everywhere. Terrorists in particular
have used the mass media (especially television) to by-pass traditional
negotiators to aim at the hearts of decision-takers. President Reagan
is said to have been seriously affected by this technique when it was
effectively applied by the Beirut hijackers of a TWA jet in 1985. IRA
and Protestant extremists are no strangers to using television to make
a point.

It is this form of self-censorship that has in the past hog-tied the
BBC. It has certainly led to much agonising over Northern Ireland.
Locally, Northern Irish BBC executives claim with some justification
that they are doing their best to get programmes on Northern Ireland
on the air. There are extremely complicated guidelines for film and
television crews out of the mainland who seek to operate in the
province. These derive as much as anything from a genuine and
sensible concern, locally, that naive London-based 'firemen' should
not end up being taken for either a metaphorical, or a more
dangerous literal, ride by local loyalists or nationalists.

The result, however, because the BBC is such a huge bureaucracy,
is that since the early 1970s the number of 'guidelines', references up,
'must inform' points have multiplied – producers might well say
beyond reason. Anyone in the BBC now contemplating making a
programme about Northern Ireland has to decide to commit him or

herself in advance to a complex and drawn out process of internal negotiation. Creative staff find this difficult and irrelevant to their avowed purposes. The levels of resentment built up have grown dangerously so that BBC managers might have expected that their own staff would try to massage the system.

The exact details of what happened may always remain a little unclear. The then head of Documentary Features, Will Wyatt, claims to have known what was happening with the production team concerned, the *Real Lives* programme-makers. So, subsequently, did the Controller, Northern Ireland, Jimmy Hawthorne, who had however been on sick leave until June. The unanswered question remains as to how far either Wyatt or the producer tried positively to inform the Assistant Director-General, Alan Protheroe, or the Director-General, Alasdair Milne. Whatever the truth the programme ('At the Edge of the Union') was made, edited and titled ready for transmission.

The format was simple. Two men, one a Protestant extremist, one a nationalist extremist, were filmed in their homes in Londonderry. They separately discussed the 'troubles' and the causes of them. They were invited to meet; both made their excuses and refused. They were at this point shown walking round the same cemetery at different times. In the original scenario the Protestant, Gregory Campbell, is shown at another moment loading a revolver before leaving with his wife and daughter for Sunday church. Martin McGuinness is shown being stopped by an army patrol, at another stage, and attending an IRA rally where guns are openly carried.

McGuinness, never convicted of a terrorist offence, but widely believed to have been the IRA's chief of staff, is quite clearly the more personable; Campbell sounds and acts much more like a bigot, and appears to be more openly in favour of violence as the means of solving the problems of Northern Ireland. The cutting of the final film is unremarkable. A range of people who saw the original in August were universally agreed that it was a fairly straightforward if unexciting contribution to a necessary, if still inadequately presented, debate.

The programme was scheduled to be screened on 7 August. Two points have to be made here. The first is that August is in the middle of the Protestant marching season, an annual flashpoint in Northern Ireland. The second, more significant in view of what happened, is that the British and Irish Governments were putting the finishing touches to the Anglo-Irish Agreement, finally signed in November.

On 26 July *Sunday Times* reporters in Washington planted a

hypothetical question on Mrs Thatcher, knowing, as she did not, that the programme had already been billed in *Radio Times*. They asked her what her reaction would be if the BBC were to show a film of an interview with a leading IRA terrorist. Mrs Thatcher, who had only recently demanded that the world's Press starve terrorists of what she called 'the oxygen of publicity' reacted with predictable fury.

The Sunday Times subsequently tried to justify its action by suggesting that it could not have asked the Prime Minister a simple question about the programme because it would have lost them the 'beat' on rival newspapers. The then editor of *The Sunday Times*, Andrew Neil, was reckoned to be hostile to the BBC. The main issue, of course, is not over Press treatment of the BBC.

Immediately following the newspaper reports the Home Secretary, Leon Brittan, wrote a letter to the BBC Board of Governors saying that to transmit the programme would not be in the national interest. He wrote this letter despite pressure from his civil servants not to do so. He also had the letter released to the London *Standard* before it got to Stuart Young, the BBC Chairman, something for which Young never forgave Brittan. It was this letter which may have formed part of the reason why Mrs Thatcher subsequently sacked Leon Brittan from his post as Home Secretary. Stuart Young, aware that a letter was about to arrive and, worse, that it was to be published, telephoned Brittan to beg him not to send it. Brittan refused. Young believed it was the sending of the letter that ensured that the Board of Governors had to act as they did. It is, perhaps, worth pointing out that Brittan and most other protagonists had not seen the film, nor even a very clear-cut précis of its contents, at this stage.

Following the receipt of the Home Secretary's letter the BBC Board of Governors held an emergency meeting (on Tuesday, 30 July). They normally meet on Thursdays, every fortnight. This meeting argued all morning about whether to preview the film and thereafter to take not an unprecedented but a very unusual step (see Briggs, 1979). After much pressure from the Vice-Chairman, William Rees-Mogg, the Board agreed to see the film. Constitutionally, this is the point at which the Governors crossed a critical line. It has been said that had the Chairman, Stuart Young, turned to his left and not his right, thereby allowing Rees-Mogg as first speaker the chance to start the discussion with a resounding attack on the programme, a more cautious judgement would have prevailed. To suggest 'more cautious' does not mean the programme should have been left untouched.

Context is all. If the programme had been shown in the autumn (as it finally was) minus the publicity (or, conceivably, when it was originally scheduled minus that same publicity) it would have gone largely unremarked. There is, with hindsight, an inevitability of cause and effect. Of course, say programme-makers, the Governors should have refused to see the programme.

But the Board said – and Young was particularly emphatic on this – that their words *were* carefully chosen. Had the hysteria not been there, he said, his statements to camera about what the Board had tried to do would have been accepted. This seems, even much later, to be naive. On at least one occasion Young, who was not used to live television other than at annual award ceremonies like 'Sports Personality of the Year', said he was going to see the Home Secretary to tell him the BBC would not be cowed. This was after the decision to ban the programme (at least temporarily).

The Board probably believed, in August 1985, that they had erased the programme from the schedules. The real 'row' stemmed from the Governors' decision, because they had in many eyes usurped a function of the Board of Management even if it was their absolute prerogative so to do. The subsequent resignation of David Holmes, at that time the BBC Secretary, was in part due to his belief, written in a long memorandum to Young, that the Board had exceeded its powers. It had not done this but what it had done was to throw into sharp relief the extremely uneasy relationship between BoG and BoM: a disaster looking for an opportunity to happen.

Again with hindsight, it looks like a storm – if not in a teacup – then in a summer hothouse where judgements were clouded by holiday absences. Young says that it was after all the silly season, and the story ran and ran because of that and because the BBC in trouble was a theme of the Press for 1985. It was, however, very bad news indeed that the BBC should have been seen by anyone to be in an internal management struggle at precisely the moment the Peacock Committee were beginning their deliberations.

Why did the Board of Governors do it? Stuart Young subsequently made the point that the Board, constitutionally, *were* the BBC. Why, then, was this decision nevertheless so wrong? The Royal Charter is specific: the Governors can do what they want under very broad terms of reference indeed. It has been the device of the Charter which has given the BBC down the years its freedom to operate, untramelled by the restrictions imposed by the Broadcasting Acts on commercial broadcasting. But such constitutional niceties mask more than they reveal. On a higher plane the Monarch is the institution in whose name all laws are enacted. Few would suggest modern British monarchs would try to put that into actual operation. There is a neat analogy to be drawn here between the two bodies. Bagehot in his classic work on the British constitution says that the three functions of the monarchy are to dignify, to advise and to warn – but not to enact. An exact parallel may be drawn with the BBC Board of Governors.

In the previous most similar case, in 1970, when a row developed over the transmission of a programme about ex-Labour Government ministers, 'Yesterday's men', the BBC Board did view the film. But in that case they were viewing it to see what defences could be erected to protect its transmission, particularly as injunctions were being threatened. The small cuts made were as much as anything to defuse those threats. The programme was shown. In 1985 there was again a threat – Brittan's letter – with unspecified penalties. There were other major differences. In 1985 the BBC had been battered by financial constraints, had just received a smaller than asked for licence fee increase, and was under indirect threat through the Peacock Committee to take advertising. The morale of staff was low.

Perhaps the most telling reasons from the Governors standing against external pressures come from the internal 'Letter to a New Governor' written by Sir John Johnston, a former diplomat member of the Board, who tried to codify the informal operations of the Governors. *Inter alia* he says that the Governors are trustees of the 'public interest' and, pointing out that this can conflict with a possibly narrower, political, definition of the 'national' interest, he states that by and large it is the public, not Government, that BoG represents.

He says that the formal documents are of little help, and that the Charter merely talks about the Governors providing broadcasting as a public service. The Charter does make clear their responsibility to Parliament, via the Annual Report. Apart from the Board's resolution of 1981, which stated their concern to maintain programme standards, there is nothing.

So what, asks Johnston, should they do as Governors? He says that an anomaly of the BBC is that creative energy is located at the bottom, not at the top where management exists to lead and to encourage. It would not be possible, he says, for managers to supervise the output in detail. It follows, therefore, he says, 'from such a system of devolution that the general government of the BBC must be by retrospective review'. Although, legally the BoG is the BBC, 'in conceptual terms, they have made a single huge act of delegation, by which they have entrusted the Director-General and his staff with the implementation of the purposes for which the Corporation has been established'. He continues:

> This is not just an academic concept. It is important, because it establishes that the Board and the staff of the BBC are parts of a whole: they are not *countervailing, but complementary*, and must live in partnership. [emphasis added]

Johnston explains that the Board have a general power to call to account, but that at all times the participation of the Director-General and his staff is vital. He says 'we are not editors ... it is on this principle that the Board does not ask to see programmes before transmission (though it formally retains the right to do so)'. Equally, he says, they are not managers either, and although he concedes that there are, from time to time, outstanding issues of political or public importance, by and large they should steer clear of day-to-day decision-taking. And, he adds, despite the fact that there are those who would wish to cast them as BBC censors, the implication throughout the document is that the Governors should never tread that road.

The Johnston 'letter' is one view; but it is one thoughtfully based on the reading of an ex-diplomat with a long career as a civil servant and is therefore highly sensitive to the nuances of organisational politics. It does throw into relief one problem for BBC Governors. Who are they representing? Johnston gives three possible answers and merely divides the Board's loyalties in twain; most have discerned that BoG, like Gaul, is potentially divided into three.

First, they have a legal and constitutional role within the British political system, a role thrust upon them whether they like it or not. They do report, annually, to Parliament. Second, as Johnston would have it, they are representatives of the public interest. He sees this as the crucial role, not least because the BBC itself has started to justify its public service position by talking of the licence fee as a shareholding. The public, therefore, are shareholders. But, thirdly, do the Governors 'represent' the programme-makers – and should they, as these latter are their employees, their workforce? Again Johnston says yes, we should and, he says, we do.

On these counts the BoG let down both its important constituencies in August 1985, choosing to tread the narrow conformity defined by a part of the political system. Johnston, for the record, finally voted to ban the programme, after earlier indecision.

I have concentrated so far on the Board of Governors as it was they who took the decision to ban the programme. What, however, of BBC senior management? Given the time of year at which this crisis arose, there is some evidence that, effectively, the Board of Governors achieved a *coup d'état*. Some BBC senior managers were away, others had been managerially emasculated, or were new to the job. Stuart Young's role, as the first four-day-a-week Chairman of the Board, had already been a cause for some concern among those managers worried that there would be a problem over roles between the Chairman and the DG. Publicly all this was (and is) vigorously denied on both sides.

If BBC managers had privately wondered what his role might be, the events of August have seemed to confirm their worst fears. Young seized the organisation on 30 July, relinquishing it by degree as August wore on. Milne, the Director-General, was on holiday. Checkland, the very recently appointed Deputy Director-General, did not take immediate action. The Assistant Director-General, Alan Protheroe, normally a man of action and – sometimes hasty – decision, had been effectively downgraded by Checkland's appointment, following on the fiasco of an interview of Princess Michael by BBC *Breakfast Time*, copied without permission, for which he was blamed. None of the other Board of Management members were likely to have carried the weight needed with a Board badly scared by Government pressure. None tried although Hawthorne, the Controller, Northern Ireland, made a brave gesture (subsequently retracted) when he resigned over the programme.

It has been said that the Board of Governors of the BBC in 1985 were a mediocre group of the 'great and the good', possibly reflecting Government attitudes, possibly put there to weaken the BBC's political front or, at least, to curb what some Conservatives believed to be its innate bias in programme-making. Fewer of the Governors than hitherto had had serious 'political' experience. Too many, like Rees-Mogg, now retitled by Government as Chairman of the Broadcasting Standards Council, were likely by disposition to toe a careful, if not overtly Government, line in which phrases like the national interest could be delivered as a *fait accompli*. All, by 1985, had been appointed (or re-appointed) by Mrs Thatcher.

The process of picking governors for the BBC is well established if not very well known. In brief the names are fielded to the Home Office by the BBC after 'soundings'. It has been the case that the HO have added names, usually after consultations with the BBC. Mrs Thatcher takes an 'unusual' interest for a Prime Minister – as she does with all such appointments. The emergence of Marmaduke Hussey as the chairman of BoG to replace Stuart Young, following his death in the autumn of 1986, was a surprise to the Corporation. His name had been added at the last minute – possibly by Lord Whitelaw. The BBC's first choice would have been the Deputy Chairman, Joel Barnett. But Barnett was unacceptable to a Government quite plainly bent on getting its way with top appointments. If Whitelaw did pick Hussey it was probably an inspired choice. Hussey was acceptable to Mrs Thatcher as an apparent scourge of Fleet Street print unions (more in fiction than in fact); but he had a good public record and undoubtedly had the right Establishment connections – including ones to the Palace; Whitelaw had an old Tory affection for the BBC and had been anxious for its future. Hussey plus Barnett are a formidable team. But the appointment process is more usually directed – if not controlled – by the BBC. When George Howard retired as Chairman in 1979, some people in the BBC had lobbied unsuccessfully for a senior ex-civil servant, (they wanted Lord Franks) to take over when George Howard retired.

They got Stuart Young – who, however, was a choice of the Board of Management – amiable, intelligent but politically naive. By 1985 the two Conservative governments had succeeded in 'subverting' or using the system, in putting a very right-wing group of Governors in post as well, naturally receptive to what they would judge to be a higher authority. This Board of Governors faced a much weaker Board of Management in the BBC than had previous Boards. This was a process of attrition going back years. The slow but sure cutting of BBC finances through inflation and the saturation of the licence fee; the effects of increasingly good programme competition and opportunities to use the excess of money awash in ITV, all had led to many of the best potential leaders of the BBC leaving for richer pastures. Those who remained tended to be naturally cautious men who stayed because the BBC acted like, and in many ways was, a comfortable bureaucracy. (This description of caution did not apply to Alasdair Milne, whom many saw as suffering those he thought fools not at all.)

In order to understand further the roots of what was a major organisational problem we have to look at the general organisation of the BBC. Beneath the Board of Governors is the Board of Management. The physical link between the two is the Secretary's Department. The Board of Management (BoM) is headed by the Director-General, described in the BBC's management training document as Chief Executive and Editor-in-Chief. Beneath him (never yet a her) come the Managing Directors of television, radio and the external services, the Deputy Director-General, Directors of Programmes for television and radio, the Directors of engineering, of finance, of personnel, and of public affairs.

The present BoM changed in July 1985 when a degree of reshuffling of top management took place. These shifts resulted in a re-creation of the post of Deputy Director-General, and effectively down-graded the post of Assistant Director-General. This change was due to two immediate problems faced by the corporation. First and most urgent, finances, following the licence fee settlement of March 1985. By moving Michael Checkland, the Director of Resources, Television, into the DDG post the BBC hoped to demonstrate that a new tough line on accounting was being taken by the management. Checkland had just completed an urgent financial review for the Director-General, with three colleagues (the so-called 'Black Spot' group) which had been specifically asked by Alasdair Milne, the Director-General, to look at what could be cut.

Checkland, having produced in record time for the BBC a report of some reasonable fierceness, was then invited to oversee its implementation. At the same time the re-organisation gave the Board of Governors the excuse to make an example of the ADG, Protheroe, who had taken the brunt of the blame for *Breakfast Time*, the BBC show, illegally copying an interview with Princess Michael from *Good Morning Britain*, their TV-am rival. Protheroe, as the most senior executive on duty, had made the monumental blunder (as seen internally) of 'losing control' of the BBC. He had done this by not referring up to Milne the decision whether or not to go ahead with the taping. Protheroe prided himself on being a journalist first and foremost, in the old school tradition; Milne would almost certainly have refused permission. But Milne had, ambiguously perhaps, delegated control of the editor-in-chief part of his function to Protheroe who, on this occasion used his power to the full – and over-stepped the mark. In a system which puts so much store on the quasi-mystical process of reference up this was a mistake which had to be registered by more than the formal admonition (already delivered by the Board of Governors to the Board of Management).

The Board of Governors sits uneasily as an executive board of control. It is clear, with hindsight, that they were moving in this direction by summer 1985. The Board, responsible for approximately 60 top posts in the BBC and thereby powerfully able to influence its long-term management direction, had perhaps seen that its appointments were weak. There is, too, the probability that the weakly constituted Board were appointing less imaginatively and in their own image. In the past it was true that papers prepared for BoG through BoM were aimed at redressing whatever 'balance' towards the middle ground was perceived to be needed. Thus, early in the 1970s when the BoG were deemed to be very right-wing, paper-drafters made their submissions more 'left' to ensure that the resulting amended documents would sit, as usual, in the magical circle of the BBC's definition of the centre.

From the outside this process had gone astray by the mid-1980s. The consensus at large was cracking from both left and right. The BBC found itself in philosophical trouble as a result. It was this general destruction of the middle ground that led one ex-BBC executive unkindly to suggest that the BBC no longer had corporate wisdom residing in its senior staff. The truth might have been that such wisdom was no longer accessible – or applicable – to the circumstances of the 1980s.

Whatever the reasons, by the mid-1980s the BBC was run by two weak bodies in growing competition for primacy. A series of minor financial problems (although some 'overspend' is 'normal'), some just part of the inaccuracies associated with the financial control of large organisations, compounded by the external pressures, began to put the Governors in a stronger position. This was *de jure* but not *de facto* a reasonable position. What BoG might have done was to take control for the time being in order to get the BBC back on course. That would have meant defending it in August, not blowing a massive hole in its defences.

Young, as Chairman, was by nature an interventionist. The corporate 'wisdom' is that having been foisted unexpectedly upon them by a Prime Minister who thought she could repeat the Harold Wilson trick with Lord Hill, Stuart Young had been 'turned' by the BBC into a stalwart defender of the BBC as it now is. Some of this gossip can be dismissed as institutional comforting but by no means all. (The truth is that BoM wanted Young as much as any outsider.)

Stuart Young spent a great deal of time aggressively defending the BBC. At times his words sounded remarkably like those of the chairman of many other British companies: the representation of the public interest is lost – unless the BBC believes its interests necessarily coincide with the public. The BoG admonishment of BoM over the first 'affair' of the Princess Michael interview, was seen in the Press as unprecedented: nothing sharpens the focus of the BoG/ BoM problem more than the belief by the Press that BoG exists to defend the BBC rather than hold it accountable for its actions. The second issue was much more serious; as I have suggested it amounted to a *coup d'état*.

The BBC has never properly faced out the problem: who really runs us? It is clear that there have always been tensions between the two bodies; Briggs (1979) says this is both inevitable and fruitful. But the relationship between BoG and BoM is made uneasier by far than, say the relationship between the ITV programme companies and the Members of the IBA, because the BBC Governors see their position as being quite different. Although by no means all are 'active', those Governors that are take a considerable interest in the BBC and all its works. The national Governors, for Scotland, Wales and Northern Ireland also chair their National Broadcasting Councils, powerful semi-executive bodies in their own right. Because the BBC makes programmes within its corporate framework the Governors have a much closer relationship with producing departments, in potential if not in fact; they are able to react more quickly, to create a climate of fearfulness or of creative freedom.

They, like BoM, also have an advantage in that they exist at the centre of the web. While it is easy to exaggerate their day-to-day power, what is not easy to over-estimate is their ability to frustrate. This is hard to pin down but it suggests that BoM may well spend such an inordinate amount of time trying to manipulate BoG meetings, second-guess any potential problems, or simply react to BoG-raised issues, that it has less time than it ought for raising strategic matters on its own account. It has been said that a major problem of the BBC is that too many of its top committees spend too much time interpreting and re-interpreting corporate wisdom. Annan described this process thus:

> ... these rulings ... must be consistent, and all serve to endorse and reinforce a transcendental abstraction called 'The BBC' ... compel[ling] the Director-General to assume a papal role, while

creating an extra layer of hierarchy which hovers brooding and numinous over both radio and television.

Members of the Board of Governors say, in unguarded moments, that BoM frustrates their real purpose, which is with long-term and strategic issues, by insisting that they should get involved in the tactical details. That, further, BoM members use the device of swamping to keep control of the Governors. The main point, however, is that both bodies spend too much time in inter-committee skirmishes; rather than support each other, they have begun to circle each other. One positive result of the 1985 summer may be that it has cleared the air: BBC staff at the centre say it has and that both BoG and BoM have recognised they have to work together or the BBC is in the short-term in deep trouble. But it is also possible to discern a running away from the central long-term question of how the BBC is to run itself efficiently from the top.

Below the Board of Management come all the major corporate divisions: radio, television, engineering, administration. The BBC has, over the years, spawned a myriad offspring. Directorates, divisions, departments; the centre, the regions; at home and abroad, the BBC extrudes a presence in the most unlikely places. The resulting sprawl is the reason why many people in and out of the BBC, former and present employees, say it is too big; worse, that it is failing to deliver at the front door what it is supposed to deliver, namely programmes. The proposed re-organisation, dated July 1985, which aims to put more finance into programmes, is a belated recognition that this indeed is part of the malaise. This proposal has immediate staff implications, a problem the BBC now hopes to attack on two fronts: by contracting out a large number of in-house services; and by encouraging young producers to take the option of going freelance – in short using a version of Channel Four's commissioning process.

As well, the BoG have finally pushed through what they regard as far-reaching proposals to advertise a number of BBC senior posts outside. This is extremely controversial to many BBC staff as it implies that sooner or later a manager of a biscuit factory could be running it. An absolutely fundamental myth in the BBC is that it is better than anyone else for programme-making because, and precisely because, its senior staff are all ex-programme-makers.

New posts like those of Heads of Broadcasting are advertised at large. Jobs for life are out; if this change works the BBC will at least look very different in the 1990s. Whether or not the incoming staff can persuade the BBC to change or are themselves changed into BBC men and women remains to be seen. As part of the more open management that the BoG wants to establish, a scheme is also emerging which will offer BBC staff secondment to other industries for managerial experience.

But the new style BBC had, by late 1988, gone much further than simply opening itself up a little. Checkland, as the new DG after Milne's abrupt dismissal, inherited a dispirited, unwieldy organisation which had begun to lose faith in its ability to survive what seemed to be endless external assaults on its programmes, personalities, and policies. Within a short time he had managed to make what the BBC were claiming was a truly radical re-structuring from the top. The Board of Management was reduced in size from twelve to ten members. Directors of Programmes for television and radio were lapsed and a new post, Managing Director, Regional Broadcasting, was created. The latter post finally gave the regions the recognition they had struggled to obtain for years, and it carried under its banner the critically important financial independence it had to have. Up to £175m were henceforth to be made available for regional and local broadcasting. A Director of Corporate Affairs was created out of the elderly Public Affairs empire.

Other changes, no less significant, were in train. A new Deputy Director-General was appointed. In the lexicon of BBC corporate mythology (not swept away in all this) the overtones of 'deputy' carries greater weight than 'assistant' and the old ADG post was abolished. Milne, Checkland's predecessor, was fired and dispatched after decades in the BBC, with a few hours' notice. Protheroe, another victim of the 'revolution' has been excised from the corporate memory with a totality which equals the 1930s Soviet purging of Bukharin or Trotsky.

Along with changes to BoM, all approved at great speed by the Board of Governors, have come changes further down the corporate structure. News and Current Affairs have been merged (it has all happened before, of course); and a new think-tank has been created out of part of the sprawl that used to be Public Affairs. The changes are meant to focus the BBC management on the immediate issue: holding the financial ring against the pegging of the licence fee to the Retail Price Index. This move, by the Government, affects the BBC badly as broadcast cost inflation invariably runs way ahead of the RPI. Checkland's own background as an accountant has been

TABLE 9.1 *BBC Public Affairs Directorate organisation*

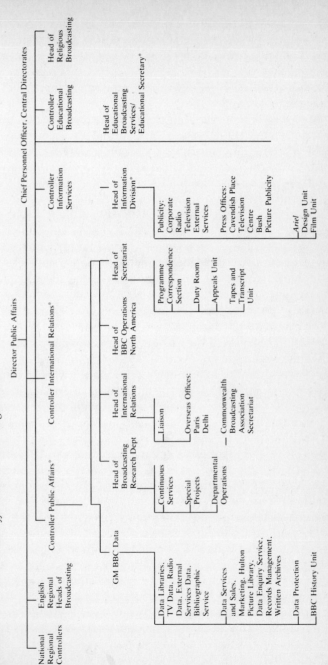

*Head of establishment
CPA is also DPA's Deputy

invaluable here. But the BBC has a habit of not conforming to neat plans. Its very size militates against it. Further there are going to be real cuts, real losses. Some of the speeches made by Checkland in 1987 committing the BBC to programmes above all else have sounded like shouting in a rising wind – not yet a gale but with the hint of worse to come.

The BBC was not the first target for Government or right-wing opinion by 1987. The monopoly of ITV suddenly overtook the Corporation's pre-eminence as a broadcasting target, along with suggestions that Channel Four should be sold off by the IBA. It gave the BBC the space it needed to re-form and re-formulate. By autumn, 1987 the BBC was exuding an air of confidence – at the top – which was redolent of the 1960s. Whether that mood was spread throughout the programme-making divisions below was more problematic. The prevailing dictum appeared to be that if you repeated and expressed an air of confidence enough the troops would respond. However, times are still changing and the BBC has only put a first foot on a long road.

Among the knotty issues still to be faced – perhaps the most potentially divisive of all, internally – is sponsorship. The BBC, in its Five Year Plan published in October 1987, has already shifted its ground. That, along with the haste with which the Plan was devised, does not augur well. The BBC in the market place is the clarion call: many see this as the beginning of the end and, as I have argued, although the BBC may survive, voices are beginning to ask: as what?

The soft underbelly of the BBC remains, to this date, more than just its management. There is as well its bureaucracy and its geographical spread. Purely on grounds of size or of numbers employed, the BBC can be and is often defended. The argument is that considering all its has to accomplish it is not particularly large. Already in 1985 the BBC had begun sharply to cut back: in radio, from the spring of that year, all staff posts coming up for replacement had to be argued for; the emphasis was on BBC local radio management finding reasons for *not* filling rather than for filling posts. But BBC senior management, like all good bureaucrats, tend to see the issue as one of holding the current range of activities while paring back where they can. Fundamental reviews (and the output review ordered in the spring of 1985 and chaired by Michael Checkland still does not count) have not taken place. Even the much earlier McKinsey review of the late 1960s has been described as a catalyst more than anything else.

McKinsey's men reportedly found to their astonishment that the
BBC could not be reduced to the dozen or so real decision-takers that
the management consultants team expected to identify in an organisation of the BBC's size. The best they could do was to get from
around 23 000 to 1400. BBC executives were still relaying this tale in
1984. It was joined by spring 1985 by a new one, the product of the
Peat Marwick Mitchell 'value for money' report. The new apocrypha
said that PMM had been unable to understand why output departments with roughly the same staff or programme requirements had
vastly different budgets. In local radio, for instance, why could not all
BBC stations be as cheap as Radio Guernsey? The BBC attitude was
that this was pure accountant mentality, a good example of why it is
impossible to measure one set of programmes against another, one
department against another. In short, the argument ran, no non-
programme-maker can hope to appreciate what it is involved in the
costs of making a set of programmes; in any case, how can you judge
the 'value' of one set of programmes against another? This confuses
three quite distinct things. First, it suggests that programme costs are
something akin to magic: they appear from nowhere; second, that
their control, as with magic, lies outside normal accounting methods;
third – and this is quite a different point, that there is a philosophical
problem in measuring value.

There is an interesting footnote here. When the Peat Marwick
Mitchell report was published at the beginning of 1985, the BBC view
was that it cleared the Corporation of anything other than minor
organisational (and financial) slackness. But even within the BBC
there were many who believed the report was extremely damning.

The report was commissioned by the BBC who asked for a 'value
for money' review of their activities. The pressure of the Corporation
to demonstrate, as publicly as they might dare, that there was not the
profligate over-spending hinted at by much of the Press, had grown
with the knowledge that there was likely to be a fight over the licence
fee. The BBC must have believed it would pre-empt any Government
moves to sugest that they could tighten their belt by using the PMM
report. The final report, delivered in late February 1985, is generally
condemnatory of the BBC's accounting systems. Although at the
time the BBC suggested it had got a clear bill of health, this is not
indicated in the report.

While the dedication and commitment of the BBC's staff and
managers was to be applauded, said PMM, and despite the com-
mendable resolve to identify and achieve more effective and efficient

ways of working, what they discovered was that 'current processes of
resource allocation ... tend ... to encourage an expectation ... that
the status quo represents a base on which new activities and expansion can be built. We are not confident that there is sufficient pressure
or that adequte mechanisms exist everywhere in the system to ensure
that the best value is obtained ...' The report pointed out that there
was not always adequate justification of costs and benefits when new
projects or ventures were under consideration.

Management skills, they also said, were lacking and accountability
was poor. This report came twenty years after the 1960s McKinsey
Report had recommended that the BBC make those responsible for
spending money accountable; despite moves in that direction the
BBC was still unable to demonstrate that its management system
worked in 1984. PMM said also that 'many managers do not have key
information on (for example) expenditure commitments and few
make use of information on key performance indicators. In some
parts of the Corporation managers do not have a clear view of their
objectives and information flow needs to be improved'.

BBC managers have long been aware of their inadequate performance, overall. One very senior manager admitted in mid-1985 that
management training in the BBC had been 'very inefficient – just
people talking to each other in rooms without any workshops or so on
... It has got better since the earlier PMM report (in 1982) but I
would not say it was anything near as good as it should be'. Heads of
department were badly trained. No wonder, he said, notice boards
often had messages to staff saying that X or Y had relinquished an
HoD job to return to production. Peat Marwick Mitchell had
undertaken a previous study. This had suggested various changes; at
least one senior manager who was asked by the PMM consultants in
1984 about the effect this previous report had had on his department
had to confess he had never seen it. Whether lapses like this are
'policy' or result from the size of the BBC is hard to tell. The BBC
has an immense capacity to shoot itself in its own feet. It moves using
bureaucratic methods of memo and meeting: but many do not tie in,
many overlap. Many senior executives appear at least to make it up
as they go along; disagreements are rife and constant. Some are
surprised at meetings at what others announce is or is not possible.
There is a storm growing outside and, to use an atmospheric
metaphor, the creaking in the rigging sounds ominous.

Thus the BBC corporately moves slowly to a conclusion because it
has to take cognisance of the dead weight of history. Like an

enormously long-running soap opera it has to keep checking the cast list and the cast biography in order to make sure the viewer cannot catch it out. Yet its business, as one of the leading journalistic organisations in Britain, push it time and again over the brink of public controversy. As Annan rightly points out BBC staff have lost their former commitment to the corporation. Because of changes to broadcasting at large the whole structure is now identified much more as an industry: although many BBC employees have not, nor could, work for anyone else, and are individually highly motivated by the ethos of the BBC, they are among the first to say that this does not commit them to the present management. The BBC was always prone to pomposity in its public face; it now appears to have compounded that in its private, internal face. Again, this partly has not been its fault. If we take as given its propensity for defensiveness, as the money has got tighter so it seems to have taken a defensive line against its own staff. This has been partly because, again following industry outside, there has been a growth of unionisation.

But BBC management – and this is mostly applied to London, and to television management – are still perceived by too many BBC personnel as remote, indifferent, somewhere other than with the programme-makers. Despite loud and long protestations, even the truths of historical fact, programme-makers in the BBC are reaching a point where they have little faith and no trust in their own management. If there are ways to describe this management style then they reside in the three elements mentioned above: the sheer size of the BBC, its management systems and its geography. As broadcasting is a creative business it needs constant renewal: both the growth of trade unionism and the growing financial crisis have shut off much of the natural supply. People in the BBC are now worried about hanging on to their jobs. The bureaucratic structure (and the infamous grading system invented by it) lead to a civil service mentality. Growing numbers of people (up to mid-1988) have never been near a programme and hardly seem to be aware (other than with a talismatic wave of the hand) that that is what the BBC does.

Additionally, the byzantine management system which has added layer after layer of new ideas on to the already overloaded bottom, has made the organisation too vertically-separated. The BBC – and this is a metaphor as well as a fact – also indulges in the most extraordinary private management language. All based on acronyms, it creates a climate of impenetrability to anyone not desperately interested in who exactly makes the decisions. Thus, all managers are known by their titular initials. We find, among this arcana, CDBS, Acq and Prog; GMO & SLG; and the wonderful S Pers OXP Ops & Eng. These, the BBC might care to recall, are people. There is, of course, a published index for those who forget.

In the course of time the BBC has also spread its geographical wings, creating in physical space a similar sense of labyrinth. In 1985 the BBC telephone directory, itself a sizeable volume, listed 64 separate sites in London, a number that is being drastically reduced with the concentration of all BBC central functions at White City. The BBC has very large establishments in Glasgow, Cardiff, Belfast, Manchester, Birmingham, Bristol (being greatly expanded); it has establishments of some size in many other places: Edinburgh, Newcastle, Leeds, Norwich, Southampton, Plymouth, New York. There are thirty or so local radio stations. Burns, again, commented on the size of Television Centre in London and the difficulty (remarked upon by long-standing staff) of finding one's way around. This problem in TC, incidentally, was nothing to the old Langham, opposite Broadcasting House in central London, now closed.

It would be unfair to suggest that the BBC has made itself untidy as a policy; what all this proliferation does suggest is that the BBC, in its expansive heyday, never really planned as it might, never appeared to wonder where all this was leading. In short it was able to be sloppy and wasteful. The BBC is long in the tooth in these internal and external battles. It has managed, against the odds, to continue to grow when others have had to hold or cut back. We have already seen that much of that growth was due to the continuous natural growth in income until the 1970s. Its posture has always been to expand into whatever new feature of the broadcasting landscape has been discerned in the distance.

All this is illustrative of one of the more difficult aspects of the Corporation to grasp – even to see; difficult for an outsider, that is. It is the BBC's quite uncanny instinct for survival. Doubtless this is in part due to its history for it has been under sustained attack one way or another for most of its life. Its pivotal place, still at the centre of much of the cultural and political heart of the nation, is testimony to its expert, if ponderously performed, ducking and weaving.

Since the 1985 licence fee settlement, having lost the case if not the arguments, the BBC immediately set about changing direction – what the then Director-General Milne called a 'hard wrench on the tiller'. At the same time it began denying those mooted changes had anything to do with the next set of obstacles: the Peacock Committee and its report. As part of those changes it claimed it was moving the centre of gravity away from the bureaucracies and into the programme departments: a partial decentralisation. There was little evidence that any of the central bureaucracies were about to offer themselves up for sacrifice in this process (unless one counts the ending of the executive dining-suite privilege at Television Centre and even over that there was a considerable amount of local 'ducking and weaving').

The present study has looked in detail at the way the current management of the BBC operates accountability. It has become clear that it works in two principal ways. There are those, mostly of the older school, who look at the systems for dealing with the public as a form of control on programme-making staff, albeit a mild form, and as a means of countering various pressures, be they from government, industry, the scientific community, of from lobbies of any kind. This results in accountability being used as a defence of broadcasters and as a defence of management. It would be wrong to see this as a cynical exercise, although some senior managers more or less openly admit that it can be so; more, it is the product of a system of managing broadcasting which has failed to move as fast as it might to keep up with changing public demands.

The best of the BBC, ironically, can be likened to a commitment to the best of the old values (Reith's ethic in part); but this has meant an atrophy of the means to measure change – the BBC has clung too long and too defensively to that part of Reith's *Weltanshauung* which demanded paternalism. The corporation manages itself by this means (dictatorship tempered by assassination); it alienates many of its staff by so doing and it is palpably not accountable to them either.

The other principal use of the mechanisms of accountability is a form of public relations. BBC managers try to use these mechanisms, too often of late, as a demonstration that they are in touch. Meanwhile they alienate, for instance, many advisory council members, by failing to give them much room to operate, and by quite breathtaking dismissal of any conclusions they reach which can have a real impact.

The question is what future do any of these mechanisms have? The BBC set them all up: it has never had to bow to public pressure in this area – of any important kind. But, having set them up, it all too often fails to use them to capacity, failing to process the intelligence they each provide. I have argued that this is a management failure, and that it is consistent with management failures more generally in public (and private) organisations in the UK.

Part III
Boldly to Go

10 Channel Four – Challenges of Commercialism

CHANNEL FOUR: THE BBC OF THE 21st CENTURY?

The BBC still dominates discussion of British broadcasting. That this should be so, sixty years after its formation, and in the teeth of change, both technological and cultural, is a reminder of how powerfully the BBC has embedded itself in our lives. But it would be completely false to regard the past sixty years as the unfolding of a planned growth.

The BBC, as we have noted, has been more or less continuously under scrutiny of one kind or another; more or less continually under fire, sometimes sporadic, sometimes sustained. The BBC has had its monopoly broken twice: in television first in 1955 and then in local radio in 1973. In the late 1980s the BBC is being asked, not for the first time, to think about alternative means of financing itself. It faces a much deeper challenge, in the long term, from both cable television and direct satellite broadcasting. But back on earth in the here and now, the BBC faces another kind of challenge: from the fourth terrestrial television service, Channel Four, which began transmission in 1982. Channel Four appears to offer a model of commercially financed public service broadcasting, cutting away at a stroke the old BBC argument that public service broadcasting and advertising-based programme revenue are incompatible.

In fact Channel Four's revenue base is more subtle than that. The channel is a subscription service, but the subscribers are limited to existing ITV programme companies. Their right to sell advertising space on Channel Four guarantees they retain the monopoly of television advertising in Britain; it also supposedly helps to guarantee that Channel Four's programme-making policies are safeguarded from direct commercial pressure.

All this presupposes what is little spoken about in commercial broadcasting. First, that ITV, for example, cannot by definition be public-service orientated; and that commercial pressures *are* brought to bear on programme-making policies. That is, in commercial broadcasting, it is audiences who are bought and sold, using the programmes as hooks to appropriate advertisers. Commercial broadcasting programme-makers concur with part – but only part – of this scenario. They argue in private that if the BBC, with its detached (from hard money) programme-making policies did not exist, and was not an equally strong bidder for audience time, then they in commercial broadcasting could not argue for a high proportion of 'good' – that is culturally significant – programmes. 'Brideshead Revisited', 'Jewel in the Crown', *First Tuesday, The London Programme*, all these and many more simply would not be made, without the existence of the BBC.

The immediate contrast, inevitably, is with the USA. Many questions are begged by these arguments. The most important is whether cultural and political differences are not more important, in the context of attitudes towards programmes, than mere money. Among others is the relationship of the programme companies to audiences. But the plain fact is that the BBC did get there first; has had an enormous impact on all British broadcasting. Change it might, but it is unlikely to go away.

To return to Channel Four: it becomes part of the development of both the structures of British broadcasting and of its programme-making philosophies. It also poses new questions about the relationships people as individuals, as well as groups, as a mass, have towards television and its programmes. In the legislation setting it up much was made of the requirement that Channel Four should not become the fourth part of what had gone before.

Channel Four had been argued about for twenty years – ever since the Pilkington Committee, reporting in 1962, advocated that ITV should not get the third television channel – the 'logical' course of action as it was still struggling to form a truly competitive system. ITV believed it had a right to the fourth channel, especially after the BBC got the third. It would, by that curious British notion of fairness, balance the system.

It was well known too, by the mid-sixties, that there would only be four UHF-band terrestrial television channels in the UK; after that the answer would lie in cables and DBS. The ITV companies, bullish by this time, thought they could make a considerable financial success by having a second channel into which they could decant repeats and much of their 'brownie point' programming – education, documentaries, religion.

But since the coming of ITV, and notwithstanding Conservative

Governments' requirements for more and more competition, the prevailing policy attitude has been that any commercial part of the broadcast system has in some way or other to be regulated, or toned down. This began in the 1950s when it became apparent that the early ITV promises of culture with adverts had been ditched for popular and down-market US imports – games shows, westerns, cops and robbers thrillers. By the time Roy (later Lord) Thomson, proprietor of Scottish Television (and the only bidder for that franchise), made his now notorious remark about ownership of an ITV franchise being a licence to print money, establishment attitudes, including those inside the then Conservative Government, were that they had created a monster.

The Pilkington Committee put an official seal on this, saying, among other things, that 'the general judgement is unmistakable: it is that the service (ITV) falls well short of what a good public service of broadcasting should be'. The Committee had been appalled at the unconcern expressed by ITV executives at their output; and, more, at the casual way they appeared to treat with the Committee itself. The BBC, by contrast, and long in the tooth, made no such mistake.

The main gift the Committee had was the third television channel on VHF – never in fact developed. The third channel was begun on UHF, necessitating an expensive period of changeover between the old VHF domestic sets and the new 'dual standard' sets – all this immediately before the next technological change to a colour system. It is arguable that, had the third channel been given to ITV they would have bankrupted themselves through this awkward period when audiences had to make, in the course of just ten years, considerable outlay in buying new sets. The BBC, in starting BBC2, were able to ignore this problem. Small audiences for the new service were both expected and planned; the licence fee, still on an annual rising curve, continued to pay for developments. Pilkington had already firmly pointed out that ITV was an unsuitable home for the next channel:

> The disquiet and dissatisfaction with television are, in our view, justly attributed very largely to the service of independent television. This is so despite the popularity of the service, and the well-known fact that many of its programmes command the largest audiences ... it is a success which can be obtained by abandoning the main purposes of broadcasting ... We conclude that the service of independent television does not successfully realise the purposes of broadcasting as defined in the Television Act.

By 1970 colour television had arrived, all on 625-line UHF. ITV companies, re-grouped under new franchises, were now beginning to provide a better service all the time. Financially curbed by the operation of the Levy on excess profits, the ITV programme companies badly wanted the fourth channel, the last terrestrial channel in the UHF band.

The Levy had created a curious effect in ITV. It meant – and means – that while they have to be careful not to make too big a book profit the companies can lose the excess revenue in excessively expensive programmes, and in excessively expensive salaries. Over time, therefore, they have put enormous resources into programmes and into buying-in staff. A fourth channel would not only provide an additional market place, the argument went, and therefore competition as originally demanded in the first Television Act, it would also enable the required dumping of unwanted programmes. The fourth channel would also create more wealth, if not immediately more profit.

Publicly, the arguments tended to revolve around the equity of deciding in favour of a two-two split between the BBC and ITV. It was also well-known that the BBC did not want a third television service; BBC2 had proved a crippling burden to the BBC and by the mid 1970s it was over-committed to a national service of local radio.

But also by the early 1970s new voices were emerging. One was that 'small is beautiful', an attitude held by the great and the good as well as by the humble. Although perhaps not particularly humble, programme-makers were beginning to wonder in public whether or not they might be creatively better off by detaching themselves from direct employment by large broadcasting organisations. Some argued that television was too monolithic, now divided into what Annan would shortly neologise as the 'duopoly'. Among the first public voices raised in this debate was that of Anthony Smith, who had previously worked as a producer on the BBC's *24 Hours* programme. Smith believed he could make a living as an independent producer only to find, upon leaving the BBC, that there was rather less freelance work than he had supposed.

Out in the cold he wrote a masterly book on the relations between broadcasters and the State – *The Shadow in the Cave*, at the end of which he appended an idea for a National Television Foundation. This idea had already been floated by, among other groups, the Association of Broadcasting Staffs, then the BBC house union. This proposal was eventually submitted to the Annan Committee, but by then a number of individuals and groups had seized upon its possibilities, including the Independent Television Companies Association, several newspapers and Sir Hugh Greene, the former BBC Director-General. The central proposal envisaged the NTF as a publisher of programmes, introducing the public's right to broadcast without damaging the good qualities which are built into the existing institutions. The doctrinal base would be openness instead of balance, expression rather than neutralisation. There would be no regular scheduling. The whole idea contained an implication that a powerful independent production sector would emerge.

The Annan Committee embraced the idea wholeheartedly. The Committee's solution was to suggest the creation of the Open Broadcasting Authority which would act as publisher for the fourth channel. It would raise the money – they had a number of new, and quite a few old, ways in mind. The Annan Committee reported in 1977, while a Labour Government was in power. It had a mass of detailed plans for the reorganisation of British broadcasting, snipping bits here and there off existing organisations, creating new ones. The rather cavalier way in which the Committee made these suggestions led to much adverse comment. More significant, and in keeping with the more academic nature of the Committee, members were allowed frequent notes of dissent. The overall picture, therefore, was one of confusion.

In general the complications of this (or any other report on broadcasting) meant that the Home Office, since 1974 responsible for broadcasting policy, took a year to produce a White Paper based on the Committee's conclusions. By then the Government had a major economic crisis on its hands. The White Paper itself was complex and contentious, arguing, for example, that the BBC should have Service Management Boards as a kind of additional public control.

As had happened so often in the past the Labour Government had tried to manipulate the organisation of people rather than structures in the system. Once again, they failed to get legislation about structures through Parliament before they lost the 1979 General Election. Broadcasting, in 1979, faced a very different future. But the Conservative Government of Mrs Thatcher accepted, eventually, one of the principles of Annan, that the duopoly should be broken. Part of the reason lay with her desire to break all monopolies, all cartels. Part – and it is an important part – probably lay with William Whitelaw, then Home Secretary.

Whitelaw was strongly in favour of allowing television more room for debate. He was known to like the BBC and to have reservations about the monopoly of ITV. This suited many in the Cabinet too: the new Conservatism was to encourage small business – what better than to have that policy demonstrated in a most public way by independent producers on the fourth channel? None of this was new: it was a similar spirit which had moved the 1951 Conservative Government. The new Government wasted little time. In May 1979 they announced that the fourth channel would be introduced under the IBA. In September, speaking at the Biennial Royal Television Society convention at Cambridge, the Home Secretary, outlined how the fourth channel might look. Already it was clear that the Government was going to accept much of what the Annan Committee had suggested. In effect, Whitelaw was proposing an Open Broadcasting Authority under the tutelage of the IBA. He wanted, he said,

> to give new opportunities to creative people in British television, to find new ways of finding minority and specialist audiences and to add different and greater satisfactions to those now available to the viewer.

He was against competitive advertising because this would merely ensure that the channels fought for a maximum audience at all times. The main source of funds would be spot advertising, although he did not rule out block advertising or sponsorship. At the same time he thought it possible that the budget for the channel need not be constrained by its advertising revenue.

Accountability figures little in this whole debate. Direct audience participation in the fourth channel was never a serious possibility. What the arguments came to was that professional broadcasters ought to have more room to work, more freedom to decide what they would make programmes about. Even in the likelihood that the output of the fourth channel would be radical, probably broadly left, nonetheless it would be 'professionally' left.

The eventual creation of Channel Four Television Ltd marks a moment of great importance in British broadcasting history representing as it does the continuance of two historical 'facts' in British broadcasting policy. The first is that of the Annan Committee, that broadcast media must have clear-cut and separate sources of income. The second, older one, is that the BBC's own dominance will be eroded by the process of commercialism.

Channel Four's existence *is* something new: the question now is whether in providing a new side to terrestrial television it has in any way provided a new form of public accountability within its own terms of reference.

COPING WITH SUCCESS: MANAGING CHANNEL FOUR

The final arrangements for Channel Four are confusing to the layman, difficult to all but the most determinedly interested party to grasp. The Company is a wholly-owned part of the IBA. The best short description of its position within the commercial broadcasting system is given in the IBA annual guide to broadcasting where, curiously, Channel Four is given a slot in the reference section between Central Television and Channel Island Television (that is, its unique position is not recognised, at least in the formal book of rules). The *Guide* says:

> The Channel Four Television Company Limited is a wholly owned subsidiary of the IBA, charged with the responsibility of assembling the programme schedule for the channel but *not* with making programmes. Apart from a weekly 'answerback' [*sic*] show for viewers, the channel makes nothing itself but commissions or buys programmes from a diversity of sources, including the ITV companies, programme suppliers and film distributors worldwide. But the company is also required to commission a 'substantial' proportion of programmes from independent production companies.

Channel Four is financed by subscriptions levied on the ITCA companies. These subscriptions are set according to the maximum audience reachable by each company; thus the two London stations pay the most in any one year, Channel Islands Television the least. In return ITCA companies have exclusive rights to sell advertising time on Channel Four, subject to certain conditions, for instance on co-scheduling advertisements.

The Welsh Fourth Channel, S4C (*Sianel Pedwar Cymru*) relays most of Channel Four's UK output but adds to it about 22 hours weekly of Welsh language programmes, supplied jointly in an arrangement unique in British broadcasting, by BBC Wales and Harlech Television.

The IBA is thus in legal terms a parent to Channel Four. In practice this means that they oversee the channel at two levels: the

TABLE 10.1   *Channel Four organisation, early 1988*

Board	Sir Richard Attenborough CBE	Chairman
	George Russell	Deputy Chairman
	Michael Grade	Chief Executive (& Director of Programmes)
	Justin Dukes (now left)	Managing Director
	Sir Brian Bailey OBE	
	Ms Carmen Callil	
	Ms Jennifer D'Abo	
	Paul Fox CBE	
	James Gatward	
	John Gau	
	Anthony Pragnell CBE DFC	
	Peter Rogers	
	Michael Scott	
	Professor David Vines	
	Mrs Eleri Wynne Jones	
Executives	Liz Forgan	Deputy Director of Programmes & Head of Current Affairs Group
	Mike Bolland	Assistant Director of Programmes & Head of Arts and Entertainment Group
	Gillian Braithwaite-Exley	Head of Programme Planning
	Ellis Griffiths	Controller of Technical Operations
	Colin Leventhal	Head of Programme Acquisitions and Sales
	Pam Masters	Head of Presentation
	Frank McGettigan	Head of Admin. and Industrial Relations
	David Scott	Controller of Finance & Company Secretary
	Sue Stoessl	Head of Marketing
Commissioning Editors	Adrian Metcalfe	Senior Commissioning Editor, Sport & Head of Features Group
	David Rose	Senior Commissioning Editor & Head of Fiction Group
	Naomi Sargant (now left)	Senior Commissioning Editor & Head of Education Group
	Peter Ansorge	Commissioning Editor, Drama Series and Serials
	Farrukh Dhondy	Commissioning Editor, Multi-Cultural Programmes
	Alan Fountain	Commissioning Editor, Independent Film and Video
	Stephen Garrett	Commissioning Editor, Entertainment and Arts
	Nick Hart-Williams	Commissioning Editor, Single Documentaries
	Michael Kustow	Commissioning Editor, Arts
	David Lloyd	Commissioning Editor, Current Affairs

Gwynn Pritchard	Commissioning Editor, Education
Rosemary Shepherd	Commissioning Editor, Children's Programmes
Caroline Thomson	Commissioning Editor, Finance and Industry, Science and Technology
Bob Towler (now left)	Commissioning Editor, Religion and Open College
Joyce Jones	Editor, Purchased Programmes

apparently straightforward relationship of a parent to its subsidiary company, and as the broadcasting 'authority' responsible for all output on its transmitters. The first relationship is only apparent because the IBA has never been involved in anything like this arrangement before. To have to take legal charge of the fourth channel has not been easy, given that the IBA's natural institutional attitude is one of control; that of Channel Four's own legal brief, one of relaxing controls.

The main method of formal control is through the Channel Four board meetings on which an IBA representative sits. There are, though, informal meetings between Channel Four's chief executive, its managing director, and the Director-General of the IBA which are augmented every second meeting by the attendance of the chairman of Channel Four's board and the chairman of the IBA.

Although at least one Channel Four commissioning editor maintains that the channel would not begin to look as it does in the late 1980s unless there had been much assistance from the 'pin-striped radicals' in Brompton Road, the known facts suggest the relationship has created a number of very real difficulties. The IBA has had to insist on changes to a number of Channel Four programmes, one, ironically, itself dealing with censorship.

The problematic nature of the relationship is borne out by reference to a set of papers circulating in Channel Four nine months after it began transmission, on the critical issue of 'balance'. Sometimes difficult for laymen to grasp, this single issue continues to lie at the heart of the regulation of all British broadcasting.

In 1982, when it came on-air, Channel Four was in the unique position of being told it need not 'balance' its programmes under the same rules as either ITV or the BBC. Nevertheless this was not, as thought by some people outside broadcasting, a charter for never balancing; only for balancing differently. What problems that led to are instructive to investigate. A senior commissioning editor tackled this issue early on, in a memo sent to Channel Four's chief executive. The central question, the memo said, was that although Channel Four had been told it might not have to follow the same rules regarding balance and due impartiality, it had hardly started a revolution:

> At the start we fairly publicly hoisted our flag to a libertarian mast, saying we thought the addition of an extra channel ought to bring with it, automatically, some loosening of the interpretation of balance and due impartiality as a concept of plurality started to take over from a concept of central regulation or censorship . . . Ten months in, what have we achieved?

The answer, according to this memo, was very little if measured in programme terms. Part of the problem, the memo suggested, was that the channel had operated in a classically pragmatic form, fighting each battle with the Authority as it had arisen, rather than being able to organise on the basis of a properly thought-through written-down policy document. The solution was either to take the whole issue on board and direct a full-frontal assault on the IBA – which might mean taking on Channel Four's own board; or to continue to fight piecemeal; or to think through a definition of balance behind which the C4 board would be prepared to unite.

The memo's author favoured the last option but, within C4's own structure, this meant that the first arbitration of what the definition of balance would be fell to the individual commissioning editor. Thus, were an editor to identify that a programme were likely to fall into the category of strongly partisan, then it would be up to them to nominate a balancing programme. If they could not find one within their own planned output they would have to look for a 'pair' programme in someone else's. The Programme Review Board would be the forum where all this was discussed. The memo pointed out that the board of Channel Four got involved too late and then in a piecemeal way. Unless there was a coherent picture to present, then the board were put in a difficult position. Finally:

> I greatly dislike the idea that we should be seen to bundle all kinds of rudery and one-sided propaganda onto the screen and wait for the IBA to slap our wrists before we exersise [*sic*] any kind of scrupulousness of our own . . . It does the Channel no good to be seen first wanting to plonk [them] on the air regardless and then impotently stand in the corner while the IBA tells us we can't show them . . .

Two replies to this document are worth quoting. One, from a member of the Channel Four Board, the other from a fellow commissioning editor. Both point to two continuing tensions inside the channel. First, these are between the equivalent (at one remove) of the creative staff and the company orthodoxies which exist in C4 as much as in any other company. The other is between the definitions of the relationships between C4 and the IBA as given by the Channel Four senior management and as perceived by many commissioning editors and programme-makers.

The Channel Four Board member reply says that although the paper has value it nevertheless smacks of simplistic analysis, dealing with the relatively small (against total) output of factual and documentary programmes, where particular problems arise. 'As you are aware, balance is about flow of general themes in our output (and the audience response to them) much more than it is about individual programmes within ·the schedule ...' This is no different from attitudes about balance which might have been expressed in either the BBC or ITV. Of course, with some exceptions, Channel Four was staffed with broadcasters who had come from these two sources. British broadcasting continues in this way to evolve in an apparently seamless way.

The response to this internal Channel Four debate was to create a position for someone who would have oversight of the total output: the equivalent of the BBC post of Director of Programmes, Television, a senior commissioning editor with powers over all output. This deputy channel controller now exists.

The other reply quoted here relates to a longer, more philosophical, look at the problem of editorial control. It points out the requirements under the Broadcasting Act which set up the channel, and the assumption that Channel Four should 'present a wider range of opinion, interests and subjects than has been the norm and somehow reconcile this with the requirement to balance. We have ... fallen into a trap by thinking that the greater range inherently involves lack of balance and are therefore actively ourselves encouraging that lack of balance.' The author here agreed that the commissioning editors needed to have a professional approach to balance and a clear grasp of what a programme was offering. He pointed out that what the Annan Committee had proposed, that the fourth channel should merely publish programmes, had not been taken up: they had a direct editorial responsibility for their output. The suggestion here, also not taken up, was that commissioning editors ought to have their names published in the programme credits, thereby identifying them and, to some extent, their editorial role.

The whole commissioning process, and its problematic position between the dictates of Channel Four management policy and programme-makers, is central to the company and the way it works and was set up to work. Commissioning editors are very much like mediaeval barons: they have client fiefdoms who rely absolutely on their patronage and although a programme maker may appeal if he or she cannot get on with a particular commissioning editor, none have overtly done so, so delicate is the relationship.

Programme makers have berated the system for this aspect, as they have lamented the way in which they are tied to one channel and its output, and to its programme policies. Where programme companies have been dropped there have been angry public recriminations, all of which will make it more and more difficult to reject current incumbents of programme strands as time passes.

The centre of the Channel Four system is the Commissioning Editor. They remain a small group, effectively heads of output departments and responsible for major areas like drama, arts, education and current affairs output, the rest dealing with parts of that output or with smaller programme areas. A number remain from the beginning of the channel (having been appointed well before it began transmission); more and more new faces are appearing as internal promotions and changes are made and as some of the first group leave.

The commissioning editors have enormous power which they have to delegate in various forms of brokerage with their selected programme-makers. There are no rules, only guidelines, hunches, prejudices. The nearest equivalent in the rest of British broadcasting is the relationship between producers and heads of output departments, particularly in the BBC, whence indeed came some of the Channel Four commissioning editors. But the big difference is that independent producers dealing with Channel Four do not have anything like the security of staff producers in the BBC, or in ITV. They have also to run and maintain a company in the knowledge that it may not outlive any series it is currently producing. This creates a peculiar tension between commissioning editors and their producers: the CEs are constantly aware that they have the power to cut off a principal, possibly only, source of income for a programme-maker. Indeed the channel philosophy actively encourages this by reinforcing the notion that creativity – and equity towards the numbers of new programme-makers trying to get through the door – insists that there can never be a contract for any one programme strand stretching into the future. Even the specific contract with ITN for the main news on the channel is vulnerable to this pressure, although because of the importance placed by the IBA on national and international news it is unlikely that this contract will not continue to be renewed.

Commissioning editors also have to think in terms of audiences: what is required in their output strand according to the Act and according to 'local' guidelines laid out in various programme committees. But it is important to stress that more or less from the start such has been the response from the independent sector to provide programmes that there has been less obvious need to direct or cajole programme-makers; merely to pick up ideas that have come in and accept or reject them.

Within three years the company had moved from brickbats to acclaim. However, executives at Channel Four remark that morale was highest when the pressure was on. Since the channel has settled down and this public pressure has eased, more local difficulties have arisen, more latent industrial disputes have come to the fore. The Board of Channel Four have, like any board, clear-cut duties. The composition of the Board reflects the compromises inherent in the setting up of the channel. It has a representative from the IBA, four members of the ITCA, two members from the independent production area, and a member of the Welsh fourth channel authority. The rest are executives of Channel Four or independent directors. All are chosen by the IBA.

Channel Four is run as a commercial company; that is its rationale and although it does not directly make money it is in business to ensure that money is made through advertising revenue for the ITCA companies who have to subscribe to it. This simple fact of life has often been forgotten in the euphoria over its mere existence. Forgetting what it is there to do has afflicted people working for the channel as well as those outside. Channel Four is run very tightly indeed, a kind of Thatcherite economism rules inside what the first chief executive, Jeremy Isaacs, once said was 'the last of the Reithian channels'.

The company gains greatly by being – and consciously remaining – small, employing only about 230 people full time. Its accountants run the independent programme contractors on a very tight leash, ensuring thereby that average programme costs per hour are lower than for any other part of UK network television. Beneath board level, in the mid-1980s, Channel Four was being run in parallel by Justin Dukes and Jeremy Isaacs (managing director and chief executive respectively). Isaacs' own impact on the channel cannot be overestimated: it was his channel and most of his staff instantly recognised his stamp upon it. In the long term this may well create an organisational crisis. The reign of Michael Grade is still young and judgements must wait; already, however, it is clear that he is wrenching the channel into new and possibly unhappy paths.

Isaacs' attitude to broadcasting was liberal, although his attitude in running Channel Four was often authoritarian. He was convinced he knew what the channel was for, and how it should provide for its audiences. He laughed off any notion that it was in any way 'accountable': that, he said 'is an aspect of broadcasting that I have never seen fulfilled'. He defended the small size of Channel Four and the desire to encourage a high turnover of staff thus:

> The constant movement of people ought to make them adventurous; we have yet to be proved right on that. By bringing in new people all the time we make them more cautious. (That is, they are made nervous by high staff turnover.) Size is not a protection today. We put the emphasis on people working very hard for short periods.

His attitude to Channel Four's perceived success remained cautious:

> The public acclaim the channel now gets marks a success. We keep getting told how marvellous we are. The trouble is that the acceptance and approbation is not for the old and adventurous in what we do but for the ways in which the public perceive Channel Four conforming to their ways of what they think a television channel should be.

Beneath the level of chief executive, managing director and programme controller, lie a series of regular meetings in which policy is laid down, guidelines for commissioning set out. These committees also discuss current and future projects and past performances. There are weekly Programme Review Boards; fortnightly Programme Finance Committee meetings, monthly Management Committee and Programme Planning Meetings. As Channel Four is so small most managers and most commissioning editors are able to attend most meetings, although those who do complain that this wastes time; others come more rarely and are complained about. The potential degree of information exchange is thus high and this is further added to by the physically small environment in the Charlotte Street base.

PEOPLE'S CHANNEL, PRODUCERS' WORLD: CHANNEL FOUR AND THE ACCOUNTABILITY GAP

It was an orthodoxy of the radical chic by Channel Four's second year that it was an 'open' channel, a breeze, if not a gale, of fresh thinking in the musty halls of traditional broadcasting. There is some truth in this belief, insofar as Channel Four has introduced new thinking about the ways programmes can be made, and what they can be made about; how far audiences can be taught positively to use television and how much they can be fragmented before the notion of broadcasting to them becomes the wrong way to reach them.

In all these ways Channel Four is different. It is not, however, *that* different (as Isaacs said before it began). As we have seen it is a commercial company with a highly motivated sense of its commercial origins, purpose and direction. It is much closer in organisational size and attitude to a small ITV company than to the BBC. Although hard to place – because it has genuinely broken moulds – it is clear that in a crisis its commercial instincts would probably override whatever other operating principles it has. Survival in the commercial system would be all, not some abstract moral principle about audience choice, or a commitment to remain 'open'. None of this denigrates its achievements nor its purposes. But it does throw light upon one curiosity: Channel Four's indifference to notions of formal public accountability. Strictly speaking, it is probably the least accountable part of British broadcasting, with the most freedom to go its own way untrammelled by any tradition.

Channel Four does have some standard means of taking its audiences into account: what I have dubbed the 'mechanisms' of accountability. These are the Duty Office, audience research, a feedback programme, an officer equivalent to the Education Officers in the BBC and, through the IBA, advisory councils. Some have been overtly copied from BBC practice although perhaps the biggest surprise is that the Channel Four board rejected early on any notion that there would be advisory councils within the channel itself.

There are also the commissioning editors who have a continuing interest in assessing, in broad terms, the audiences for their own area; the informal system of accounting which takes various of the staff to meetings, conferences, ceremonies, seminars, as observers and speakers; and the structures within and between Channel Four, the IBA and the ITCA; and the IPPA – the Independent Programme Producers Association (among others).

AUDIENCE RESEARCH

Channel Four has a constant problem with its audience research: the BARB system cannot accurately measure below 250 000; many Channel Four audiences fall within the margin of error generated by the data; in any case BARB research was set up to deal with the requirements of the advertisers, ITCA and the BBC, all anxious to see what size of large-scale audience they could achieve. Channel Four was set up to cater for much smaller, more specialist, audiences. For the channel controllers and the CEs, then, quality of audience was always going to be much more important.

Research, an early discussion paper by a commissioning editor said, 'will be needed to follow and understand the implications of the new technologies on people's use of leisure and viewing habits'. The question, shortly to be asked, would not be 'which channel do I watch?', but 'do I want to watch anything at all?' The same paper also suggested that much more formative research needed to be done to help plan series and to help the programme-makers. The need to research into the effectiveness of programmes was critical, especially in education.

The problems thrown up by the BARB system mean that Channel Four commissions a lot of research for itself. Some of this research is at variance with BARB. For instance, Channel Four research in 1985 suggested that its share of total audience was rather higher than BARB's figures said. On patronage (the numbers turning to the channel at some time during a week) the Channel Four figures also contradicted BARB.

BARB suggested by March 1985 that Channel Four's share was around six per cent of the total weekly audience; their own figures suggested nearly 14 per cent. On patronage, BARB was saying Channel Four got about 60 per cent; the latter said they got 75 per cent weekly, 89 per cent monthly. Channel Four research on attitudes towards output also showed a growth of audience loyalty, and a belief that the programmes were as professional as any other channel's. Only a minority, however, said they enjoyed most programmes.

These data have to be taken in conjunction with our knowledge of the television audience. Although Channel Four was set up to break a mould, to give specialist audiences their kind of programmes at better, more accessible, times than the other channels, all television programmes attract a general audience. So even when a programme is 'marked' by a producer, mentally or in editing, as an 'up-market documentary', that programme will have an audience profile close to the national social class and education level pattern. At one level this makes a nonsense of the very idea of Channel Four, although it does suggest that where programmes are different they will reach out, perforce, to the general audience. The problem, of course, is that that audience may hate the programme.

COMMISSIONING THE PROGRAMMES

Channel Four staff, as unconsciously as those in the BBC, say things which imply that they have a moral sense in what they do – that is, a very strong belief that the programmes they are commissioning and putting out are exactly what their audience *need*; this has the smack of Reith about it and can lead a commissioning editor to say that the mere existence of the C4–IBA connection ensures that peoples' needs are catered for. Another commissioning editor is less sanguine:

> Most people in tv would be bothered by the lack of reaction. Most people would rely on the Duty Log, the Video Box*, the Press (like most people would anywhere), or your neighbour, or your taxi driver ... Personally, I am very dubious about surveys. I rely on people I meet casually – I don't always tell people what I do.

He continues:

> In fact it's a combination of all these things – it is not satisfactory and maybe it never could be. The old idea is that tv is just about putting programmes out and that you don't have to do anything else. My idea, partly because of my background, is that tv

---

* Video Boxes, which now exist in London, Bradford, Manchester and Glasgow, are means by which members of the public can comment on Channel Four programmes by making a short video film, basically a talking head to fixed camera. Begun as a novelty they can be useful to producers of the 'Right to Reply' programmes who may use extracts from them as short clips of *vox pop*. Early on, the London Video Box was popular with disgruntled independent producers who used to make acerbic comments at commissioning editors they were unable to reach in any other way.

programmes have a life of their own. I think we have been better than lots of channels on this ... people can write off for leaflets, pamphlets, course. I don't think you serve audiences by allowing tv to stultify. Audiences need to have an impact on programmes ...

These editors come from a variety of backgrounds but they are increasingly recruited from mainstream broadcast production. It is they who are responsible for spending the bulk of Channel Four's money. It is they who commission, from two main sources, all the programmes which appear (the two main sources are independent producers and ITV companies; other programmes come from bought-in series from abroad, from repeats and from occasional series or programmes commissioned from non-professional companies or from 'maverick' sources). It is fair to say that the main problem for this small group is that they have little time to assess what they are doing, little time to discuss with colleagues what policies to implement. For instance:

There is no real sense in which this talking to people outside happens. It is very hard to say what C4 policy is on any number of things. Different editors work in different ways. I have tried to tell people what my policy is ... I can honestly say I never thought it would be different. Early on there were those of us who tried to say it doesn't have to be like this (i.e. traditionally based tv production within the C4 system). *** knows a lot about scheduling but there is nowhere he can feed this in. I may not see *** for three months ... [they were on the same floor of the building]

This same commissioning editor also reported that he did not have much sense of the outside. He found it difficult to make sense of audience research – what priority to put on its findings – again partly because audiences for at least one of the strands of programming for which he was responsible were then small. Like a number of other CEs one method he used to establish contact was to go and meet people at various functions. One connection he exploited was with a close friend who had many contacts in an industrial field.

The work pressure on commissioning editors can be astonishing (see Table 10.2). It is as if the payment for the privilege of working for the channel were a life sentence of very hard labour. This was remarked upon by many people working for Channel Four, not just

TABLE 10.2   *A taxonomy of tasks for a Channel Four commissioning editor*

IBA/ITV meetings
IBA Educational Advisory Council   (8 days per year)
IBA/ITCA/C4 Co-ordinating Committee   (3 per year)
ITV/BBC/C4 Liaison Committee   (3 per year)
IBA/C4 Liaison meetings   (6 per year)
Other miscellaneous functions

Industry/Awards meetings
RTS Council
RTS Awards Review Committee
RTS Training Committee
BAFTA Documentaries Jury
Priz Italia Documentary Selection Panel
HEC Film Awards Jury
Pasco Macfarlane Memorial Jury
IPPA Meetings

Internal meetings (formal)
Programme Planning Committee   (10 per year)
Programme Review   (46 per year)
Current Affairs Meeting   (46 per year)
Commissioning Meetings   (20 per year)
Budget/Finance Meetings   (46 per year)
Education Group Meetings   (46 per year)

Overseas trips
NRK Norway
RAI Italy
PBS Stations, USA
China

Domestic trips
Visits to ITV companies
Visits/Viewings – independents outside London
Location visits
Speak at regional events (e.g. Newcastle, Liverpool)

Conference/Festivals
Edinburgh TV Festival
RTS, Cambridge
Health and the Media – 2nd International Conference,
    Edinburgh
Training in the Television Industry, Ripon
Social Action Broadcasting, Loughborough
Doctors or Apples?, University of Kent
Coronary Heart Disease Prevention Conference, Canterbury
Wildscreen, Bristol
EBU Adult Education Conference, Peebles
Unemployment and the Media, IBA

TABLE 10.2 *continued*

The Media and NGO's in Europe, IBT/BAFTA
National Association of Community Health Councils
 Conference, London

New proposals

General letters

Telephone calls

Individual meetings
New proposers (serious ones)
Overseas broadcasters
Representatives of organisations
ITV colleagues
Umpteen miscellaneous

Programme monitoring
Discussion of programme outlines
Discussion on budget/schedule
Meeting production team/writer/presenter, etc.
Receive progress report on shooting
View rough-cuts
Negotiate improvements where necessary
View completed programmes
Discuss publicity/follow-up/presentation
Co-ordinate to co-productions with overseas partners
Arrange viewings for PB or IBA when necessary
Thank-you letters

Acquisitions
View cassettes submitted 'on spec.'
View acquired programmes (e.g. Vietnam)
Liaise with Contracts Dept. on purchases

Reports/Papers
Report on educational output (contribution)
'Food For Thought' – case history!
WHO paper on 'Health and the Media'
Biennial Progress Reports
Miscellaneous internal papers

C4 Consultations
Environmental/Conservation seminar
Mental Health seminar
Meetings with individual advisers/consultants
Project Planning/Liaison meetings (e.g. Sex,
 Environment, Mental Health)

Press and Marketing
Press/producer/follow-up planning meetings
Press launches for commissioned series

Seasonal launches
Interviews with journalists
Regular liaison with press office
Liaison with marketing on BMRB research
Liaison on other research projects, e.g. Well Being
Plan special seasons (e.g. Worldwise, Decade of Women)
Organise competitions (Photography, Amateur Naturalists)

Business development/distribution
Liaison with LC on forthcoming series
Liaison with SY on possible books/spin-offs
Liaison with SD on off-air recording
IPPA Seminar on distribution
MIP
London Multi-Media Market

Educational follow-up
Planning and liaison with Derek Jones (C4 Education Officer)
Meetings for major projects (e.g. Information Technology,
   Cautionary Tales, etc.)
Planning posters, leaflets, etc.
Liaison and contributions for C4

Scheduling
Compile lists of projects awaiting Tx
Liaise with PB/JI/GBE
Convey latest information to suppliers
Plan special seasons

Social functions/Awards dinners
e.g.   BAFTA
       RTS
       EMMYs
       Wildscreen
       ITV functions
       IBA functions
       IPPA functions
       FBU functions
          etc. etc.

---

the CEs. The first chief executive, Jeremy Isaacs, was said to be a workaholic.

This company is run by one man: he's very interested in programmes which is fine at Thames (where Isaacs was before) but not here. He's eclectic, he's the most open person I have ever worked for in tv. He is also someone who will like an idea one moment then heartily dislike it the next. The real problem is when your programme makers have a chief executive saying their idea is the best thing since sliced bread one minute, then saying the next that we can't afford it.

Another CE went further than this detection of inconsistency and talked of the 'inadequacy' of the bosses and the developing battle which he detected 'between Jeremy's team and Justin's [Dukes – the managing director] team'. This was a complaint, much heard in 1985 when Channel Four was becoming highly successful, that the reason was a gradual erosion of idealism by straight commercialism.

Some staff in Channel Four believed it was only by *not* being critically acclaimed that they could be said to be fulfilling their original brief. This was how one commissioning editor put it:

> Channel Four will come under pressure from ITV because it is not likely to obtain its share. ITV will start to say we will give you three hours a night, non-commissioned stuff. Money really is very scarce – money now spent on investigation and experiment will be spent on security: if you can sell it you can have it.

Channel Four, then, had begun to develop new ways of making television programmes. It had developed a unique way of getting the ideas from drawing board to transmission, often at a remarkably low price. Its schedules, however, began to reflect a more traditional approach by 1985, adding in repeats in peak time and, despite keeping a strand of education in the early evening, beginning to look much like BBC2. The advertisements intruded of course, but the BBC had for many years used 'fillers' lookalike advertising for its own future programmes or for *Radio Times* or, increasingly, various merchandising spin-offs, so that BBC2, at least, looked sometimes like C4. Channel Four, however, cannot be said to be publicly accountable to any great degree. Indeed, the pressure of work on a small staff ensured that they could deal rather less with the public than their equivalents in the BBC – or much of ITV.

Was it responsive to the audience? Again, on the whole no, taking the corporate view that what it provided, using pressure groups and lobbies to argue its case, was a liberal and paternal system of a kind of 1980s version of moral uplift. It was indeed the last of the Reithian channels, at a time when, arguably, the BBC was beginning at last to dismantle the heartland of its Reithian ideals in order to pursue more commercial interests.

The challenge of Channel Four was that it was able to demonstrate a form of public-service broadcasting financed, however indirectly, by advertising revenue. The challenge of commercialism was that the BBC began to see a future in which many aspects of commerce – like merchandising from programmes, or selling video tapes – were not so bad. As soon as that aspect of the 'modern' BBC was proclaimed there was no real reason why it should not least toy with direct commercial funding, most obviously through advertising. That it continued to proclaim, in the words of its former chairman, Young, that 'you cannot be a little bit pregnant' suggested it still was holding, however tenuously, to its original brief.

Part of that brief had always been to educate. Both Channel Four and the BBC took the term in its broadest sense. Many of Channel Four's early appointments had come from BBC Education departments, disillusioned with financial cuts and what some saw as a diminishing commitment by the BBC to that broad definition. But BBC Education remains a potent force for public-service broadcasting ideals. It also demonstrates that audiences – in one form or another – can be involved with programmes, even to the point of insisting that they take one direction rather than another. Educational programmes contain some of the seeds of a 'true' and workable accountability. To this area we finally turn.

11 Beyond the Fringes

Both educational and social-action broadcasting have developed the direct relationship with their audiences that other parts of the broadcast system has failed to develop, or have rejected as impracticable. In the case of educational broadcasting this 'closeness of fit' came very early and has remained an integral part of the way programmes are made. Put simply, educationalists, in various guises and including the classroom teacher, have effective veto powers over programmes at the planning stage and beyond, if the product does not suit. By and large this works, and works well, because both sides acknowledge the importance of the central relationship. Educational broadcasting only can work, in its own terms, if there is co-operation and consensus.

In social-action broadcasting, a younger partner in what might be described as social-responsibility broadcasting, a similar if generally less formal agreement has come to exist. The extreme end of this newer, but no less significant relationship between audiences and programme-makers, lies in the BBC's Community Programme Unit, which was set up to hand over editorial control. Educational broadcasting, including schools and the Open University, and a host of continuing (the old 'further') education programmes, combined with a unique 'advisory' structure which is much stronger than elsewhere, keeps BBC Education among the most important present guardians of British public-service broadcasting. Major undertakings, like the literacy campaign or the computer-literacy project, may be cited as evidence that right into the 1980s the early commitment to education has been sustained and seems likely to continue.

The most important point about the BBC's education services, pertinent to one of the themes of this book, is that BBC Education is in an entirely different relationship with its clients – indeed it is perfectly reasonable to see them as clients with the implications imposed by that word, rather than as audiences. If, as has been argued, the BBC has moved *de facto* from paternalism to professionalism in its guiding ethic, and if, as has been also suggested, there needs to be a new informing ethic to public service broadcasting, educational broadcasting provides at least part of the model.

That model is one where broadcasters identify a client population using a variety of techniques, adapt programme ideas to that group, discuss the programme's potential with advisory bodies and, subsequent to the broadcast, undertake extensive follow-up procedures for continuing to interest the client/audience, and to evaluate that client/audience's response. Locked into the schools broadcasts are powerful advisory bodies with what amount to veto powers.

Of course it would be equally fair to suggest that this model might not fit at all well into general programming. But it might up to an agreed point fit news and current affairs, which continue to attract much public interest and often opprobrium, and it might fit many documentary programmes as well. Most of all it might be fitted to *general* guidelines attachable to *all* programmes, where those guidelines could affect, for instance, racial jokes, sex scenes or violence.

THE PREFECT SYSTEM: EDUCATIONAL BROADCASTING

Educational broadcasting, as Robinson (1982) points out, was early recognised as a great potential of the new medium. Reith created a National Advisory Committee on Education in October 1923. By the summer of 1924 the British Broadcasting Company had already a full-time Director of Education (J. C. Stobart), seconded from the Ministry of Education. Many people, who in the 1920s saw great hope for change in broadcasting, also saw its educational output as the most significant part. Britain in the twenties was a society in transition: social, economic and political changes were all happening apace; at the same time the old social and economic divisions were painfully obvious. Reith certainly was aware of this and believed that a part of broadcasting's divine mission was to help heal, to bind up, to consolidate the nation. Adult education could be a part of this as well as school-based learning. Indeed the potential for adult post-school learning was well-established outside broadcasting.

Among the bodies concerned with the development at large of adult education, the British Institute of Adult Education were in 1923 regularly including broadcasting as an item on the agenda of their executive committee meetings and had approached Reith. Stobart, writing in an early issue of *Journal of Adult Education*, outlined the importance of radio to education in this field and went on to say 'wireless must flow into the vacant spaces of continuing education . . . providing a stimulus, an auxiliary . . . something complete'. He imagined these radio talks followed by 'illustrations, guides to reading, some easy system of contact with libraries, tuition by correspondence . . . None of these developments is impossible'.

By far the most important early major development in adult education broadcasting was the Hadow Report of 1928, *New Ventures in Broadcasting*. The report made the folowing main points:

1. Broadcasting has the potential for widening the field from which students are drawn, by being able to touch and stimulate a mass public; it can put listeners in touch with experts and can lead to more formal study.

2. It is not necessary to appeal all the time to large audiences . . . but that a much larger proportion of listeners than is commonly supposed have particular interests to which special items might appeal.

3. There was a hazard in one-way communication; discussion groups, formal and informal, might increase the value to be had from broadcast talks.

To get all this under way the Hadow Report recommended the establishment of a national organisation to encourage group listening and discussion with a central council for broadcast adult education with area councils, served by full-time officers. Pamphlets would be published and a weekly journal should be started, all aimed at strengthening two-way communication.

By November 1928, the Central Council for Broadcast Adult Education had been set up. Area councils took longer and only four (out of 14 proposed) ever started. But six education officers were appointed and by 1930 there were 530 listening groups. The proposed journal took longer and came up against much violent opposition from the magazine press. *The Listener* – the magazine concerned – eventually started in 1929.

Broadcasting, through radio in the 1930s, transformed serious music understanding and playing in schools, just as it was able to bring many other aspects of the outside world before children. Adults were able to look forward to many direct learning programmes, like those on languages, as well as being offered programmes which gently pushed them into wanting to find out more. Educational broadcasting has always emphasised that it is only a stimulus to other activities, not a substitute for them.

BBC EDUCATION IN THE 1980s

BBC Education today provides about 2000 hours of television (21 per cent of the output) and 1700 hours of radio (six per cent of the

TABLE 11.1 *Educational broadcasting: organisation charts for television and radio: A*

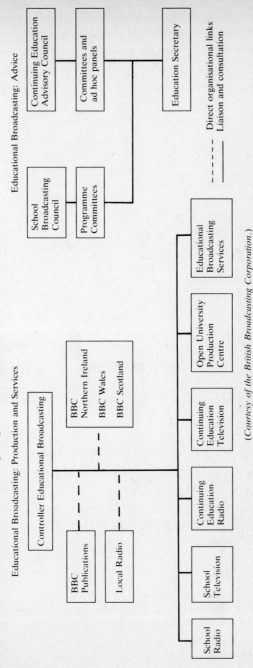

(*Courtesy of the British Broadcasting Corporation.*)

TABLE 11.1   *Educational broadcasting: organisation charts for television and radio: B*

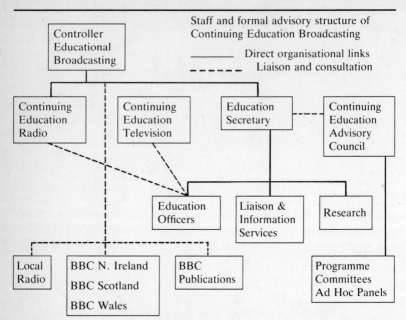

output) a year. It is organised into five major departments to do this (see Table 11.1): school radio, school television, continuing education radio, continuing education television and the Open University Production Centre. Programmes are also provided by Scotland, Wales and Northern Ireland and by many BBC local radio stations (20 of them have an education producer).

Schools Broadcasting

BBC schools broadcasts are used by up to 95 per cent of all UK schools (BBC Education Research). There have been many changes since these broadcasts began in 1924, notably the advent of means of recording programmes off-air by tape recorder and now video cassette recorder. For this reason BBC schools radio began, in 1983, to transmit some programmes late at night on the assumption that many schools were now equipped to record schools programmes in conjunction with a timer. This change has led to a decline in use of these broadcasts, however. Schools radio, like schools television, operates in all main curriculum areas and has moved recently into micro-electronics. Planned developments include a magazine programme for teenagers with audience participation, and more 'out of school' programmes. Radio has always been an important element in primary school music and dance classes.

BBC schools television, transmitting over 400 hours a year, has been transferred from BBC1 to BBC2, which cleared BBC1 for daytime programmes. This move was helped by the discovery that about 99 per cent of secondary schools now have video cassette recorders, and has led to changes in programme formats: more programmes are conceived as 'modular', aimed at particular parts of a syllabus; primary schools, where only 24 per cent have VCRs still view most schools television off-air.

The output departments use the same resources as other programme-makers, have access to the same production facilities on the same terms. The results is that schools broadcasts have a high quality, indistinguishable in schools drama output, for instance, from mainstream drama output. Similarly many programmes appearing on air in peak time are Continuing Education programmes.

Continuing Education

As with schools broadcasting, continuing education radio and television complement each other. For example, in the 1980s series on micro-electronics, on mental handicap, and on unemployment amongst youth, the television programmes have been directed at broad audiences while the radio programmes have aimed to reach teachers and tutors. Radio is used sometimes where events are fast-moving in a priority area; that is, if a programme-maker, or the Continuing Education Advisory Council (CEAC) Programme Committee, identify an urgent need, radio programmes can be put together and scheduled much faster than television.

About half of the continuing education radio programmes are transmitted on VHF, limiting their audiences automatically; the remainder are on Radio Four medium and long wave. Programmes go out on VHF on Sunday afternoons (language, basic education and professionally directed series) while more potentially popular series have to fight for space with mainstream programmes on Radio Four. Continuing education television produces about 250 new programmes a year, nearly 100 hours of television. With repeats, the department annually transmits around 400 hours (some 950 programmes). These can be divided into language and communications, public affairs and

history, science and technology, arts, leisure skills and health. Most
go out in off-peak times while the remainder is transmitted flexibly
and competitively.

The Open University

The Open University, very much a child of the 1960s' euphoric
attitude to expanding adult education at the highest level, was
conceived as a 'university of the air'. Since its beginnings in 1969
many have questioned the use of broadcasting in its work as an
expensive waste of time and money. Of late, faced with continuing
cuts from the DES, the OU has itself begun to pull back resources
from its broadcasting arm. The OU production centre at Milton
Keynes, opened in 1982, is the expensive result of early commitment
to using off-air broadcasting for much of the university's teaching
output. It has now to find its way in a world where the proportion of
income derived from the OU next door is going to get smaller and
smaller. The BBC has freed managerial controls to allow more
autonomy, which in practice means taking commercial work or
contracting itself to other parts of the BBC.

At first OU productions were based at Alexandra Palace in north
London (the site of BBC television's first programmes in the 1930s).
By the time the OUPC at Milton Keynes had opened the department
had 400 staff and they were producing 250 television and 400 radio
programmes a year. All fifty-five BBC producers were subject-
specialists. Currently, the OUPC provides 130 Open University and
40 continuing education courses with material.

ADVICE OR CONTROL? THE ROLES OF THE SCHOOLS
BROADCASTING COUNCILS AND THE CONTINUING
EDUCATION ADVISORY COUNCIL

For schools, the BBC believes it should ensure that its programmes
are 'sponsored' by a body which represents the 'professional network
of use'. This body is the Schools Broadcasting Council: like the GAC
a ponderously large organisation bringing together educationalists
from all over the UK. There are related (and much smaller) bodies in
Scotland, Wales and Northern Ireland.

The main council has around 40 members drawn from a variety of
educational organisations and representing teaching at all levels and

across all subject areas. It meets twice a year to consider policy and the overall balance of the output. It also appoints members of the Primary and Secondary Programme Committees whose work is concerned with the purposes, nature and suitability of planned series. These programme committees are the real power in the system, the central part of educational broadcasting accountability. At the meetings of these committees proposed series are taken apart line by line. The Committees do refer programme ideas back, they also reject them, ask for major amendments, question the logic of why that series; why now?

Production departments are supported further by the Educational Broadcasting Services area. It is from EBS that the education officers are drawn, whose job it is to go about the country assessing the use of current series in schools and colleges and the viability of future series. Education officers will talk to individual teachers as well as groups of them. They will carry out various kinds of *ad hoc* research, supplemented by the larger scale research undertaken by the EBS's own research department. This department annually and every term surveys the overall use of both BBC broadcasting and independent television series.

Education Officers also organise conferences, meetings and courses and provide information to the centre on programme needs, both to programme-makers and to the Schools Broadcasting Council. It was the Education Officers who first identified a major national need for adult literacy in the early 1970s. EBS also have responsibility for giving out information on transmission times, for distributing an annual programme, and for getting out to schools and the relevant bodies, all information, back-up material, publications (like teachers' notes) and pupils' pamphlets on series. There is a Technical Advisory Service which gives advice on reception and on recording.

In Continuing Education a similar arrangement for advice holds, although the Council (CEAC) has rather less powers. The Continuing Education Advisory Council (CEAC) represents the adult and further education world. Staff from the educational broadcasting councils (UK, Scotland, Wales, Northern Ireland) act as a secretariat to this committee.

Again CEAC provides links between programme-makers and programme users. The main function of this secretariat is to study trends in educational practice and to show how these may best be used by broadcasters. The staff also pre-test series, inform users of what programmes are available and in the pipeline, to discover how programmes have been used and what their impact has been. CEAC, like the SBC, has a programme committee which closely monitors programme plans and progress.

THE SYSTEM IN COMMERCIAL TELEVISION AND CHANNEL FOUR

ITV and the IBA

Commercial television was the first to introduce schools broadcasting on television in the UK and although the commercial part of British broadcasting has been much criticised in aspects of its programming this is one field where it has retained a high reputation. ITV produces rather less than the BBC, about 50 annual school series and an average of 26 half-hours of adult education. Channel Four has transformed the overall picture but as it had a specific brief to commission and show rather more education programmes it has to be considered as separate from ITV.

The role of the IBA in attempting to gain more education time on ITV has been ambiguous. Commercial television companies have been anxious not to clutter day-time schedules with schools programmes, or any obviously educational output (but then so has the BBC). The IBA, as with its more general role, has had great difficulty in holding on to what relatively small output there has been. In programme companies education departments have always been among, if not actually *the*, most marginalised, most open to threat of closure. The IBA has an Education Advisory Council. From the beginning of 1985 a new structure was brought in, reflecting dissatisfaction with the previous arrangements. The new council had fewer members responsible for advising the Authority on educational policy and for monitoring educational programmes. Most ITV companies have their own education advisory panels, however. As with the BBC, ITV companies have appointed education officers, (CCEOs – continuing and community education officers). Since the last franchise renewals the IBA has also required ITV companies to show evidence of local education programmes as well as network ones. The 1984 IBA Annual Report suggests there has been less than full progress in this area: 'Uneven as the developments are bound to be in a federal system such as ITV', the Report says. However, Granada, Central, HTV, LWT, Thames, TVS and Yorkshire now all have community units of one sort or another. These units, crossing the boundary between education and social action broadcasting often call on Community Service Volunteer advice.

Channel Four

Under the Broadcasting Act setting up Channel Four the service is specifically told it must cater for tastes not otherwise catered for on ITV1. Channel Four schedules about eight hours of educational programmes a week. A report to the IBA Education Advisory Council in 1984 said:

We planned our educational output on the assumption that five and a half hours a week would be directly commissioned as 'educational' output and that a further one and a half hours would be achieved by the wrapping around of general output, in particular of the major documentary series. In the event, the quantity of output so organised has averaged around eight hours a week, rather more than the seven hours required by the IBA.

The Report says this is due to the wide range of informative programming commissioned by editors outside the immediate area of education and by the boundless enthusiasm of the education liaison officer.

As with the BBC (from whence, incidentally, came a number of key personnel to Channel Four, especially in this area) Channel Four relies in educational broadcasting on the extensive use of back-up material. Wrap-around booklets, leaflets, pamphlets, reading lists, etc., are crucial to the philosophy of C4 education programmes: the old paradox of wanting people to switch off and do something useful.

Audience reaction to many Channel Four programmes has been hard to judge as audiences tend to be very small (as they often are for Open University broadcasts). Three main sources of audience data are available to Channel Four: those BARB figures which can be used; regular series-based research commissioned by the channel from BMRB; the number of requests for back-up material. There may be comments in the Duty Log or letters appreciating or complaining, but Channel Four education make the common point of all programme-makers in minority broadcasting that, even taking Appreciation Indices into account, no one can make fully accessible what motivates an audience.

THE USE OF SUPPORT SERVICES IN EDUCATIONAL BROADCASTING

The BBC received 234 000 requests in 1985–6 for continuing-education leaflets (out of 567 000 copies of printed material). Channel Four has around 750 000 every year for its much broader categories of 'education' programmes. Education is not and is never likely to be a big audience grabber, although individual programmes and some rare series might be. This is true whatever format education programme-makers use to get their message across.

It has become part of the professional's basic kit in this area not to label a programme strand as educational (unless it is an Open University programme) as it is likely that this alone will deter many casual viewers or listeners. But programmes in the broadcasting horizons of continuing education can get surprisingly large audiences with a surprisingly high commitment. Two BBC examples illustrate this well: its *Delia Smith Cookery Course* book which accompanied the series in 1978 sold over one and a half-million copies; when the series was running the production office was getting over 300 letters a week. 'Groundswell', an environmental series broadcast on Radio Four in 1983, sent out 1000 fact sheets in response to listeners requests. Channel Four has also had excellent responses, for instance to its environmental series, *Worldwise*, which culminated in a six hour marathon 'The Longest Running Show on Earth'.

The BBC Adult Literacy Campaign began in 1972 as a result of advocacy from the BBC's own education officers who informed the then-named Further Education Production Department that there was growing evidence that very large numbers of adults in the UK were illiterate – maybe as many as two million. The EOs believed that broadcasting could reach these people where other means would fail because broadcasting uniquely did not require literacy for understanding and because it was received in the non-threatening home environment.

Initial scepticism among BBC staff was high. One reason was the concern that even if a television series could be devised for non-literates, how could the necessary network of voluntary centres for follow-up be created and cope with a possibly huge demand? Nevertheless the BBC decided to submit plans for a series to the Further Education Advisory Council and further discussions took place at a conference organised by the British Association of Settlements in November 1973. When a plan for both television and radio series was put forward in the BBC in January, 1974, it significantly recommended that the television part of the overall operation should effectively confine itself to reducing anxiety and stigma, rather than engage in instruction. It was also suggested that the programmes (ten minutes long) should be transmitted in peak time, rather than in educational slots. The programmes had to be made in such a way that the mass literate audience would find them acceptable.

The plan was accepted by BBC management and costed at an initial outlay of £800 000 for staff, transmission and studio time. It was agreed by the FE Advisory Council in May 1974. During that spring the plan was widely talked over by the BBC and local education authorities, and voluntary schemes. A further £200 000 was considered necessary by the broadcasters for non-broadcast activities, including a telephone referral service, contributions towards training tutors, research into the design and distribution of associated printed material and research into the effectiveness of the whole project. The 'Right to Read' campaign was an enormous undertaking altogether and involved far more organisations than just the BBC. A year after the project was planned the BBC moved to recruit volunteer tutors, using airtime to do it. The address people were asked to write to did not mention the BBC at all, on the grounds that this would avoid inhibiting all the other media from publicising it. The first programmes, *On the Move*, were recorded in September 1975, while BBC Radio began the series *Teaching an Adult to Read*. In October the referral telephone number was given on *The Jimmy Young Show* from which there was a massive response, and *On the Move* was first broadcast in the same month.

The BBC contribution to the national literacy campaign may not have been absolute but it was clearly decisive: television demonstrated its social usefulness, while radio showed its educational potential at a different level, for tutors. Both helped to alleviate a hidden and large social problem. The literacy campaign has been one of the BBC's outstanding success stories all round. In the late seventies and eighties a similar effort was made at an entirely different level with computer literacy. In the high excitement over the microprocessor and the silicon chip induced in the UK by sensational (and often wrong) media coverage, the BBC joined in with a programme transmitted in 1978, called 'Now the Chips Are Down'.

The BBC's Continuing Education Department decided to back a further three major documentaries in this area (*The Silicon Factor*), and as a result of these and increasing social and Government awareness and promotion of the microcomputer the BBC commissioned a series of ten programmes, *Hands on Micros*, in the autumn of 1979. Expertise in the BBC was limited in this field and it turned to a number of outside agencies for assistance and advice, among them the Department of Industry. The DoI agreed to put up money for consultation, piloting and pre-testing, educational liaison and information, all of this on offer not least because the DoI had planned to make 1982 the year of the micro. The research, devised with the help of the BBC's BRD, aimed to find out what level of interest there was likely to be in any programmes: questions were added to the BBC's Daily Survey (this was in the pre-BARB days). A second study was designed to provide guidance on content, style and format. This study asked four groups of 30 people, selected by age, sex and class, representative of the groups already identified as most interested from the first study results, what they wanted to see in a computer series.

The most controversial part of the planned series was the BBC microcomputer (set up through BBC Enterprises) – controversial in retrospect because it took the BBC inevitably into a highly competitive commercial arena in which it could be, and has been, accused of using a oligopolistic position to promote a single product. None the less, the BBC believed that in helping to design and promote the BBC micro it was doing a major public service. The machines which resulted from awarding the development contract to Acorn Computers have been widely praised.

In the event the series was called *The Computer Programme*. Delays, endemic to the microcomputer field, meant that the series was put back by three months; supply of the BBC micro created many problems for a long time. Most unhappily, from the BBC side, production of the micro hit snags just before the launch of the programme, in January 1982. The computer had been designed to perform to the limits of known microtechnology and this proved hard to reproduce in volume.

Research subsequent to the first series showed that seven million people had watched at least part of *The Computer Programme* during one of the three transmissions in 1982. Analysis of the audience showed a remarkable evenness. Up to 80 per cent thought the programmes had provided a good introduction to the subject, explaining the basic principles very clearly. Only 5 per cent thought the programmes too difficult to understand. Among those already owning a microcomputer most also agreed the programmes were a good introduction. The associated materials had also been heavily sub-scribed. *The Computer Book* had sold 60 000 copies by late summer 1982 and there was heavy demand for the National Extension College's self-study course (over 100 000 copies up to October 1982). More than two thousand colleges and schools had used the course; a very low drop-out rate was reported.

Channel Four has attempted to do similarly educational programmes across a wide range. The biggest effort so far has been towards the environment. As with the BBC the importance of back-up and study material has been recognised. Channel Four has limited resources but it has devised ways of producing study material cheaply. At the margins they will often simply recommend a booklist for viewers.

Both the BBC and Channel Four use Broadcasting Support Services (and their Scottish and Northern Irish equivalents) extensively. Broadcasting Support Services grew out of the adult literacy campaign, beginning as a telephone referral system to put teachers and would-be learners in touch with each other. It has become a back-up service needed to distribute the mass of literature now emerging from many programmes on many different channels. Its growth is an indication of the extent to which broadcasting can become much more than a passive activity involving no more than sitting down and staring or listening.

But educational broadcasting at large is proof of that. The underlying questions that remain are: how far can broadcasting, especially television, deliver much more than an introduction to a subject; and how far ought it to try?

SOCIAL ACTION BROADCASTING

Social action broadcasting has existed more or less as long as the BBC. But its most recent manifestations have come in the past ten years or so. Community Service Volunteers (CSV) suggest the turning point for social action broadcasting came with a report by Francis Coleman, under an IBA fellowship, which looked at *Social Action in Television* (1975). The report examined the Dutch agency Werkwinkel, which had pioneered the use of television to motivate viewers into doing things for the community. Until this time most programme-makers outside education had tended to believe their audiences were passive.

Alec Dickson, founder of CSV, says he believes the mass media
have been through three distinct stages since 1960 with respect to
Voluntary Service Overseas (VSO) and CSV. The first was one of
undisguised hostility and scepticism about the ability of young people
to deal effectively with social problems. The second phase was
brought when producers and directors began to be interested in social
problems: 'Cathy Come Home', 'Edna the Inebriate Woman',
'Johnny Go Home', all played their part in altering broadcasters'
attitudes to social problems and their solutions. But, says Dickson,
viewers were left with a feeling of 'impotent grief'.

The current phase in Dickson's schema is where agencies like CSV
and programme companies have met to consider and implement
ideas relating to involvement of viewers and listeners. In the ten years
to 1985 six television companies and the BBC, and 20 local radio
stations, have been involved in social action broadcasting of one kind
or another. The coming of Channel Four has greatly reinforced the
philosophy behind social action broadcasting by making much more
airtime available. Programmes about and for the sick, the disabled,
the illiterate and the unemployed can be found all over the output at
various times. The BBC and ITV majors like Thames have contributed through various forms of 'telethon' like 'Children in Need'.
Expansion seems now to depend on the extent to which likely growth
in broadcasting can be matched with sufficient broadcaster concern·
about the importance of social action broadcasting as an integral part
of the output.

The development of ideas like 'Live Aid' and 'Sports Aid' help this
considerably. Because these types of social action attract very large
audiences they can easily be slotted into peak-time schedules – and at
short notice. The competition for time is crucial: too many worthy
programmes can be marginalised by the exigencies of audience-
grabbing – for ratings, for advertisers. If British broadcasting is to
become more competitive, and at the same time to fight itself for
advertising and sponsors' revenue, social action has little hope of
achieving much more than its output levels of the mid-1980s.

ACCESS PROGRAMMES: OPEN DOORS AND OPEN SPACES

Access programmes, said the Annan Committee report, now appear
in many shapes and forms. This, written in 1977 or thereabouts,
was more sanguine than it might have been. For genuine access

opportunities the viewer or listener will search the airwaves mostly in vain. Broadcasters are generally extremely unwilling to allow free or even restricted access to people not schooled in professional broadcaster norms. Part of this unwillingness to let the public get too near the microphone or camera may be a recognition by broadcasters, however inchoate, that much of what they do is artifice rather than art. Today, technology supplies the means for many more people to get on-air. The twin arguments used against this: first, that they would not know what to do; second, that they would not know what to say (and therefore drive audiences away), both miss the point.

Access implies just that: it provides a channel for members of the public to say something: the necessity for it to be particularly professional or particularly interesting is entirely relative. Of course professional broadcasters have a vested interest in keeping their audiences watching or listening and, therefore, not allowing anything on-air which will drive them to switch off. There is too a desire not to let the public suppose that what they see or hear is produced by professionals when it is not.

This underestimates audiences. There will always be a percentage who will misunderstand; it is the height of élitist arrogance to assume that, whatever minority or majority these constitute, programmes have to be made to take them into account at all times. In practice programme-makers do not bother to trouble themselves about this unknowing and unknowable part of the audience, continuing to make the programmes they want to make. Although mainstream television and radio is just that, more and more programme-makers are prepared to take risks at certain times. This is perhaps more true of drama and arts programmes than of, say, situation comedies.

Ultimately, it could be argued that access programming challenges the right of the professional programme-maker to be on-air at all. Although it would be ludicrous to suggest that access programmes ought to be scheduled for prime-time or take a large proportion of programmes on-air, there is point in asking why there are not as many as Annan implied. Part of the answer is that Annan lumped together a number of different types of programme – notably adding phone-in programmes to the access category. This is not what is normally meant by access, and neither is it what professional broadcasters mean, although they may use phone-ins as an easy example of access when pushed to name an access programme.

In fact there is only one identifiable access programme strand currently in British television: the BBC's *Open Space* run by the

Community Programme Unit. This slot, scheduled for early evening viewing on BBC2, represents a genuine attempt by the CPU to give audiences a chance to make programmes and get them on-air. However tiny this effort, measured against all UK television, it is a breakthrough and it has now the advantage of having lasted well over a decade.

HTV and Tyne Tees have in the past run genuine access programmes but, as with much of ITV, these programmes come and go as season succeeds season; the commercial imperative of only continuing series with the potential for large audiences, or series which gather the 'Brownie Points' for the IBA, tends to act against what are bound to be small minority programmes.

The BBC Community Programme Unit began life in 1973. It has had an internally stormy existence ever since within the BBC, sometimes in public controversy outside it too. Senior management are frequently exercised by its output, and have often resorted to direct or indirect pressure to change, delay or, less frequently, ban programmes.

Two examples are a programme by doctors seeking to explain the probable effects on the medical service of a nuclear attack, which was held up for a long time by the then Director of Programmes, Television, on the grounds it was not 'balanced', a nonsense term applied to access programmes. Second, a six-week delay imposed on a programme made by Sheffield Police Watch on police tactics during the miners' strike of 1984–5 which showed the police in a particularly bad light. In the case of the Sheffield Police Watch programme, *Panorama* senior staff queried the veracity of the films inserted as they had been unable to get hold of such material. This was one reason given internally for holding up the programme. CPU staff said the reason they were given the film footage was because they were 'trusted' to be sympathetic. The Establishment team from *Panorama* were not.

Incidentally, this episode also provides ammunition for those who attack the BBC's own insistence on there being 'one' BBC. The desire to show a single corporate face flies in the face of creative reason and points again to the tensions which have developed over the years between the bureaucracy and the programme-makers. The fact that management are usually ex-programme-makers has not lessened this tension. In some ways it has heightened it, as programme-makers can be frustrated by senior staff who understand only too well the tricks used to circumvent the 'rules'. Yet rules applied too rigorously to broadcasting stifle its potential. The CPU itself, set up to take some of the heat away from broadcasters who were accused of élitist arrogance, now takes an exceptional amount of heat internally for not conforming. The key question is: to what should it conform, given that it is meant to be non-conformist?

The Community Programme Unit operated outside Television Centre in a house in Hammersmith Grove for many years. Staff deliberately kept their unit out of any building obviously devoted to broadcasting and to get established in the local area in an unobtrusive building. This itself led to continuing pressure on them to move back into the part of the Television Centre they now occupy, where, unstated, an eye can be kept on them. But considerable effort goes into maintaining an image of 'not professional broadcasting' although the impact of unit staff on programmes can be considerable.

The Unit advertise for and receive hundreds of applications from people and groups who wish to make a programme. These are made out on pro formas giving a certain amount of detail of the proposed programme and of the person, persons, or group proposing to make it. These raw proposals are sifted by staff into groups of impossible, possible, etc. Staff choose which of the various proposals to take under their wing often because they have a personal, if general, interest in the subject proposed. It is at this stage that choices are being made by unit staff, leading to the accusation that even here we do not have real access programming. In short, the professionals in the CPU look for 'balance' over a series, for lighter and heavier interest programmes; for, in fact, exactly what channel controllers want when they come to examine programme offers. The CPU would be highly unlikely, for instance, make two or three programmes for women's groups, however striking or worthy the respective causes, however important the single issues.

Critically, CPU staff engage in a similar debate over what to schedule for the advisory meeting as do network controllers pondering the scheduling of the network. Although none would put it this way in the CPU, what their actions imply is that they are seeking to hold a large audience, the largest possible, while ensuring that audience will stay loyal by not over-killing it with the same topic. The staff cite, in conversation, an 'Open Space' programme on why men go to watch striptease artistes in pubs (made by a stripper and including sequences of exotic dances). It came as no surprise that the programme got into the BBC2 Top Ten for audiences in that week. Although CPU staff know why that was the case they still quote this as evidence that the programmes can get big audiences. Programme-makers even in the CPU are showmen (and women). Unit staff sometimes despair because, they say, a particular group will not co-operate – that is agree to be guided by the professionals on what *is* televisual. Women's groups are said to be the worst (and one hardly has to wonder why).

Editorial control is handed over to those groups chosen. What is not handed over is professional control. It is often hard to determine where the line is drawn between the two. Editorial control means that a group wishing to make a sreries of points can do so in any way it likes, within the law. Professional control was originally meant to be professional advice. Over time this appears to have mellowed into something rather stronger. CPU staff will point out that the 'problem' groups are those who do not follow the 'advice' given. In truth this advice is handed out by broadcasters, self-chosen, sympathetic to access: they want the programme being made to be successful. They also know the pitfalls amateurs will fall into. There is at no stage any chance that the programme-making group will be allowed to handle cameras, lights and sound.

But professional control means editing control: apart from what is originally shot, the critical moments come in the editing suites and here professional judgement can often clash with amateur desire. Who wins largely depends on the will-power of the antagonists. It is also true that direct conflict is rare. Nevertheless the professional adviser will know that his or her own career will be judged on the result. That judgement is not based on how much advice was given and accepted (unknowable) but on the programme itself. If it looks professionally done it will be judged a success. If it looks a mess but the programme-making group loved it, that will not help the professional. It is in editing that the crunch often comes in this business, for professionals *qua* professionals. It is the arena in which the amateur is most vulnerable. Many have turned a camera these days. Almost none of the public have used a professional editing suite where sheer technology can intimidate, where the decisions about why to edit at one point rather than another can be crucial. Editing mixes pragmatism, aesthetics and technology. It is the domain of the experienced and of the decisive. On all these counts the outsider is likely to defer to the insider.

The fact that the CPU have moved to a position where, for at least some of the time, they can take back full professional and editorial control is significant. It is not doing the staff in the Unit a disservice to say that, as with so many other worthies in other contexts, they lament the inability of the non-professional to see where his or her best interests lie. It is the old aid syndrome, believing that we in the West – in this case west London – know best.

Access programming has to let go further if it is to become what it always threatened to be: letting the public unchaperoned into broadcasting. New technologies make that much more feasible. Educating young people in how to make television, how to edit programmes, makes feasible true, complete access, just as that access *is* available to any literate person through writing for the Press. Broadcasting is reaching a moment when it can no longer fall back on professionalism (or intransigent trades unions) as the reason for not letting the public in.

ACCESS PROGRAMMES AND BROADCASTING MANAGEMENT

All 'Open Space' (or other access) programmes are subject to veto by senior television management. There is ample evidence that this veto is frequently threatened and has been used. CPU staff are well aware that their activities are, *per se*, considered to be potentially subversive of the whole of the BBC output as it stands because their working method challenges two fundamental principles: editorial control lies with the professional; and only professionals have an understanding sufficient to justify broadcasting a programme in the first place. But senior management in the BBC have frequently found that the CPU is a useful mechanism of accountability. At public meetings the CPU will be cited as evidence that the BBC does let the public have access to microphones.

In terms of a BBC career, time in the CPU is not thought to be a good route to anywhere else. (Exceptions prove rules here as elsewhere: Paul Bonner, Channel Four's first Controller of Programmes, was an early and enthusiastic CPU member, eventually running it.) All of those working there have volunteered; in so doing they have labelled themselves in a particular way. The Unit is considered peculiar by many other broadcasters: why work in broadcasting only to hand over the bulk of one's skill to amateurs to exploit? Yet the CPU is on to something which most broadcasters have missed: for all its faults it stands as an example of how broadcasting can act as a facility for the public to raise a debate.

It is perfectly true that most of the audience cares little for the CPU's programmes. But were an enlarged CPU, with vastly increased resources, multiplied throughout the land perhaps, to publicise its facilitising role to many more, then it might be that access programmes, dealing with both large and small matters of public concern, could become part of mainstream broadcasting.

CHANNEL FOUR: ACCESS THROUGH PROFESSIONALS?

It is possible to see a large part of Channel Four as a giant Community Programme Unit, committed to letting minorities have much more airtime proportionately than their numbers would ordinarily permit. Channel Four is instructed in the Broadcasting Act, but vaguely as befits British broadcasting legislation, to 'ensure that the programmes contain a suitable proportion of matter calculated to appeal to tastes and interests not generally catered for by ITV . . . and to encourage innovation and experiment in the form and content of programmes'. But as with the CPU, only much more so, Channel Four does this most of the time by using existing professionals. (There have been a number of examples of new entries into programme-making but most of these have come from other professions or other media.) Where there has been a change is in the way larger minority groups have formed into organisations capable of putting up programme proposals. Among the most successful of these is the International Broadcasting Trust (IBT), consisting of a large group of bodies with an interest in development education – a partnership between education, television and the fight against world poverty, as their literature puts it.

This was set up in response to Channel Four's own conception. It 'announced the end of one-way television' upon its launch in 1982 as a lobby of various voluntary bodies anxious to secure airtime. Originally, the IBT wished to secure a protected percentage of Channel Four's airtime. In the event it has had to bid against all comers but has maintained a highly sucessful record.

In 1983 twenty-two new programmes were broadcast apart from repeats. Although this level of programming was not achieved in the following year as Channel Four began to move away from simply renewing extended contracts for early programme providers it did continue to secure a reasonable level of on-air output. IBT now has about 75 organisations under its umbrella. It sees its use of television more instrumentally than it did: having programmes on Channel Four enables IBT to reach many more people more economically than through any other means. This parallels attitudes among many independent production companies who use their limited C4 output as a showcase – an advertisement to say they exist and are available for work.

IBT has been tempted just to make television programmes, rather than use television as one outlet for its message. This was discussed by the IBT board and rejected. Much of its work is involved in spreading the message by follow-up to television series like *Utopia Limited*. This work is carried out by Broadcasting Support Services.

There have also been continuing problems with Channel Four: the IBT felt early on that they were being pigeon-holed into one kind of relationship with one commissioning editor and that this was not what they wanted. In fact they had identified the problems of the commissioning editor process. IBT believe they have programme ideas to offer in at least three Channel Four areas: education, multi-cultural and current affairs programmes. Mostly they have been confined to the education slot.

IBT's expectation of television, like many others before and since, was too high. They felt, again in common with many other groups, that access alone would bring about change, that if the message could be put across to enough people the problem would become understood and people would act. Needless to say, they have been disappointed. But the follow-up material has been taken by a large number of viewers and, in conjunction with non-broadcasting activities, IBT now has begun to set the television output into a more sophisticated (and probably more accurate) context.

Community broadcasting and community programming shades at this point well away from access into both educational broadcasting and 'social action' broadcasting. Educational broadcasting has long had a different relationship with its audience, a relationship that social action broadcasting has sought to extend in the past decade. Both recognise what a recent Thames Television advertisement develops as a theme: that there are an awful lot of people in the audience who want to do something, to get out of their seats and get involved. This may mean taking a course, engaging with a new – or old – sport, playing a musical instrument, helping neighbours, the deprived, or the community at large.

Along with these desires, programme-makers have begun to see ways of feeding information back to audiences. This can be done directly through the telephone or indirectly through mail-outs and study material. Channel Four has developed this enormously but it had already been around through BSS for years. Or it can be done through school-based projects like the Media Literacy Project which aims to get school-children fluent in being able to 'read' mass media, especially television. In all these ways, those connected with broad-casting – and not just the professionals – are slowly bringing changes. The general direction of those changes is towards giving audiences more information, if not yet access, to broadcasting. In part it has meant more access but, as we have seen, this is still circumscribed by that same professional concern for the integrity of the show that informed the earliest broadcasts. It is, too, a concern for the maintenance of a professionalism (including all kinds of technical and artistic status codes) which, in this area as perhaps no other, is beset with definitional inexactitude. In the last analysis 'professional' broadcasters will try, like all other groups with power, to hang on to what they have got, come what may. That is perfectly natural; but it needs to be tempered – more, much more, than it is now.

12 The Continuity of Change

The BBC by the late 1980s represents what we might designate as the moral model of public service broadcasting. It was the very first in the world to be established on principles which were not orientated towards profit or propaganda; it was, by 1988, among the last left more or less intact. Those principles were that:

- Broadcasting should be universally available;
- It should in its output, cater for a catholicity of tastes;
- There should be universality of payment;
- Broadcasting should be distanced from Governments;
- Broadcasting should be distanced from commerce.

To those basic first principles others, less important, have been added. As time has passed it has become more and more difficult for the BBC to fulfil its own brief. One reason has been finance. If, as the BBC still argues, it has to provide under the first heading – for everyone, everywhere – then the costs are horrendously high.

But, as I have argued, another more significant change has taken place in the land. Consensus is under threat, if not already executed, by larger social change. The principles on which the BBC was founded, although not necessarily dependent on consensus, are nurtured and fed by it. In its absence or demise – however slow – the BBC will be permanently under some form of threat. Its energies will be sapped.

But the BBC itself has been guilty of exercising policy choices which have led to accusations that it no longer fulfils its own original brief. Among these accusations, for example, are those which say that when the BBC abandoned mixed programming on radio for generic programming, it threw away principle number two. It did this because in putting all of one kind of programmes on to one service it appeared tacitly to accept that consensus was a myth. That is, there are audiences who will never be willing to listen to expand their own choices by listening to other than what they know they like.

Generic programming is inherently divisive, inherently narrowing. Although it appears to give more choice, the choice is in not having to choose. Although this has not happened on BBC television in the

same way – frequencies in short supply forbid it – the damage has
been done.

The fourth principle has also been limited by the BBC's need to
return to Government time and again in the 1970s for more money.
The extra boost given to strike action by BBC employees in 1985 over
the *Real Lives* programme was probably in part due to a recognition
by BBC staff that this last principle has become one of deep importance at a time when all else is less obviously adhered to. The
BBC still survives on the licence fee. The problems this creates are
well known. But the corporation has inevitably strayed into commercial waters with an increasingly aggressive management (and Board)
backing these forays. The sale of programmes abroad is the most
legitimate; the venture involving the BBC computer perhaps among
the least acceptable. It is not that the BBC ought not to be
commercial, more that its unique position in British broadcasting
makes it peculiarly vulnerable to attacks of unfair practice. Again it
can be argued that the BBC is put in an impossible position: enjoined
either to save money or to make more, then berated when it is
successful at either (because in the former case by saving money the
result may be less worthy programmes). But the BBC did not come
into existence to grace a fair universe and it is sufficiently canny to be
able to fight its own fights.

The plain truth is that the BBC has lost its way in the jungles of
decisions it has had to take on all fronts in the last twenty years. With
a weaker and weaker management, and a weaker financial base,
beset by increasing costs and audience demands, it has become too
close to governments, too easily picked off in often inconsequential
fights. Its own history (and its own often pompous sense of that
history) have not helped, bogging it down with precedent when it
needs, corporately, to be liberated and free, able to make hard new
choices. As an organisation it has correctly perceived that it has to
change its attitude to its audiences. It has not gone far enough in the
right direction, preferring too often to make populist 'pally' noises
when it ought to be engaging seriously in intelligent dialogue. But the
first moves have been made and with more serious purpose it could
bring onside that most powerful of lobbies – its own consumers. ITV
(and ILR) almost by definition can never do this because they have to
deliver these same consumers to advertisers; to permit them access
would be to destroy the contract with their ultimate paymasters. But
for the BBC the paymasters are really those same consumers – not
the Government.

As it has developed in sophistication, ITV in particular, and recently the IBA, have begun a campaign to suggest that they too are public service broadcasters. They are not, nor can they be. Commercial television in the UK does an excellent job, much better than almost anywhere else, of providing a good programme mix, even at peak times. ILR, incidentally, does a generally dreadful job, providing the kind of unadulterated pap that even US radio stations long ago abandoned. But, and ITV executives admit it, without the BBC as a constant reminder – and threat to their audiences – the best ITV programmes would be rarely made. Producers in commercial television unashamedly use the BBC to argue their case for the equivalent of public service programming. No one should ever forget, however, that ITV boards have hitherto backed the making of these programmes because they have somewhere at the back of their minds the renewal of their franchise – and of their monopoly right to make a fortune.

Channel Four seems, at first sight, to break the rule about commercial finance and public service broadcasting. In reality it does not. Channel Four is not public service broadcasting. It is minority broadcasting, thereby perpetuating and improving on one aspect of what, collectively, amounts to public-service broadcasting, but it in no way constitutes it within its own corporate identity. It is also financed commercially, which puts it potentially within the influence of one interest group; finally, as it happens, it is largely unaccountable – much less accountable than the reformed ITV system. If the moves still being canvassed in 1988 to detach Channel Four from ITV were successful, Channel Four would then become just another commercial network – the most powerful one in Britain, because fully national.

The BBC, then, is both the only public service broadcasting service system in the UK and the most accountable. Its mechanisms of accountability have been charted throughout the previous chapters. At the same time it has been badly managed; even now there is still confusion at the top. It had still, late in 1988, little sense of future direction, although it was beginning to argue furiously that it had. It was still over-staffed, expensively run and needed urgently to be much more open and accountable – but not to governments.

In the last count it needs, if anything, to be much further away from the centre, both the political centre and its own bureaucratic centre. It has to have more financial room to manoeuvre and it has, paradoxically, to slim down. This author, unfashionably, has decided it does not need to lose any services currently run. The manpower saving should come from a better-run administrative system, and from real devolution, not devolution plus central *duplication*.

The 'new' structure devised during 1985 and finally introduced by late 1987 went a little way down this road, but nothing like far enough. The BBC is adept at re-inventing the wheel, only the tracks these make continue to deepen the ruts of old pathways. Much of the 'new' structure had been tried before in a different context, a more settled world. Now what the BBC needs is a powerfully thought-through vision of the future: that was still not forthcoming, and the death of the BBC Chairman of Governors after a long illness, in the autumn of 1986, threw many assumptions to the wind. After three years of uncertainty the BBC was back where it had started: on the long hard road to establishing itself all over again.

Some changes have happened but probably not fast enough. Even now, there is still far too much talk of the 'best of all possible worlds' – that is, all change is change for the worse. A good deal of this is to do with the common fear in organisations undergoing difficult times, that any movement will rock the boat. The BBC is amazingly entrenched in many things. What can be a strength in good times has nearly capsized it. The confusion at the top – between Board of Management and Board of Governors – has in part been a fight over control at a time when who gets control has suddenly become crucial.

Apart from deflecting yet more energy from the real battle going on, this internecine warfare betokens more evidence of the failure on all sides at the top to come forward with a re-statement of the BBC 'principles'. This is urgently overdue. Much loose talk now abounds between broadcasters – including some academics – over what public-service broadcasting is. The BBC, once, could cogently argue and be believed, when it said psb is what we say it is; no longer. Nevertheless, now the BBC needs to say: psb is this: discuss.

It is perhaps symptomatic of the creeping malaise over public service broadcasting that the BBC appears to fear this debate. Of course it will throw up awkward questions about BBC (and other) practices. But we are in danger of bringing to a whimpering end one great achievement. Britain invented the system which has sustained the BBC and its ideals and idealism. We should not now lightly chuck it in the bin.

OF PEACOCKS AND PUBLICS

Remember that the most beautiful things in the world
are the most useless; peacocks ... for instance.

(John Ruskin)

The Peacock Committee reported on 3 July 1986. Remarkably, its report was on time; more remarkably, its main conclusion was hidden from view, lost in a welter of Press comment that it somehow vindicated the position of the BBC. The other immediate response to the report – that it would not be implemented – suited many interested parties, including the Government, by now more worried about the next general election.

The main point seized upon was that the report did not recommend advertising on the BBC; as most commentators had assumed this was why the Committee had been set up to start with the fact that it came out against such a financial solution was news. But Peacock's report, although likely to be shelved by the government which commissioned it and subsequent, including Conservative, governments is important. It may not set *the* agenda of discussion of the future shape of British broadcasting; it certainly sets an agenda – and one which public-service broadcasting and its advocates cannot ignore.

It returned to the philosophical concerns manifest in the 1962 Pilkington Report – which in part it resembles. Peacock – an economist – is clearly exercised throughout with the effort of trying to pin down the 'real' basis of public service broadcasting; he is, too, anxious to establish its philosophical roots in economic terms: value for money, in one sense. In these matters the report is important, for it stands, much more closely than Annan nine years previously, at the gateway to technological change which must affect the way broadcasting is organised. The technological change argument has been around for so long now that it has lost its force. Many of those who were hottest for its impact a decade ago have now lapsed into silence as the reality of slower incrementalist alterations in innovation have apparently gainsaid the earlier enthusiasms. But changes there have been and the Peacock Committee have lit upon their longer-term impact as reason for much of what they suggest should be done now.

The central question remains: what is the nature of public service broadcasting and is it susceptible to economic analysis in the way other, more tangible, goods are? Peacock, much like this author, sees consumers as the key to any possible change. Unlike this author, Peacock imagines two conditions pertain with broadcasting which are true in life at large. These are that consumers can be sovereign and that a free market in broadcasting ought to reign, with marginal adjustments.

Peacock examines the proposition that, as many supporters of the present say, it is not the same as any other consumable. Is the consumer the best judge of his interests? The report says he is, because mistakes made in 'mis-viewing' a programme can be easily rectified – 'at no cost' says the report. This is arrant nonsense: the major irretrievable cost is in time wasted, which most audience members would regard as very important. It is for that reason we know that consumers are willing to read and take note of programme-guide advice in magazines and newspapers. The main argument advanced for a move to a subscription service in the future, says Peacock, is that by pricing programmes consumers will rapidly learn how to get value for money. This carries an astonishingly large assumption about the continuing range of programmes available although most of the argument has raged over precisely this problem in a non-licence-fee based system.

The report rejects advertising on the BBC, in this part of its own deliberations, unclearly. That is, by its own admission the report's rejection of the BBC being in part or wholly advertising-finance funded is *not* based on what is best for the consumer (who might in fact benefit by having a wider choice of goods to choose from, through that advertising).

The report does note that one argument in favour of the current arrangements is that the public may not know what its own best interests are: value-judgements cannot be kept out of the analysis – neither have they been in the report. That is, we do by and large support institutions and establishments for reasons other than pure self-interest. Art galleries, education, all kinds of major activities, which as individuals we might not need or use, are given public funds, by and large graciously, by a public which acknowledges their intrinsic value to society.

The chief difficulty with the report is its internal inconsistencies and its insistence that the medium to long-term future is what will count – against the advice of that older economic adage that in the long-term we are all dead. The biggest leap in the dark comes when the committee tackle the question of subscription financing. Their limited research data are poor, lending weight to the view that the public would be heartily opposed to a subscription service.

Although the BBC publicly welcomed the 'idea' of subscription broadcasting, when the report was published, it seemed that, once again, its own desire to rush a judgement into the public domain had overcome common sense. Subscription broadcasting would bury the BBC as constituted in the mid-1980s, at best condemning it to a minor role on the fringes of broadcasting. One reason for this is that the level of subscriptions payable for the popular programmes would have to be set high enough to pay for the rest of the output. If this were so, would the public be prepared to pay?

The prior existence of ITV ensures that the public's perception of commercial broadcasting being 'free' would be mightily reinforced. The issue – whether the bulk of a population can be persuaded to pay for a range of services they might not individually use – is still there. Identified by Peacock it lurks hidden by the welter of technological flim-flammery that the report dazzles its reader with – including a mass of largely unreadable econometric data and a curious layman's appendix on the technical background to broadcasting, probably the single most irrelevant addition ever made to an official report.

Peacock boasts that his report was delivered on time. But it has not been tardiness which has meant previous enquiries into broadcasting have taken up to three times as long: it has been care and attention to detail. Even then most have been consigned to the wastepaper bin by governments not at all anxious to legislate in such a difficult field. Peacock laments the lack of a communications policy, as have others before.

But so many current communications policies confuse technology and the broader issues of culture. To try to encompass all of them inside a law, or sets of laws, is to try to legislate for all life. In the end Peacock is a failure – as it had to be. It fails because it cannot second-guess the future and because it raises issues which it then stubbornly fails to address. Principal among them is whether in the end the BBC should stand as an institution whose importance to British society is at least as important as, say, the Royal Family or the Church of England (arguably much more so than both). And if it is so to stand, how to prevent institutional morbidity through an arrogant acceptance of received and out of date wisdom; how to enhance its future through new technology rather than undermine it?

By late 1986 Peacock and its deliberations had been lost to view by a much more publicly debated problem – the question of BBC bias. Only the most naive would believe this had nothing to do with the Conservative Party's growing desire to sell off parts of the BBC at almost any cost. This along with a belief that the Corporation was biased against the Right – and not just in its coverage of events like the US bombing of Libya.

As this book has argued at length, by the late 1980s it was perfectly possible to see the BBC as a main part of the political opposition in Britain, and on two counts. First because with a Labour party in disarray the official opposition was stifled; in its absence the BBC continued to put the alternate case willy-nilly. Second, and perhaps much more damaging to an ideologically based government, the BBC represented day after day the kind of consensus the Conservatives wished to eliminate. Ironically, the more ideological members of the Labour party lost no sleep over the decline of BBC support among MPs and others.

THE BRITISH BROADCASTING CORPORATION

I have argued, some would say with great perversity, that the BBC ought to continue. I have not suggested, neither does my research data bear out, that the BBC should remain unchanged. As everyone now indulges in telling this public body what it should do next, I shall put forward a plan. I have little doubt it will not be indulged although some parts might be examined with care.

First the BBC has to re-align itself. By this I mean it has to re-establish its commitments to the political system and its parts. It has lost much support – certainly from the Right but also, by default, from the Left. Many of its political supporters continue to argue for it because they can think of no better way of doing things, rather than from conviction.

The re-alignment would come very quickly if the BBC were able to reorganise its central decision-taking processes so that decisions could be taken more quickly. Since the Peat Marwick Mitchell report of 1985, and since the setting up of the Peacock Committee (as the report drily notes) the BBC has shaken itself into better shape. There is more hard accounting going on; more outsiders are being brought in; morale is slowly rising. But BBC staff still live in a vast sprawling organisation where decisions are mysteriously taken elsewhere. These same staff – down to the cleaners – are the front-line when members of the public (audiences, in short) confront them with the latest BBC scandal, usually over costs. These unfortunates, when faced by angry consumers in the local pub, equally usually have no solid answers.

Most – perhaps all – communications organisations have poor internal information systems. The industrial relations of these systems are often notorious, witness national newspapers; they are not alone. The reasons why this should be so are easy to find. Communications in the modern world is a speedy affair where the excitement and creativity of the doing override or completely swamp the mundane but vital functions of just keepings channels open. The BBC is probably no worse than any other broadcast organisation in this respect. But it is among the world's largest. Curiously because it is probably also the best its staff worry about it more – as do its public. We are most intrigued to know what is going on.

If the corporation has, as a matter of great urgency, to revise its attitudes to its own staff, then it has to do so to its audiences. My conclusion has been that the BBC represents the only proper model of public service broadcasting in Britain; that commercial broadcasting inadequately measures up to this, although it is positively affected by the model of the BBC. But even so the BBC has failed so far to find the right form of relationship with its audiences. There is an overlap with the past which creates an awkward hybrid of populist present and paternal past. The BBC should now engage in a better dialogue with the general public in which open 'government' is the ruling voice. If it really is to become 'our BBC' we, the consumers, have to be able to see more of the processes which go to make up the products we consume, and to have stronger rights over their production and consumption.

A part of those rights is access and access is always easier to small, rather than large, bodies. Half a life-time ago the Beveridge Committee suggested that the BBC need to devolve; what it said even before the advent of regional commercial broadcasting proved the point, is more true now. The BBC has to devolve if it is to survive. That means not duplicating its regional and local services at the centre. It does mean serious – more serious than presently planned – local production for local television and radio, a parallel to ITV, in fact.

The regional reorganisation in England by the BBC is a welcome step in the right direction although once again, the BBC has failed to come up with a proper south-east region. The best models are the national regions in Scotland, Wales and Northern Ireland. Would that poor old England could – in the BBC – get its own forms of true independence, networking where appropriate but not being obsessed by it. This is not just a BBC problem, but the BBC has remained stuck with its sense of being a 'national' broadcaster, as if ITV, despite its strong regionalism, does not have (at least as far as its audience is concerned) a national character and distinct identity. Regionalism also reinforces the audience's awareness of what services are available and of the extent to which a particular service of broadcasting serves an area. As the BBC, uniquely, relies on its special relationship with its audiences, this latter point is vital.

I have not mentioned finance. It is my belief that the licence fee ought to continue into the foreseeable future. With Peacock I endorse the need to untie it from any one government: linking it to some form of retail index is the way. It would benefit in its collection by being quarterly rather than annual. More important, it should be axiomatic that the State should make it clear that its collection, whether by the BBC or not, is for the BBC. That is, unlike the present arrangements, the licence fee should be seen to be for the BBC alone. Governments have argued that only they have the right to taxation. But the mechanism is clear. The State should now give the BBC its frequencies – in my view in perpetuity – but only if certain other conditions, all in the Royal Charter, continue to be met. By this means the BBC will be freed of a number of minor but trammelling legal and constitutional trip-wires.

It should also be the case, bearing in mind recent events, that appointment to the Board of Governors should be made by an all-party committee of the House of Commons – a procedure which should be extended to the IBA and the Cable Authority (and could be usefully extended to all similar public bodies). Mrs Thatcher has disgracefully abused her powers of patronage; although all Prime Ministers are prone to nudge these appointments in particular directions she appears to have come close to constitutional trans-gressions. Of course this reflects the consensual lacunae in British public life, a theme which has shadowed much of my central discussion.

What, then, am I arguing for? I do believe that technological changes will alter what is potentially available to audiences; that such changes may be regulated, even slowed, but that in the current state of international trade, can no longer be stopped. But we in Britain, while known externally for the continuity of our traditions, possibly to our economic detriment, have of late opted for a form of technological double-speak, especially in the field of communica-tions, which leaves us vulnerable.

Leaders of political parties, in Government, in industry – even in the BBC – have appeared to suggest that if only all these wonders of the so-called new industrial revolution are allowed free rein our own economic and industrial future is, if not assured, then likely to be buoyant. This misses the lessons of history completely; it even misses the very carefully structured (by government) economic and industrial policies of one of our greatest rivals, Japan.

Most of all, if we rush at the future without examining what in our past and present we wish to take, as a necessary part to make that future liveable, we will destroy the continuity of our culture. The result will be chaos. We have to decide not what to throw away but what to change and in what directions. This is never easy and we have, through our various social and cultural problems (I identify social class and inherent secretiveness as the two most damaging still), a long way to go before we can sensibly decide priorities.

Meanwhile it is worth hanging on to those institutions which have contributed to the light: the BBC is unquestionably one of the most important, although one of the youngest. What we have to remember is that all bodies can be changed and, if we deem it worth the effort, should be in the circumstances that prevail. The BBC could be changed by outsiders; we, its owners, can push it hard. But it is in the nature of the BBC, at the heart of its best philosophy, that it knows when change is needed and responds positively to it. As one of its current staff (and a supporter) said, early on in the BARRTA study: 'what you have to remember is that the BBC is not its current management, or its Board of Governors; it is far more than that, and far more important than them'.

It is indeed. The decisions to be taken about it, and therefore about public-service broadcasting in the 1990s, have to go far beyond the immediate and trivial questions to do with who scheduled what, when and why. They have to do with our desire and requirement as a society to have a means of communication which will provide as near as possible the best – in information, education and entertainment – in the world. They have, too, to do with the necessity to keep the aim of consensus alive as a means of political, economic and social discourse: not, perhaps, ideal but the least bad means we have yet devised of remaining a democratic society.

Postscript

The bulk of the research for *Beyond the BBC* was undertaken between 1981 and 1984. Since then many things have changed in broadcasting; more have remained the same. Although Government policy is now to expose British broadcasting to largely US and other foreign competition via a weakened national system, as well as permitting more or less unlimited access to the British market through satellite, it does seem as if substantial elements of the current arrangements will survive.

Government policy is contradictory: although the 1988 White Paper suggested radical changes in some directions, it held back from a completely open market. Structures do remain – some, indeed, are reinforced. Although the IBA is now a target of a Government apparently determined to show it is anti-regulation, there will be bodies like the Broadcasting Standards Council, as well as the continuation of the Broadcasting Complaints Commission.

The principal attack – and that, I believe, is the correct word – is on what Mrs Thatcher clearly thinks are the twin evils of British broadcasting, writ small from her brief for the country as a whole. These are an over-cosy oligopoly between the BBC and ITV (with Channel Four straddling the middle); and that public service broadcasting is philosophically close to her definition of 'socialism': anti Government and pro the notion that society is real.

The contradictions in Government policy in this area are vitally important. First, because in them are sown already the seeds of final destruction of the best broadcasting system in the world (and that has to be said, *pace* all the faults it displays). Second, because if there are contradictions, there is some faint hope that they will enable that system to outlive this Government and Thatcherism is general.

The research for, and writing of, *Beyond the BBC* spans most of the Thatcher years: they have to be taken into full account now because, although a theoretical base is almost entirely missing, and the mish-mash of slogans and conundrums espoused in their name often seems little more than raving, their collective impact in ten years is considerable. It is for that reason alone that the often bullish pronouncements by BBC staff, though private, are misplaced. Mrs Thatcher has profoundly affected the BBC and its immediate future. She has driven it back, forced it into a defensiveness which many of us outside find *offensive*, not least because it is couched in a ghastly kind of populist bonhomie, extremely unbecoming to an organisation as established as the BBC. Part of that bonhomie suggests that the BBC has changed itself into something new, and that part of that change has encompassed its audience – a positive realisation of public accountability. If the BBC at the top believes this then delusion is now endemic in the Corporation, a Pavlovian product of these years of attrition by the Government. If they privately recognise that much of the change is cosmetic, waiting on the day when things begin to look up again, the Micawberism is forgivable.

The reality may be bleaker. The BBC has shaken out many of its old guard in favour of newer, brasher minds. These are, perforce, concentrated on the balance sheet. Exercises like the presentation of the annual 'accounts' in a two-hour television programme are, on this scale of things, like the glossy but generally uninformative annual reports from public companies.

The truth is that the BBC does not have the wherewithal to mobilise public support in such a way that would, under the current arrangements, also engender a real move towards public acountability. The central theme of this book – that the BBC needs to think more about the nature of its *responses* and of its *responsibilities*, rather than continue to address the impossible – stands more starkly than ever. In truth it is becoming an indictment. Where the BBC has strength – in its history, in its prior commitment to the truth at all costs – it is now making dangerous compromises. In a political system as potentially subvertible as ours, where imbalance can so easily be tilted to become permanent, a body of knowledge which, like a beacon in the night, can illuminate what debate there is left – might even affect public opinion – such a library of wisdom as this could be used as a bench mark of liberal democracy. Instead the BBC has become a hostage to fortune: in its journalism it is failing, seeking increasingly to play jazz tunes in the maelstrom.

As the senior partner of impartiality in British journalism the BBC ought, in the name of public responsibility, to be fighting with all its might against the ever increasing encroachments against the liberty of the Press. It ought to be fighting from the centre, in public. Instead, there is silence. When even judges in Northern Ireland begin to complain that the Government has gone too far, the public might long ago have expected the BBC to have made some pronouncement on the way that Government has eroded freedoms, both in the Province and out. Certainly, in the former case the BBC has suffered

– witness the *Real Lives* débâcle. But on home ground, its own standards, the BBC has suffered a humiliating defeat (over its Libyan coverage). Its own 'vindication' is forgotten: Tebbit's unwarranted and inaccurate attack is what is remembered – and what has been acted upon in the BBC.

The BBC will argue and protest loudly that all this is unfair, that things really have changed. Of change there is no doubt: the question is – in what direction? Is the BBC in 1989 more or less of what it was ten years ago? Is it financially secure? Is it resolute for truth, for impartiality – at all costs? Is its morale good? Is it led by men (and very, very few women, still) who believe in its future as a public service organisation? Is it of good heart, courageous – or afraid?

What is true is that many of the old songs and the old singers – senior BBC staff particularly – have gone: Alasdair Milne, Stuart Young, David Holmes, William Rees-Mogg, Alan Protheroe, Brian Wenham, Dick Francis, Michael Grade, Ian McIntyre (Controller, Radio Three) – as the list lengthens it reads like a roll-call of a distant battle.

But although there is a new regime, although the newcomers have begun to try to change the BBC, most of what I have said in these pages remains as true of the BBC today as it was when I began. It does in truth change slowly: indeed, part of my argument has been that changes still come far too slowly for the changes in the world outside the portals of Broadcasting House.

Despite Michael Checkland, despite Marmaduke Hussey, even despite the *bête noir* of BBC journalism, John Birt, the BBC is still largely what it was before: an extraordinary mixture of artistry, creative thrust, arrogance, bureaucratic nonsense, uncertainty, one of the most inspired ideas of the twentieth century anywhere in the world, and one of the least publicly understood; loved, but as a distant, dare one still say it – Aunty.

In their present mood the British public will cheerfully see it destroyed, along with a great number of other inspired British ideals (like the NHS and our museums), not because a government of philistines will assault it from the front but because long ago they have begun to whittle it away from the rear (privatisation being but one of the poisoned chisels brought into play). In broadcasting that process had begun before the foundations of this research project were fully set. If I have made attacks on some of the practices I have uncovered – notably on mediocre management – then those attacks are based on my desire to see the BBC survive into the twenty-first century more or less intact and not, as I and many others currently fear, as a tattered remnant of a brilliant idea.

As things stand the BBC appears to be conspiring with its enemies to ensure its own destruction. The 1988 White Paper which the BBC appeared to welcome contained its death warrant – the lunacy of a legally enforced subscription, rising year on year, as an increasing proportion of the BBC required revenue, set against a diminishing licence fee. Along with ITV – equally integral to the total broadcasting system in the UK – the BBC is apparently allowing itself to be picked off, bit by bit. And if, as I seem to hear, voices whisper 'don't fret old boy, we're all working secretly together to stop this madness', then another nail may shortly be heard penetrating the coffin, driven in by the dancing feet of laughing Government supporters.

The present Government has long been adept at using the British obsession with secrecy for its own ends. Keep quiet, perhaps they will go away; even, shut up, we'll outlast them. For the BBC, in one respect, that may prove to be true but only, I now fear, as an emasculated adjunct of the State.

At the centre, meanwhile, the accountant's mentality (all things may be measured in the balance sheet) mirrors the Thatcher economic policy. A few years on, and the caution of hoping that the BBC may outlive the wild and weird antics of a Government wishing itself as a permanent fixture on its electorate, may seem somewhat misplaced.

Part of the problem is that the BBC is still so important – not just to the cultural heritage of this nation, but as part of its democratic processes; part of the constitutional arrangements, jejune as they are, which ensure that at least some semblance of reality penetrates into public life. That the BBC is lamentably failing to carry the banner for Press freedom, now more threatened than at any time since the French Revolution and the Napoleonic Wars is, again, a measure of its timidity, after ten long years of sustained attack from those in authority.

If one comment made to this author stands out it is that the BBC 'dies the thousand deaths of the coward': would that it were untrue. In the end, the coward may live on, but can he live with himself? This canker of cowardice is eating the heart out of a great public institution while those within either deny there is a sickness at all or simply wring their hands and ask: what can I do?

So, at the beginning of 1989, we may surmise that the BBC will still be around in the year 2001: we may even hope that it will be strong, resourceful, complete and viable; but in our nightmares grow the fear that it will be no more than an enfeebled voice, crying in the wilderness among a Babel of commercial pap, in large part served out by the monstrous regiments of the few multinationals.

References

Annan Committee (1977) *Report of the Committee of Enquiry into the Future of Broadcasting*. Cmd 6753 (London: HMSO).

Beveridge Committee (1951) *Report of the Broadcasting Committee*. Cmd 8116 (London: HMSO).

Briggs, Asa (1961, 1965, 1970, 1979) *History of Broadcasting in the UK* (vols 1–4) (Oxford University Press).

Briggs, Asa (1985) *The BBC: the First Fifty Years* (Oxford University Press).

Burns, T. (1977) *The BBC: Public Institution and Private World* (London: Macmillan).

Cathcart, R. (1984) *Most Contrary Region* (Belfast: Blackstaff Press).

Crawford Committee (1926) *Report of the Broadcasting Committee*. Cmd 2599 (London: HMSO).

Curran J. and Seaton J. (1986) *Power Without Responsibility*, 2nd edn (London: Fontana).

Drinkwater, J. (1984) *Getting It On* (London: Pluto Press).

Eckersley, P. P. (1942) *The Power Behind the Microphone* (London: Scientific Book Club).

Glasgow University Media Group. (1976) *Bad News*; (1980) *More Bad News* (London: Routledge & Kegan Paul).

Gunter, B. (1985) *Dimensions of Television Violence* (London: Gower Press).

Hobson, D. (1982) *Crossroads* (London: Methuen).

Kumar, K. (1977) 'Holding the Middle Ground', in J. Curran, M. Gurevitch, and J. Woolacott: *Mass Communication and Society* (London: Edward Arnold).

Leapman, M. (1986) *The Last Days of the Beeb* (London: George Allen & Unwin).

McKinsey Report (unpublished BBC internal report).

McQuail, D. (1969) 'Uncertainty about the Audience', in P. Halmos (ed.) (1969) *The sociology of mass media communicators* Sociological Review Monograph (Keele University).

MacShane, D. (1979) *Using the Media* (London: Pluto Press).

Mander, J. (1980) *Four Arguments for the Elimination of Television* (Brighton: Harvester Press).

Middlemas, K. (1979) *Politics in Industrial Society* (London: André Deutsch).

Peacock, Committee (1986) *Report of the Committee on Financing the BBC*. Cmd 9824 (London: HMSO).

Pilkington Committee (1962) *Report of the Committee on Broadcasting*. Cmd 1753 (London: HMSO).

Postman, N. (1986) *Amusing Ourselves to Death* (London: Heinemann).

Reith, J. (1924) *Broadcast Over Britain* (London: Hodder & Stoughton).

Robinson, J. (1982) *Learning Over the Air* (London: BBC).

223

Scannell, P. and Cardiff, D. (1977) *Social Foundations of British Broadcasting* (Milton Keynes: Open University).

Smith, A. (1973) *The Shadow in the Cave* (London: George Allen & Unwin).

Sykes Committee (1923) *Broadcasting Committee Report*. Cmd 1951 (London: HMSO).

Taylor, L. and Mullan, B. (1986) *Uninvited Guests* (London: Chatto & Windus).

Tracey, M. (1978) *The Production of Political Television* (London: Routledge & Kegan Paul).

Ullswater Committee (1936) *Report of the Broadcasting Committee*. Cmd 5091 (London: HMSO).

Wedell, E. G. (1968) *Broadcasting and Public Policy* (London: Michael Joseph).

Index